Front cover: 'Leander' class frigate HMS *Arethusa* on STANAVFORLANT duty in July 1982. This ship was converted to carry the Ikara missile system in April 1977. *Michael Lennon*

Back cover, top: Leader of the 4th Frigate Squadron, HMS *Avenger* was the last Type 21 to return from the Falklands war and is photographed entering Plymouth on 10 September 1982. Note the extra 20mm gun mounted on the flightdeck. *Mike Lennon*

Back cover, centre: HMS *Magpie* at the Coronation Review in 1953. Note the uniform light AA armament consisting of single 40mm guns in the bridge wings and twin 40mm mountings and associated directors abaft the funnel. Most ships of the 'Black Swan' class were so equipped in the postwar years although the number of 40mm guns fitted varied. *Skyfotos*

Back cover, bottom: HMS *Broadsword* was the first Type 22 frigate and is seen here entering Portsmouth in 1979. The Type 22s carry the most modern weapon systems, but no main gun. However, later Type 22 frigates currently on order to replace ship losses in the Falklands war will have gun mountings. *Mod Navy*

2

Powered by gas turbines, carrying two helicopters and having a guided missile main armament, the Type 22 is the latest frigate to enter service with the Royal Navy. The photograph shows the third Type 22, HMS *Brilliant*. *Yarrow (Shipbuilders) Ltd*

ROYAL NAVY FRIGATES

1945-1983

LEO MARRIOTT

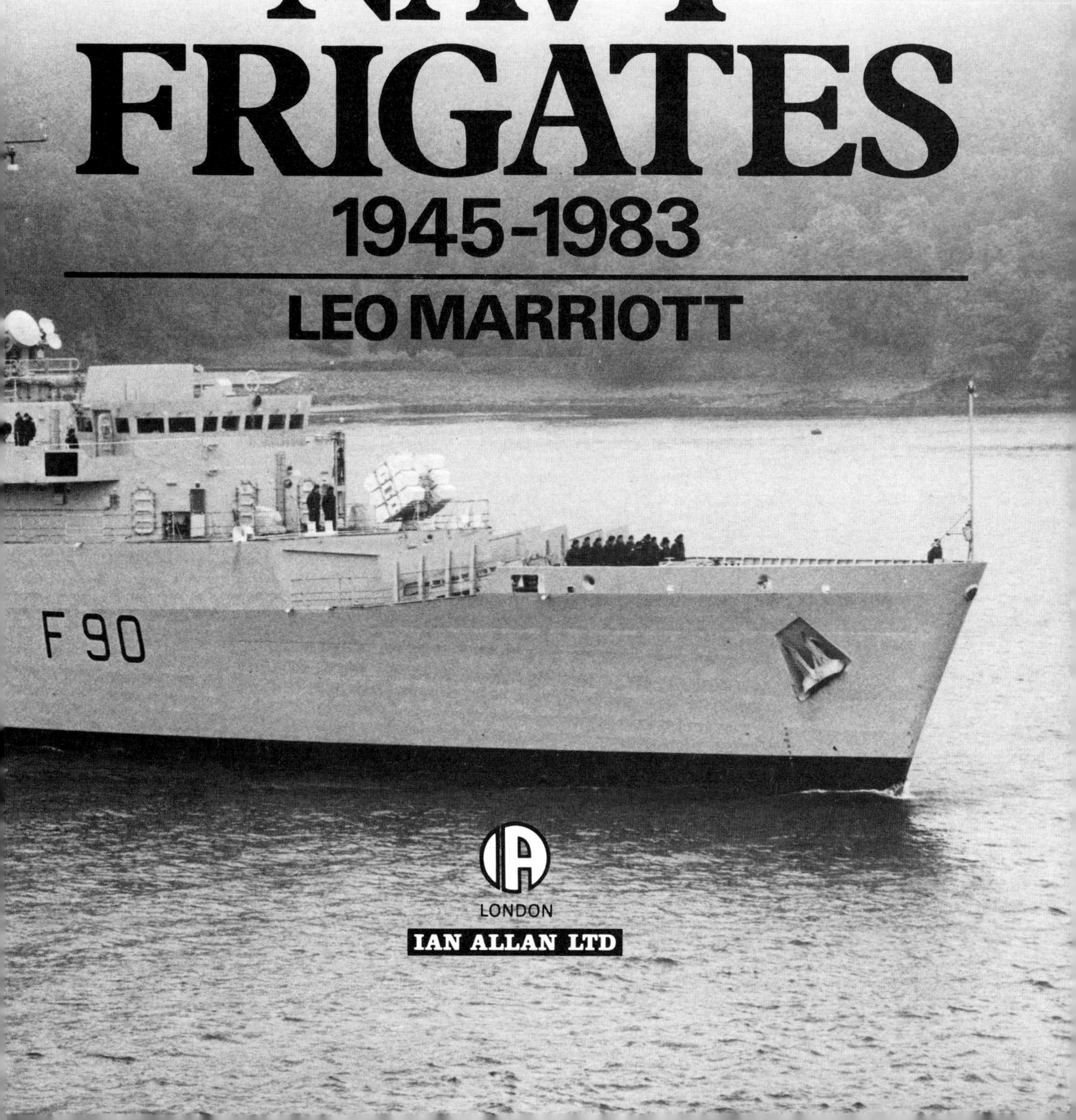

LONDON

IAN ALLAN LTD

Acknowledgements

One of the joys of writing a book like this is the realisation that there are a wide variety of people who are only too willing to take the time and effort to help out by providing photographs, information and personal knowledge. It gives me great pleasure, therefore, to take this opportunity to thank the following people and organisations who have contributed in some way to the compilation of this book and hope that they will find the end result worthy of their efforts: Wright and Logan, Naval Photographers, Portsmouth; Mike Lennon; Mr T. C. Bickerton, Public Relations Manager, British Aerospace Dynamics Group, Bristol Division; Fleet Photographic Unit, HMS *Excellent*; Photographic Unit, HMS *Osprey*, Portland; Mr J. Baird, Public Relations Department, Westland Aircraft Ltd, Yeovil; Mr D. K. Brown FRINA, RCNC, (for information relating to frigate Type designations listed in Appendix 1); Cdr F. E. R. Phillips RN, Naval Assistant to the Director of Public Relations (Navy); Mr Tom Goyer, Assistant Publicity Manager, Short Bros Ltd, Belfast; Mr Charles Hamilton, Managing Director, Skyfotos; Mr W. C. McMillan, Executive Manager, Yarrow (Shipbuilders) Ltd; Lt-Cdr E. H. Featherstone, HMS *Fearless*; Officers and Crew, HMS *Brighton*.

Leo Marriott

First published 1983

ISBN 0 7110 1322 5

Published by Ian Allan Ltd, Shepperton, Surrey; and printed by Ian Allan Printing Ltd at their works at Coombelands in Runnymede, England

3
The 'Loch' class was the standard AS frigate design evolved at the end of World War 2 and incorporated the experience gained in that conflict. HMS *Loch Ruthven* is seen here still bearing her wartime colour scheme and pendant number in April 1946. *Wright and Logan*

Contents

Glossary and Abbreviations

AA	Anti-Aircraft
ADAWS	Action Data Automation Weapon System
AS	Anti-Submarine
ASR	Admiralty Standard Range
ASW	Anti-Submarine Warfare
ASWE	Admiralty Surface Weapons Establishment
ATW	Ahead Throwing Weapon
bhp	Brake horsepower
CAAIS	Computer Assisted Action Information System
CODOG	Combined Diesel or Gas Turbine. An integrated ship's propulsion system where the ship can be driven by either diesel or gas turbine power, but not both together
COGOG	Combined Gas turbine or Gas Turbine. An integrated propulsion system consisting of two or more gas turbine units where the ship can be driven by a combination of some, but not all, units
COSAG	Combined Steam and Gas turbine. An integrated propulsion system consisting of both steam and gas turbines and where the ship can be driven by either or both turbines together
CRBFD	Close Range Blind Fire Director
DF	Direction Finding
DP	Dual Purpose
ECM	Electronic Countermeasures
ECCM	Electronic Counter Countermeasures
ESM	Electronic Surveillance Measures
EW	Electronic Warfare
Foxer	An acoustic decoy towed astern of a ship to counteract acoustic homing torpedoes
GRP	Glassfibre Reinforced Products
HF/DF	High Frequency Direction Finding
IFF	Identification Friend or Foe. A radar system designed to identify co-operating targets on a radar screen
ihp	Indicated horsepower. Measure of power output of steam reciprocating machinery
kg	Kilogram
kW	Kilowatt
Limbo	See Squid
MATCH	Manned Torpedo Carrying Helicopter
MGB	Motor Gunboat
mm	Millimetre
MRS	Medium Range System
MAD	Magnetic Anomaly Detector. An airborne device for detecting submerged submarines by measuring disurubances in the earth's magnetic field
NATO	North Atlantic Treaty Organisation
oa	Overall
RN	Royal Navy
shp	Shaft horsepower
SCOT	Satellite Communication Terminal
Squid	Three-barrelled AS mortar firing depth charge projectiles to a range of about 400yd. Loaded manually. Postwar development led to the Limbo system which fired a heavier projectile over a longer range. Could be loaded, aimed and fired by remote control
STAAG	Stabilised Tachymetric Anti-Aircraft Gun
STD	Simple Tachymetric Director
STWS	Ship's Torpedo Weapon System
TACAN	Tactical Aid to Navigation. System whereby a ship or aircraft can determine its bearing and distance from a beacon which may be land-based or installed in another ship or aircraft
UHF	Ultra High Frequency
UK	United Kingdom
US	United States
VDS	Variable Depth Sonar

Introduction

It is nearly 40 years since the end of World War 2. In that time political and technical changes have altered the status of Great Britain and the role of the Royal Navy in ways which could not have been foreseen amid the rejoicing at the coming of peace in 1945. In that year Britain was an equal partner with the other two great powers, the United States and Soviet Russia, and her Empire and Commonwealth stretched around the globe. Her navy was second only to the vast fleet possessed by the United States Navy and was tasked with worldwide commitments. Most important of all, Britain was privy to the technical secrets which shortly enabled her to construct and test her own nuclear and thermonuclear weapons.

The effort of fighting and winning a second world war within the period of 30 years had left its mark, however, and in the years immediately following the end of the war the armed forces were inevitably run down. There was no money available for the furtherance of new weapons, and, rightly, the government of the time gave priority to the domestic front, where the rehousing and resettlement of a population disrupted by nearly six years of war was a major task. Industry and transport systems needed to be re-equipped and revitalised, and in this period the welfare state was introduced in the form that we know it today.

Abroad an irresistible tide of nationalism led to the break up of the Empire, a process which had already started before the war, and even the independent Commonwealth countries such as Australia and Canada were far less dependent on the mother country than they had been before 1939. Thus, in the late 1940s, both political and economic factors pointed to a steady decline in the strength of the Royal Navy and it was obvious that it would never again hold the pre-eminent position it had held before the start of World War 2. Nevertheless, several factors contributed towards a temporary halt in the reduction of the effective strength of the Royal Navy in the late 1940s and early 1950s. The start of the so called 'Cold War', signalled by the blockade of Berlin by the Russians in 1948, was followed by Chinese communist aggression in the Far East, which in turn led to the Korean War in 1950-53. Against this background, the North Atlantic Treaty Organisation was set up in 1949 and, apart from military aid, the United States also pledged financial assistance for European rearmament. The Mutual Defense Assistance Pact (MDAP) provided funds for the purchase of weapons by NATO countries and enabled the Royal Navy to go ahead with the development and construction of new ships to meet an increasingly threatening international situation. Although many ships of the wartime navy continued their expected progress to the scrapyard, the 1950s saw the laying down of many new classes of warships and the completion of major ships laid down or designed during the war. Thus, for example, the carriers *Ark Royal* and *Eagle* passed into service during this period.

Following the end of the Korean War, the urgency for re-equipment of military forces lessened and the Defence White Paper of 1957 contained many sweeping measures which effectively cut the plans of all three services for future equipment and also established the guided missile as the prime aerial defence system. The policies of the Wilson Labour government, elected in 1964, led to a review of Britain's position in the world and a realistic appreciation of her financial abilities to follow various defence policies. This led to a decision in 1968 to withdraw all military forces from positions east of Suez by 1971 and a similarly timed announcement led to the decision to run down the expensive aircraft carrier force. This latter decision, hotly contested at the time, was possibly the most retrograde step taken in respect of the Royal Navy by any postwar government. In the event, a Conservative government elected in 1971 decided to retain the *Ark Royal* in service as long as possible and also authorised the construction of three through deck cruisers which became the current 'Invincible' class. Obviously, the foregoing decisions had a major impact on the size and structure of the Royal Navy. In 1970, the Wilson government had set a target of approximately 70 destroyers and frigates as the front line strength and by 1980 this figure had fallen to approximately 60. The defence review announced by John Knott, the Conservative defence minister in 1981, cut the numbers to only 50. This decision was made in the teeth of fierce protests that the Navy would be unable even to carry out its NATO commitments in the Eastern Atlantic which represent its current major task.

At the moment, the Royal Navy is the world's third most powerful navy in terms of effectiveness if not in terms of actual ship numbers. It is, however, only a fraction of the size of the powerful American and Russian navies, and may well be overtaken in the near future by other navies such as the French (which currently operates two modern fixed wing aircraft carriers as well as a force of six ballistic missile submarines with a seventh vessel approved).

It is against the foregoing background that this book sets out to study the development of the frigate in the Royal Navy during the period in question. Apart from political and financial influences, the overwhelming factor affecting warship design has been the technological revolution in virtually all fields of warship construction. The greatest advances have been in electronics and sensor systems, weapons and propulsion systems. The changes undergone in warship design since the end of World War 2 are probably as fundamental and as varied as those experienced by the Victorian navy when steam supplanted sail and iron hulls replaced the traditional 'wooden walls'.

At the end of the war, steam represented the major propulsion system in most RN escorts and frigates, using either turbines or reciprocating machinery to drive the screws. In the early postwar designs for the 'Whitby' and 'Blackwood' classes, higher operating pressures and temperatures resulted in greater fuel economies and lighter machinery. However the navy was ready to investigate and use alternative systems and the first to see widespread adoption was the diesel engine which was chosen for the 'Salisbury' and 'Jaguar' classes in the early 1950s. Again fuel economy and increased range was the objective but the resulting ships were relatively slow for their role as major fleet escorts (although considerably faster than wartime frigates). Both the steam turbine and the diesel were eventually replaced by an entirely new propulsion system which took its technology from the aircraft industry — the gas turbine. Introduced into operational service with the 'Tribal' class frigates of the early 1960s, the gas turbine proved to be a reliable and effective warship propulsion system and all major warships constructed for the Royal Navy since the early 1970s have been powered by this system. Adoption of the gas turbine has had many effects on warship design as it requires large intake and exhaust trunkings and filters. Most importantly, gas turbine-powered ships can be started from cold and be under way within a matter of minutes compared with the hours required to raise steam from a boiler. Another consideration is that the turbines are usually installed in modular form which means that they can be removed as a complete unit for major repairs and another unit substituted. Thus ships need to spend less time in dockyard hands. Most designs incorporate two or more separate gas turbines which means that the chances of a ship having a total power failure due to battle damage is considerably reduced. Finally, the modern gas turbine lends itself to remote and electronic control which in turn reduces the numbers of staff required to operate it.

Mention of electronics brings us to the greatest revolution, not only in warship design, but in the world as a whole. Computers have changed our lives and they have certainly taken over warships. Computers take up space in a warship, not because of their actual size but because the need to protect them from shock damage and to provide them with adequate ventilation and cooling. The Type 21 was the first design to be provided with a modern digital control system for the ship and its weapons, and the Type 22 has gone a stage further. Ships of the 'Leander' class have been equipped with computer-assisted action information systems during their rebuilding and no self-respecting warship can take to the seas these days without its own electronic brain. As well as controlling and operating weapon systems, computers are also found in engine control systems, communications and other departments.

Another development in the electronic field is, of course, radar. Although developed to a high state during World War 2, new research and techniques have brought continuous improvements. Again technology, in the shape of the transistor, has had a major impact on warship design. Although transmitters and receivers are much more compact and reliable than they used to be for a given power, the increase in tasks allocated to frigates has meant that these ships have to carry a greater array of radar equipment than before. The ultimate in this respect was probably the Type 61 aircraft direction frigate which carried a bewildering array of radar equipment to the exclusion of virtually everything else. The huge 'double bedstead' aerial carried by these ships weighed nearly two tons and, being mounted at the top of a tall mast, must have caused great problems to the ship designers trying to keep stability within reasonable limits.

Transmissions from any radar, as well as detecting other targets, can also be received by other ships and the direction of the signals plotted. This means that any ship using its radar can be detected and possibly located by an enemy vessel which is not using its own radar and therefore remains undetected. This has the result that strict procedures have to be enforced with regard to the use of radar and all modern frigates (and other warships) are equipped with the means to detect and locate other ships' radar and radio transmissions. This is known as electronic surveillance measures (ESM) and is something else for which the overworked ship designer has to find room.

Radar systems can be rendered useless by various methods of jamming and modern radar systems are designed to try to overcome this. Thus a whole new field of electronic counter-measures and electronic counter-countermeasures (ECM and ECCM) has come into existence. The steady increase in aerials and black boxes which have equipped postwar frigates are witness to the increasing effect of electronics in sea warfare.

The original function of frigates was to attack and sink submarines and their main weapons were depth charges and the early ahead throwing weapons (ATW) such as Hedgehog and Squid. As the underwater speed of submarines and the range of sonar has increased, so the range of AS weapons has also improved. The first development was the Limbo mortar, an improvement of the Squid, but this has been supplanted and replaced by other weapons such as the Ikara missile system and helicopter-carried homing torpedoes. The helicopter has wrought a major change on the shape and layout of the modern frigate, as all designs now include a hangar and flightdeck for the carriage and operation of this vital piece of equipment.

Since the invention of gunpowder, the main armament of any ship had been its guns but, initially against airborne targets, and then almost universally, the gun was slowly replaced by the guided missile. Already under development at the end of World War 2, the guided missile appears in a variety of forms on most modern frigate designs culminating in the latest Type 22 design where missiles are the main means of defence against both air and surface targets. On the other side of the coin is the necessity for ships to be able to defend themselves against missile attack and while this has usually meant attempting to jam or disrupt the missiles' guidance systems, the Seawolf missile system now coming into service is capable of intercepting other missiles in flight.

Thus the modern Royal Navy frigate carries extensive radar and electronic equipment, is armed with guided missiles, carries one or more helicopters, is powered by products of the aerospace industry, and the whole thing is run by computers. Compare this with the typical late war frigate which carried relatively simple radar equipment, was armed with a couple of 4in guns and depth charge mortars, was propelled by reciprocating steam machinery, and was controlled by weatherbeaten men exposed to the elements whilst standing on an open bridge: the difference between these two images is what this book is about.

The recent conflict in the Falkland Islands has thrown the characteristics of our modern warships into the spotlight of topical discussion. The informed layman probably knows more about the Royal Navy's warships than he ever did in the past. Words like Exocet, Seawolf, Sea Dart, *Antelope*, *Sheffield*, *Coventry* and *Ardent* are literally household words. At the same time, the professional men of the Royal Navy and designers of warships will be taking a close look at the lessons to be learnt and these will, no doubt, be reflected in the design of future frigates. Some lessons, however, have been painfully relearnt after being forgotten in the years since World War 2. Foremost among these is the fact that, historically, a force of surface warships has never been able to defend itself effectively against concentrated air attacks unless it is provided with sufficient carrier-based air power of its own. When the task force sailed for the Southern Atlantic many observers wondered if the development and deployment of sophisticated surface-to-air guided missiles would change this state of affairs. It did not.

Although surface-based missiles took a terrible toll of attacking aircraft, enough got through to cause severe losses of ships and lives among the British fleet. Sea Harriers operating from the two carriers were more successful than could reasonably have been hoped in the circumstances but were handicapped by the need to conserve aircraft and the lack of an airborne early warning system.

Another lesson to be absorbed was the surprising usefulness and effectiveness of the gun in modern warfare. The heavy guns of the frigates and destroyers were essential in the shore bombardment role and one frigate even claimed to have shot down an Exocet with its 4.5in gun. Light automatic weapons were shown to be still a very effective means of countering close range air attack.

Finally the greatest lesson of all, which has been shown time and time again in the history of the Royal Navy, is that the finest ships and weapon systems in the world are of no use unless they are manned, maintained and operated by human beings. The men that man the ships are the greatest factor in success or failure and ultimately it is because of these men that the rest of us are able to go about our daily lives in peace and security.

1 The Wartime Frigates

Frigate Development in World War 2

The first warship in modern times to be termed a frigate was the 'River' class of escorts which came into service in late 1942. They were purpose-built vessels intended to escort and protect ocean convoys against submarine attack and they were the first vessels to be designed specifically for this particular role. There were, of course, several other classes of warship which were being used to escort convoys but none of them had been specifically designed for the particular purpose of defending ocean-going convoys against concentrated submarine attacks. It is instructive to look more closely at these escorts, because the omissions and deficiencies in their design led to the development of the first frigates.

Perhaps the most successful ships in service in 1942 were the 'Black Swan' class sloops of which 31 were eventually completed for the Royal Navy. Displacing 1,300 tons and equipped with steam turbines to give a speed of 20kts, they were heavily armed with six 4in guns in three twin high angle mountings, and several light AA guns. They were excellent ships in every way and they shared in the destruction of 28 U-boats as well as shooting down several enemy aircraft; but, despite this, they suffered from two main drawbacks. In the first place their very excellence arose partly from the fact that they were designed to full naval warship standards and therefore could only be built in yards familiar with the construction of warships. Even then building could take up to two years and consequently the type could not be rapidly produced in the numbers required at that stage of the war. Secondly, the design could not easily be adapted to carry the new AS weapons such as Hedgehog and Squid unless part of the main armament was removed. The Admiralty was loath to do this as the ships' AA armament was sorely needed at the time.

Also in service were several prewar-built sloops of the 'Bridgewater', 'Hastings' and 'Grimsby' classes, which had preceded the 'Black Swan' design. With a displacement of just over 1,000 tons and a speed of only 16½kts they were both smaller and slower than the 'Black Swans' and carried a lighter armament. Although useful ships, they suffered from the drawbacks of the 'Black Swan' class to an even greater extent and were not built in very large numbers.

The escorts available in greatest numbers in 1942 was the famous 'Flower' class corvette, which had been developed from a commercial whaler design just prior to the outbreak of the war. On a standard displacement of 950 tons the 'Flowers' made 16kts and carried a 4in gun, a few light AA guns and depth charges. They were intended mainly for use in coastal regions and short-range escort work, and were never intended for the mid-ocean work in which they were soon employed. Although excellent seaboats they were very lively and the accommodation standards for the wartime crews were cramped, cold and damp. Their small size made it difficult to fit new weapons and radar and although a modified version was eventually produced it could do no more than nibble at the problems. The outstanding advantage of the type was that it could be produced quickly and in large numbers by normal commercial shipyards — and ultimately a total of 145 was built in UK yards with others being built in Canada. The large number built, and the rate at which they were introduced into service in the early part of the war, was a vital factor in holding off the expanding U-boat menace despite the operating deficiencies of the class.

Against the experience gained with the prewar escort vessels in the early part of the war, the Admiralty decided that a new class of vessel was required to provide effective defences for the ocean convoys. Thus plans were drawn up in 1940 for a 'twin screw corvette', which became the 'River' class and was later redesignated 'frigate'. The 'River' class, displacing 1,400 tons, was considerably larger than the 'Flower' class and was armed with two single 4in guns and several light AA. Anti-submarine armament comprised the usual depth charge racks and throwers, while Hedgehog was fitted on the foredeck in front of the forward 4in gun. The large open quarterdeck gave plenty of room for depth charge stowage (over 200 were carried eventually) and later for handling acoustic torpedo decoy gear (Foxer). The increase in size meant that accommodation standards for the crew were improved and the ship was better able to carry improved radar as it became available. Being designed to commercial standards, the 'Rivers' could be built by normal shipyards; a total of 57 was built in the UK, more were built in Canada and the design was also adopted by the United States Navy.

4
HMS *Thyme*, a 'Flower' class corvette, in 1946. The most numerous escort type in Royal Navy service during the war, the 'Flowers' were quickly phased out of service following the end of hostilities. Note the lantern aerial cover for the Type 272 radar abaft the bridge.
Wright and Logan

5
A battered looking HMS *Wear* enters Portsmouth at the end of 1945. The 'River' class was designed as an ocean going escort in the light of experience gained in the early part of the war and it was the first Royal Navy type in modern times to be designated 'Frigates'.
Wright and Logan

6
It had been intended to improve the AS qualities of the 'River' class by removing the forward 4in gun and Hedgehog mounting and installing two Squid mortars. This scheme was cancelled after the end of hostilities and HMS *Helmsdale* was the only ship of the class to be so modified. She continued in service for several years as a training ship. *Wright and Logan*

Due to the increase of size in the 'River' class, several yards which had been building 'Flower' class corvettes were unable to build the new design. In order to plug this gap an updated and modernised design was produced to replace the 'Flowers'. The new type was known as the 'Castle' class frigate and was 50ft longer than the corvettes to give a displacement of 1,100 tons. Gun armament was similar with a single 4in and several AA guns, but the major improvement was the inclusion of a Squid AS mortar just forward of the bridge and enclosed from the weather by protective bulwarks. Speed remained at $16\frac{1}{2}$kts. Although the first vessels of the class were not laid down until 1943 a total of 26 had been completed for the Royal Navy by the end of the war and others had been completed for the Canadian and Allied navies.

The final product of wartime experience was the 'Loch' class frigate, the first of which was completed in mid-1944. Although of a similar size to the earlier 'River' class, the new design was optimised for large scale production and provision was made to incorporate new weapons and equipment coming into service. Thus the armament consisted of a single 4in gun, a large number of light AA guns and, most significantly, two Squid mortars mounted just forward of the bridge. As soon as the design was finalised, all contracts for the 'River' class were cancelled and replaced by orders for 'Loch' class vessels. The efficiency of the new type can be gauged from the fact that, despite their late entry into the war, ships of the 'Loch' class were involved in the sinking of 16 U-boats.

In 1944 a requirement arose for AA escort vessels, particularly for the British Pacific Fleet which was forming at the time. The answer to this requirement was an adaptation of the 'Loch' class, involving the removal of the single 4in gun and the Squid mortars, and their replacement by four 4in AA guns in two twin mountings installed in B and X positions. The new variant was designated the 'Bay' class and a total of 19 vessels of this class was completed for the Royal Navy.

Finally, mention should be made of one other class of escort vessel which, although numerically very important, lies rather out of the scope of this book. This is the 'Hunt' class of escort destroyers, a total of 86 of which was produced between 1939 and 1943. Designed mainly as fleet AA escorts with a limited AS capability, over 60 survived the war and were redesignated as frigates in 1948. During and after the war, several were transferred to foreign navies and the rest were scrapped in the 1950s. No major modifications were made to the class after the end of the war to adapt them for modern AS warfare and they therefore played no part in the evolution of the postwar frigate. In passing, however it is worth mentioning the two 'Hunt' Type IV destroyers *Brecon* and *Brissenden*. These two vessels were designed by Thornycroft and were completely different from the other 'Hunt' class types in that the forecastle deck was extended right aft to give virtually a flush deck appearance instead of the traditional destroyer layout. A fuller hull section was adopted and a pronounced knuckle was incorporated on either side of the bow. The net result of these changes was improved sea riding qualities with no loss of performance. The extra stability of the fuller hull allowed the full 'Hunt' class armament of six 4in guns and a triple set of torpedo tubes. The Type I and III 'Hunts' had had to sacrifice one twin 4in mounting due to stability problems. In many ways these two vessels were ahead of their time and experience with some of the features of this class was invaluable in the design of postwar vessels. In particular, the extended forecastle deck became a standard feature of many postwar designs and conversions.

It is not the intention of this book to go into great detail concerning the design and development of the wartime frigates as this aspect has been well recorded and documented in other publications. However the following pages set out general details of those classes which saw significant postwar service and details of their eventual fates.

'Black Swan' Class AA Frigates

This famous class of escorts had its origin in a Naval Staff Requirement of 1937 for ocean going escorts having good AA and AS qualities. The result, a development of earlier sloop designs, produced a vessel of 1,300 tons standard displacement carrying a heavy armament of six 4in AA guns in three twin mountings as well as a quadruple pom-pom mounting and a number of 20mm single guns. Thirteen vessels were built to the original 'Black Swan' design (including four for the Indian Navy) but wartime experience and the need to fit extra equipment resulted in 24 further vessels completed to a modified design and known (naturally enough!) as the Modified 'Black Swan' class. Several of the later vessels were not completed until after the end of the war.

The modified vessels featured better provision for the light AA armament, a slight increase in beam, stabilisers and other detail improvements. As the war

7
The 'Hunt' class escort destroyers were redesignated as AA Frigates in the postwar period. HMS *Bicester*, a Type II 'Hunt', is seen here wearing a frigate pendant number and with her armament cocooned at the Coronation Review at Spithead in 1953. *Skyfotos Ltd*

8
HMS *Pheasant*, built as a Modified 'Black Swan', was the last of the class to retain a tripod mast. Note the obsolete Type 291 Air Warning radar at the masthead. *Wright and Logan*

9
One of two 'Black Swan' class ships converted to navigational training ships, HMS *Redpole* is shown here in 1958 just before she was withdrawn from service. The ship's armament has been removed and an additional deckhouse built in X gun position. Note the Type 277 radar on the lattice mainmast. *Wright and Logan*

progressed, continual modifications and additions of new and extra equipment eroded the differences between the two versions and by 1945 they could be considered as one class for all practical purposes. Radar equipment varied but, again by 1945, the standard outfit consisted of a Type 291 air warning radar at the very top of the mast, with a Type 293 'cheese' aerial mounted at the top of the lattice structure of the mast. The lattice mast, a feature of the last few ships to complete, was retrospectively fitted to all the class where it replaced the original tripod mast. *Pheasant* was the last vessel to be so fitted, the work not being carried out until some time after the end of the war. A Type 285 gunnery radar was installed on top of the director tower above the bridge. In the original design the sole AS armament consisted of depth charge throwers and rails on the quarterdeck. Later in the war those ships originally fitted with the quadruple pom-pom mounting on the quarterdeck had it removed in order to carry more depth charges and their equipment. A split Hedgehog spigot mortar was fitted forward in most ships to increase their AS effectiveness.

By the end of the war the class was regarded mainly as an AA escort due to their combination of a heavy AA armament coupled with a radar-controlled fire control system as well as a substantial secondary battery. The stabilisers fitted to the Modified 'Black Swan' class made them exceptionally good gun platforms. Because of these features, a large number of the class were sent to the British Pacific Fleet in the Far East where their excellent AA capabilities were needed against the Japanese. Thus by VJ-Day in August 1945, no less than 17 of the class were in Far Eastern waters.

Of the 37 vessels of both groups completed, six had been delivered to the Indian Navy and a further six were lost during the war which left the Royal Navy with a balance of 25 at the end of hostilities. Five of these (*Acteon, Modeste, Nereide, Snipe, Sparrow*) were not completed until after the end of the war. Indeed the last of the class to be commissioned, *Sparrow*, was not finally completed until December 1946.

With the end of the war, some of the vessels were adapted for peacetime roles. *Redpole* and *Starling* were disarmed and converted to act as navigational training ships. *Redpole* retained her original tripod foremast but a new lattice mast, carrying a Type 277 radar aerial, was stepped aft and extra deckhouses were constructed on the quarterdeck and in the position vacated by X turret. She continued in her training role until she finally paid off in 1958 and was scrapped in 1960. *Starling* retained the lattice foremast with which she had been fitted and also the Type 293 and 291 radars mounted thereon. Like *Redpole* she also had extra accommodation erected aft and also a lattice mainmast installed on the quarterdeck. This new mast was taller than that fitted to *Redpole* and carried mainly communication equipment. Following a refit in

HMS MAGPIE. 1,490 tons.
Black Swan Class Frigate.
1954.

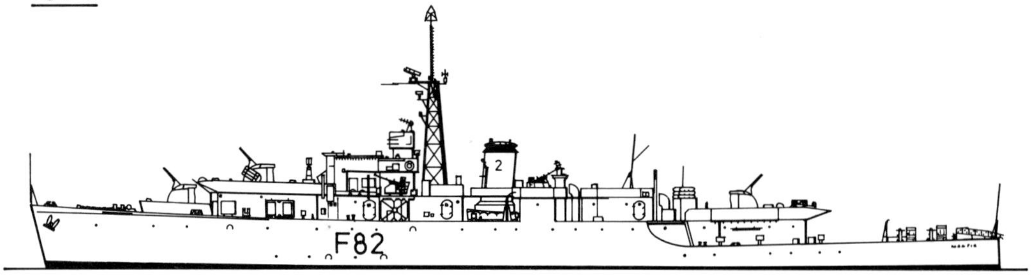

BUILDERS – J.I. Thornycroft, Woolston.
LAID DOWN – 30th DEC 1941.
LAUNCHED – 24th MAR 1943.
COMPLETED – 30th AUG 1943.

LENGTH – 299 ft. o.a.
BEAM – 38 ft.
DRAUGHT – 11 ft.
SPEED – 18 knots.

the mid-1950s, extra equipment was installed on the mainmast for trials but, following completion of the trials, the mainmast and its associated aerials were removed in 1957. *Starling*, of course, had a distinguished wartime record when she was leader of the 2nd Escort Group led by the famous Capt F. J. Walker, who was probably the most proficient AS tactician of the whole war. Sadly, he died of illness brought on by overwork before the end of the war but his memory lived on at the paying off ceremony when the ship ended her last commission in November 1959. Following a period in reserve she was put up for disposal in 1961 but was not finally scrapped until 1965.

Another ship of the class to undergo substantial modification was *Wild Goose*, one of the original 'Black Swans'. In the course of a refit during 1945-46 she had X turret removed and extra accommodation installed on the quarterdeck. The twin 40mm Hazemeyers which she had previously carried were replaced by the standard Mk V twin mounting with an STD for each position. The original tripod mast was replaced by a lattice structure and an up to date radar outfit installed. Finally, 3pdr saluting guns were added and the ship was repainted in the prewar standard Far East colours, comprising a white hull and superstructure and a buff funnel. Thus equipped she was allocated to the Persian Gulf division of the East Indies Station where she served with only short breaks until 1954 when she was placed in reserve. Apart from *Wild Goose*, several ships served in the Gulf area including *Wren*, which was also repainted in the white and buff colour scheme, although for several years she was not otherwise modified. However, in April 1949 she commenced a refit at Malta dockyard which involved the removal of the AS gear on the quarterdeck and also the twin 40mm guns and their sponsons from the waist. Again extra accommodation was installed on the quarterdeck but X turret was not removed. *Flamingo* was similarly altered prior to 1949 and both vessels also served for many years in the Gulf area.

Many of the ships of the class in commission in the Far East at the end of the war remained in the area to assist in the maintenance of a British presence. One of these, *Amethyst*, became a household name following her famous exploit on the Yangtse river in late 1949. Trapped by the advancing Chinese communist forces at Nanking, where she was acting as guardship for the British diplomatic community, she was heavily shelled and trapped in the river nearly 200 miles from the sea. After months of diplomatic activity had failed to obtain the ship's release, Lt-Cdr J. Kerrans led the ship on an epic and dramatic night-time dash along the heavily guarded river to the freedom of the sea. The exploit caught the imagination of the country and the ship was given a warm welcome when she returned to Devonport in November 1949, still bearing the scars of her action. Following a refit, she sailed again for the Far East in July 1950, where she rejoined the 3rd Frigate Flotilla in time to see more action in the Korean War. *Black Swan*, the name ship of the class, had been one of the ship's waiting anxiously off the mouth of the Yangtse from the *Amethyst* to make her breakout and was later in action herself. In June 1950 she was assigned to Task Group 96.5 stationed off the east coast of Korea and later was involved in an action when five out of six attacking North Korean gunboats were sunk. During the course of the Korean War several ships of the class had their light AA armament modernised and increased. *Modeste*, for example, by 1952 carried no less than eight 40mm guns disposed as two single mountings in the bridge wings, two twin mountings amidships and two more single guns on the quarterdeck.

Following the end of the Korean War and the rundown of forces in the Far East, several vessels returned to the UK and were laid up prior to disposal and scrapping. While the activity in the Far East had held the limelight, other 'Black Swans' were carrying out arduous duties in other parts of the world. In the confused situation following the setting up of an independent state of Israel, British ships were involved in patrols designed to prevent the flow of unauthorised refugees and arms into the area. The 3rd Frigate Flotilla, consisting of *Pelican* (one of the forerunners of the 'Black Swan' class), *Peacock, Magpie* and *Mermaid*, took part in the so called Haifa Patrol and later in the Red Sea patrolled the Gulf of Aqaba before finally returning home in 1952. In the South Atlantic *Snipe* found herself in an encounter with an Argentine gunboat as she was engaged in re-establishing British posts at Port Lockroy and Admiralty Bay on King George Island in the South Shetlands.

In 1949, *Whimbrel* was sold to the Egyptian Navy and was renamed *El Malek Farouq*. In 1954, following the deposing of King Farouq and the rise of Colonel Nasser, the ship was again renamed and became the *Tarik*. She was still in service as late as 1981. The only other vessels to be transferred to foreign navies were four ships which went to the newly reformed West German Navy in 1958 and 1959. The four vessels concerned (*Mermaid, Flamingo, Hart, Acteon*) were renamed *Scharnhorst, Graf Spee, Scheer* and *Hipper* respectively. While these were, no doubt, cherished names in the German Navy, there seemed something incongruous about small escort vessels carrying names previously borne by famous battlecruisers and heavy cruisers. However, they proved useful training vessels for the new navy and served for many years with their new owners, the last being scrapped in 1972.

Erne, one of the original 'Black Swans', was

10
Several 'Black Swan' class frigates were deployed to the Persian Gulf area and among these was HMS *Wren*, shown here leaving Portsmouth in late 1946. She has a white hull and buff funnel which was the traditional prewar colour scheme for ships stationed in the Far East and Indian Ocean. *Wright and Logan*

11
HMS *Mermaid* leads HMS *Cygnet* and HMS *Peacock* of the 2nd Frigate Squadron into Malta harbour in 1953. *Mermaid* has 20mm guns in the bridge wings and radar fit includes Type 291 at the masthead, Type 293 below, and Type 285 on the gunnery director. *Mod (Navy)*

allocated to the Wessex division of the Royal Navy Volunteer Reserve as a drillship in 1951 and served in this role until 1965 when she was sold and scrapped.

Others continued in service, particularly with the 3rd Frigate Flotilla in the Far East, until the late 1950s and early 1960s. As the new frigates came into service they were gradually withdrawn until the last ship in Royal Navy service, *Crane*, paid off at Portsmouth in 1961.

Like most of the other wartime frigates, the 'Black Swan' class saw much useful service after the war in all corners of the world where their heavy gun armament on a relatively small ship provided an economic projection of British seapower. In the postwar ASW situation their limitations as anti-submarine vessels were recognised and in 1951 it was proposed to modify some vessels to improve their AS capabilities. The modifications involved the removal of B turret to make room for a single Squid mortar and the fitting of updated radar and sonar gear. Such a modification would not have been particularly effective due to the relatively slow speed (18kts) of the 'Black Swan' type and in any case by this time all resources were involved in the construction of new types and the conversion of destroyers to fast AS frigates.

Name	Number	Builders	Laid Down	Launched	Completed	Remarks
Acteon	U07/F07	J. I. Thornycroft, Woolston	15/5/44	25/7/45	24/7/46	W. German Navy 1958. For disposal 1964.
Alacrity	U60/F60	W. Denny and Bros, Dunbarton	5/4/43	1/9/44	13/4/45	Sold Arnott Young. Arrived Troon 3/11/56 for scrapping after hull stripped at Dalmuir.
Amethyst	U16/F116	Alex Stephen and Sons, Linthouse	25/3/42	7/5/43	2/11/43	Sold Demmelweek and Redding. Arrived Plymouth 18/1/57 for scrapping.
Black Swan	L57/F57	Yarrow and Co, Scotstoun	20/6/38	7/7/39	27/1/40	Sold West of Scotland Sbkg. Arrived Troon 13/9/56 for scrapping.
Crane	U23/F123	W. Denny and Bros, Dunbarton	13/6/41	9/11/42	10/5/43	Sold Lacmonts. Arrived Queenborough 1965 for scrap.
Cygnet	U38/F38	Cammell Laird, Birkenhead	30/8/41	28/7/42	1/12/42	Sold Sbkg Industries. Arrived Rosyth 16/3/56 for scrapping.
Erne	U03	Furness Shipbuilding, Haverton Hill	26/5/38	5/8/40	26/4/41	RNVR drillship (Solent), 1951. Broken up Antwerp, 1965.
Flamingo	L18/F18	Yarrow and Co, Scotstoun	26/5/38	18/4/39	3/11/39	W. German Navy 1959. Broken up 1965.
Hart	U58/F58	Alex Stephens and Sons, Linthouse	27/3/42	7/7/43	12/12/43	W. German Navy 1958. Broken up 1969.
Hind	U39/F39	W. Denny and Bros, Dunbarton	31/8/42	30/9/43	11/4/44	Sold Clayton and Davie. Arrived Dunston 10/2/58 for scrapping.
Magpie	U82/F82	J. I. Thornycroft, Woolston	30/12/41	24/3/43	30/8/43	Sold Hughes Bolckow. Arrived Blyth 12/7/59 for scrapping.
Mermaid	U30/F30	W. Denny and Bros, Dunbarton	8/9/42	11/12/43	12/5/44	W. German Navy 1958. Broken up 1958.
Modeste	U42/F42	Chatham Dockyard	15/2/43	29/1/44	3/9/45	Sold J. A. White. Arrived St Davids on Forth 11/3/61 for scrapping.
Nereide	U64/F64	Chatham Dockyard	15/2/43	29/1/44	6/5/46	Sold P. W. McLellan. Arrived Bo'ness 18/5/58 for scrap.

Name	Number	Builders	Laid Down	Launched	Completed	Remarks
Opossum	U33/F33	W. Denny and Bros, Dunbarton	28/7/43	30/11/44	16/6/45	Sold Demmelweek and Redding. Arrived Plymouth 24/6/60 for scrapping.
Peacock	U96/F96	J. I. Thornycroft and Co, Woolston	29/11/42	11/12/43	10/5/44	Sold Sbkg Industries. Arrived Rosyth 7/5/58 for scrap.
Pheasant	U49/F49	Yarrow and Co, Scotstoun	17/3/42	21/12/42	12/5/43	Sold West of Scotland Sbkg. Arrived Troon 15/1/63 for scrapping.
Redpole	U69/F69	Yarrow and Co, Scotstoun	18/5/42	25/2/43	24/6/43	Sold J. A. White. Arrived St Davids on Forth 20/11/60 for scrapping.
Snipe	U20/F20	W. Denny and Bros, Dunbarton	21/9/44	20/12/45	9/9/46	Sold J. Cashmore. Arrived Newport 23/8/60 for scrap.
Sparrow	U71/F71	W. Denny and Bros, Dunbarton	30/11/44	18/2/46	16/12/46	Sold Sbkg Industries. Arrived Rosyth 26/5/58 for scrap.
Starling	U66/F66	Fairfield Shipbuilding Co, Govan	21/10/41	14/10/42	1/4/43	Sold Lacmonts. Arrived Queenborough 6/7/65 for scrapping.
Whimbrel	U29	Yarrow and Co, Scotstoun	31/10/41	25/8/42	13/1/43	Transferred to Egyptian Navy 1949.
Woodcock	U90/F90	Fairfield Shipbuilding Co, Govan	21/10/41	26/11/42	29/5/43	Sold Sbkg Industries. Arrived Rosyth 28/11/55 for scrapping.
Wren	U28/F28	W. Denny and Bros, Dunbarton	27/2/41	11/8/42	4/2/43	Sold Sbkg Industries and arrived Rosyth 2/2/56 for scrapping.
Wild Goose	U45/F45	Yarrow and Co, Scotstoun	28/1/42	14/10/42	11/3/43	Sold P. and W. McLellann. Arrived Bo'ness 27/2/56 for scrapping.

Data: HMS *Opposum*, 1949
Displacement: 1,490 tons standard; 1,925 tons full load
Length: 299ft oa
Beam: 38ft
Draught: 11ft full load
Guns: 6×4in Mk XVI (3×2) in Mk XIX mountings, 8×40mm AA (2×2, 4×1) in Mk V twin and Mk VII single mountings
AS weapons: Split Hedgehog multiple spigot mortar mounted on B gundeck
Machinery: 2×Admiralty three-drum boilers operating at 250lb/sq in. Parsons geared turbines driving two shafts giving a total of 4,300shp
Speed: 18kts
Oil fuel: 415 tons
Complement: 192

Note: Considerable variation in close range armament occurred throughout the class

'Castle' Class AS Frigates

The pressing need for escort vessels in World War 2 led to the maximum utilisation of shipbuilding capacity in the United Kingdom. Although the 'River' class frigates and their later derivatives, the 'Loch/Bay' class, represented the ideal type of escort vessel for the Royal Navy, it was decided that there was still a requirement for a smaller and simpler vessel which could make use of the capacity of the smaller shipyards. Accordingly the design team at Smith's Dock, which had been responsible for the original 'Flower' class corvette design, drew up plans for a new and larger corvette. The new type, to be named after British castles, was nearly 50ft longer than the preceding 'Flower' class and featured improved accom-

12

HMS *Carisbrooke Castle* was the first of the class to be laid down in 1943 and is seen here at the Coronation Review, 1953. Postwar modifications include the installation of a Type 277 radar at the top of the lattice mast which has replaced the original Type 272 and two single 40mm guns have replaced the 20mm guns aft of the funnel. *Skyfotos*

13

HMS *Caistor Castle*, completed in 1944, was one of the ships representing the Reserve Fleet at the 1953 Review and her main armament is cocooned in weatherproof coverings. Note the HF/DF aerial at the masthead and the small IFF aerial carried below the top of the lattice mast. *Skyfotos*

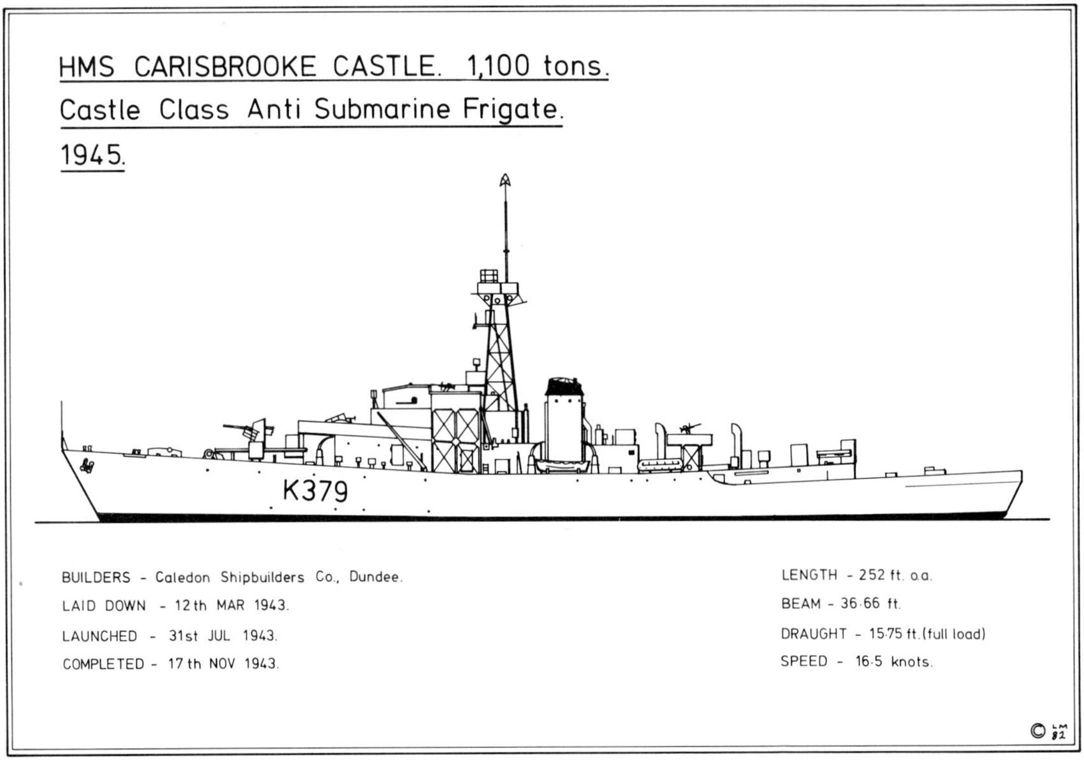

modation, more oil fuel and a modernised armament. The first vessel, *Hadleigh Castle*, was laid down in April 1943, and was completed in the amazingly short time of just over five months. The 'Castles' were good looking ships with well proportioned lines and a workmanlike look about them. Main armament comprised a single 4in gun on the forecastle with a single Squid three-barrelled AS mortar mounted behind it, just in front of the bridge. Initially the light AA armament consisted of six 20mm guns mounted as two singles in the bridge wings and two twin mountings aft. Extra 20mm guns were fitted in some vessels. At the top of the lattice mast was the aerial of the Type 272 radar with HF/DF mounted above it. Machinery was the same as the 'Flower' class corvettes but speed rose by half a knot, to $16\frac{1}{2}$kts, as a result of the greater hull length.

Following approval of the design, a vast programme was put in hand in early 1943 with 59 vessels being ordered from British yards and further orders being placed in Canada. In December 1943, a reappraisal of the whole frigate and corvette building programme was carried out. This was occasioned by the fact that the Battle of the Atlantic, while not won outright, was definitely running in the Allies' favour and that, as a result, the amount of new construction required could be safely reduced. The facilities thus freed could be used for other priority work such as the construction of landing craft. One result of this review was that future construction would concentrate on frigate types and no more corvettes would be ordered. Accordingly 15 of the ships ordered from UK yards were cancelled as were all those ordered from Canadian yards. Of the remainder, five were completed as mercantile rescue ships, one was transferred to the Norwegian Navy on completion, 12 were commissioned into the Royal Candian Navy, which left a total of 26 completed for the Royal Navy. Two vessels, *Denbigh Castle* and *Hurst Castle*, were sunk in action so that at the end of the war in 1945 only 24 remained in service.

Following the end of hostilities most of the class paid off into reserve. Already their small size and slow speed made them obsolescent as front line AS vessels, although they proved useful in various roles such as training and coastal patrol. In 1948 they were redesignated 'Frigates (2nd Rate)' and their pendant number changed to Flag F superior in common with other wartime escort classes. Also in 1948 a scheme was put forward to modernise the class. Changes would have included the replacement of the single 4in gun with a Mk XIX twin mounting, replacing the previous radar with a Type 293Q and the addition of AS homing torpedoes which were under development at that time. In the event this scheme was not proceeded with, probably on the grounds of limited cost effectiveness. Modification to the class in the postwar period was limited mainly to fitting an improved radar and replacing the twin 20mm guns by two single 40mm mountings. The original Type 272 radar was replaced in most vessels by the later Type 277 as fitted to the 'Loch' class. This programme had in fact already started before the end of the war. In the 1950s those ships in commission were fitted with the new Type 974 navigation radar, with the aerial installed on a small platform projecting forward from the lattice mast.

In 1951, the only ships in commission were *Flint Castle*, *Hedingham Castle*, *Leeds Castle*, *Oakham Castle* and *Tintagel Castle*. A few years later the class was represented at the Coronation Review by *Caistor Castle*, *Carisbrooke Castle*, *Knaresborough Castle*, *Hedingham Castle*, *Leeds Castle*, *Flint Castle* and *Tintagel Castle*. Those vessels temporarily out of reserve, such as *Caistor Castle*, appeared with their armament cocooned and were really only there to make the numbers up.

Oakham Castle was converted to an Atlantic weather ship by James Lamont and Co, Port Glasgow, and was commissioned under Air Ministry ownership as the *Weather Reporter* on 16 May 1958; she replaced a 'Flower' class weather ship conversion named *Weather Explorer*. That left three other 'Flower' class conversions remaining in service and these were later replaced by three more 'Castle' class vessels in 1960. The three new ships were *Weather Monitor* (ex-*Pevensey Castle*), *Weather Adviser* (ex-*Amberley Castle*) and *Weather Surveyor* (ex-*Rushen Castle*) and all four weather ships gave sterling service well into the 1970s before the advent of satellites made them redundant.

The vessels converted to weather ships were the last of the class to survive, the rest have been withdrawn and scrapped by 1960. One of the first to go was *Berkely Castle* which was damaged when she capsized in dry dock at Sheerness during the disastrous East Coast floods in February 1953. Up for disposal in 1955, she was scrapped in 1956 along with *Caistor Castle* and *Knaresborough Castle*. By 1958 only eight vessels remained with the Royal Navy and all of these were in reserve and due for disposal. Except for those converted to weather ships, they were all scrapped in the next two years.

Although a useful type at the time of building, the 'Castle' class was rapidly outmoded in the postwar era and had little effect on mainsteam frigate development.

Name	**Number**	**Builders**	**Laid Down**	**Launched**	**Completed**	**Remarks**
Allington Castle	K689/F89	Fleming and Ferguson, Paisley	22/7/43	29/2/44	19/6/44	Broken up at Sunderland, 1958.
Alnwick Castle	K405/F105	Geo Brown and Co Greenock	12/6/43	23/5/44	11/11/44	Broken up Sunderland, 1958.
Amberley Castle	K386/F286	S. P. Austin and Son, Sunderland	31/5/43	27/11/43	24/11/44	Air Ministry *Weather Adviser*, 1960.
Bamborough Castle	K386/F12	J. Lewis and Sons, Aberdeen	1/7/43	11/1/44	30/5/44	Broken up Llanelly, 1959.
Berkeley Castle	K387/F387	Barclay Curle and Co, Glasgow	23/3/43	19/8/43	18/11/43	Broken up Grays, 1956.
Caistor Castle	K690/F690	J. Lewis and Sons, Aberdeen	28/8/43	22/5/44	29/9/44	Broken up West of of Scotland Sbkg, Troon, 1956.
Carisbrooke Castle	K379/F379	Caledon Shipbuilding Co, Dundee	12/3/43	31/7/43	17/11/43	Broken up Industries, Faslane, 1958.
Dumbarton Castle	K388/F388	Caledon Shipbuilding Co, Dundee	6/5/43	28/9/43	25/2/44	Broken up Gateshead 1961.
Farnham Castle	K413/F413	John Crown and Sons, Sunderland	26/6/43	25/4/44	31/1/45	Broken up Gateshead, 1960.
Flint Castle	K383/F383	H. Robb, Leith	20/4/43	1/9/43	31/12/43	Broken up Faslane, 1958.
Hadleigh Castle	K355/F355	Smiths Dock, Middlesbrough	4/4/43	21/6/43	18/9/43	Broken up Gateshead, 1959.
Hedingham Castle	K529/F386	John Crown and Sons, Sunderland	2/11/43	30/10/44	12/5/45	Broken up Granton, 1958.

Name	Number	Builders	Laid Down	Launched	Completed	Remarks
Kenilworth Castle	K420/F420	Smiths Dock Co Ltd, Middlesbrough	7/5/43	17/8/43	22/11/43	Broken up Llanelly, 1959.
Knaresborough Castle	K389/F389	Blyth Shipbuilding Co	22/4/43	28/9/43	5/4/44	Broken up Port Glasgow, 1956.
Lancaster Castle	K691/F691	Fleming and Ferguson, Paisley	10/9/43	14/4/44	15/9/44	Broken up Gateshead, 1960.
Launceston Castle	K397/F397	Blyth Shipbuilding Co	27/5/43	27/11/43	20/6/44	Broken up St Davids on Forth, 1959.
Leeds Castle	K384/F384	Wm Pickersgill and Sons, Sunderland	22/4/43	12/10/43	15/2/44	Broken up T. W. Ward, Grays, 1968.
Morpeth Castle	K693/F693	Wm Pickersgill and Sons, Sunderland	23/6/43	26/11/43	13/7/44	Broken up E. Rees, Llanelly 1960.
Oakham Castle	K530/F530	A. and J. Inglis, Pointhouse	30/11/43	20/7/44	10/12/44	Air Ministry *Weather Reporter*, 1958.
Oxford Castle	K692/F692	Harland and Wolff, Belfast	21/6/43	11/12/43	10/3/44	Broken up T. W. Ward, Briton Ferry, 1960.
Pevensey Castle	K449/F449	Harland and Wolff, Belfast	21/6/43	11/1/44	10/6/44	Air Ministry *Weather Monitor*, 1960.
Portchester Castle	K362/F362	Swan Hunter, Wallsend	17/3/43	21/6/43	8/11/43	Broken up West of Scotland Sbkg, Troon, 1958.
Rushen Castle	K372/F372	Swan Hunter, Wallsend	8/4/43	16/7/43	24/2/44	Air Ministry *Weather Surveyor*, 1960.
Tintagel Castle	K399/F399	Ailsa Shipbuilding Co, Troon	29/4/43	13/12/43	7/4/44	Broken up West of Scotland Sbkg, Troon, 1958.

Data: Postwar service
Displacement: 1,100 tons standard; 1,580 tons full load
Length: 252ft oa
Beam: $36\frac{3}{4}$ft
Draught: 14ft
Guns: 1×4in Mk XIX on Mk XXIV mounting
2×40mm AA (2×1)
2×20mm (2×1)
AS weapons: 1×Squid three-barelled AS mortar.
2×depth charge throwers and one rail (15 depth charges)
Machinery: 2×Admiralty three-drum boilers. Four-cylinder triple expansion reciprocating engine driving one shaft giving a total of 2,880ihp
Speed: $16\frac{1}{2}$kts
Oil fuel: 480 tons
Complement: 96

'Loch' Class AS Frigates

The 'Loch' class of AS frigates represented the final product of wartime experience in frigate design and operation. It was basically a redesigned version of the successful 'River' class and was optimised for mass production on dispersed sites. To facilitate this, the ship was built up of prefabricated sections which could be constructed at the dispersed sites and moved by road or rail to an assembly slipway. Each section had maximum dimensions of: length 29ft; width 8ft 6in; and height 8ft 6in. Maximum weight of each section was set at $2\frac{1}{2}$ tons to suit crane capacity at the shipyards. Eighty per cent of the hull and superstructure was made up of prefabricated units, the rest of the structure being worked in by the assembly yard. The setting up of the organisation necessary to run a widely dispersed production system was a massive task, and took some time. However, once in operation, the time required to complete a frigate was drastically reduced. Whereas the average time taken to complete a conventionally constructed 'River' class frigate was in the order of 15 to 18 months, a prefabricated 'Loch' class frigate was completed in an average time of 10 or 11 months. Had the war continued past 1945, building times would probably have fallen even more as the tempo of production increased. As it was, of the 110 ships ordered under the original programme, only 28

14

Several 'Castle' class frigates served with the Portland-based 2nd Training Squadron in the postwar years. One of these was HMS *Tintagel Castle* which served continuously with the squadron from 1945 until withdrawn from service in 1957. The photo shows her as she appeared in June 1953 with two single 40mm guns aft but no 20mm in the bridge wings. *Wright and Logan*

15

HMS *Loch Quioch* enters Portsmouth flying a paying off pennant in June 1954. In peacetime service the original 20mm AA guns have been replaced by 40mm guns in the bridge wings and aft of the funnel. The ship still retains a quadruple pom-pom mounting aft and the single 4in gun forward. *Wright and Logan*

16

Loch Ruthven was one of seven 'Loch' class frigates modernised in the early 1950s. Changes included the provision of a Mk V twin 40mm mounting to replace the pom-pom and a twin 4in mounting forward to replace the single gun carried originally. Although the Type 277 radar was retained, a new Type ANU parabolic aerial replaced the earlier dish aerial. *Wright and Logan*

'Loch' class were completed although a further 19 were completed as 'Bay' class AA frigates (qv) and eight converted to non-frigate uses. In order to simplify production, curved structures were eliminated wherever possible and one noticeable result of this was that the deck sheer was reduced to three straight lines instead of a continuous and more graceful curve from bow to stern. This introduced a distinct kink in the upper deck just in front of the foremast, although the revised hull form showed no adverse performance features compared with the previous 'River' class.

As completed the ships displaced 1,435 tons (standard) on a length of 307ft (oa), a beam of 38½ft and a full load draught of 12ft. Machinery consisted of four-cylinder triple-expansion reciprocating engines driving two shafts and giving 5,500ihp, which in turn gave revolutions for 19½kts. (*Loch Tralaig* and *Loch Arkaig* were fitted with double reduction geared turbines with an output of 6,500shp.) Armament consisted of a single Mk V 4in gun, a quadruple 2pdr pom-pom and several single 20mm guns. For anti-submarine use two Squid AS mortars were mounted forward of the bridge with an all-round screen protecting the operating crews from the worst of the weather, and a depth charge thrower and rail on the quarterdeck. Sonar Type 144 was fitted for search purposes and to assist accurate Squid attacks, Sonar Type 147b depth finding sonar was carried.

A strong lattice foremast provided the platform for the Type 277 search radar which could detect surface targets out to 15 or 20 miles and aerial targets out to 40 miles. A pole extension to the mast carried the standard HF/DF aerial, and IFF interrogators and responders were also fitted.

Of the 28 vessels completed, three were transferred on completion to the South African Navy and never served with the Royal Navy. The three vessels concerned, *Loch Ard*, *Loch Boisdale* and *Loch Cree* were renamed on transfer and became *Transvaal*, *Good Hope* and *Natal* respectively. A further three vessels (*Loch Achanalt*, *Loch Alvie*, *Loch Morlich*) were transferred to the Royal Canadian Navy but returned to Royal Navy ownership after the end of the war.

Following the end of hostilities against Japan most of the class paid off into reserve with the exception of *Loch Glendhu* and *Loch Quoich* which remained active in the Far East, and *Loch Arkaig*, *Loch Fada*, *Loch Tralaig* and *Loch Veyatie* at home. In 1948 six of the laid up ships were taken out of reserve, refitted and transferred to the New Zealand Navy. The ships concerned, together with their new names and final disposal are listed opposite.

HMS. LOCH KILLISPORT. 1,575 tons.

Anti Submarine Frigate.

1954

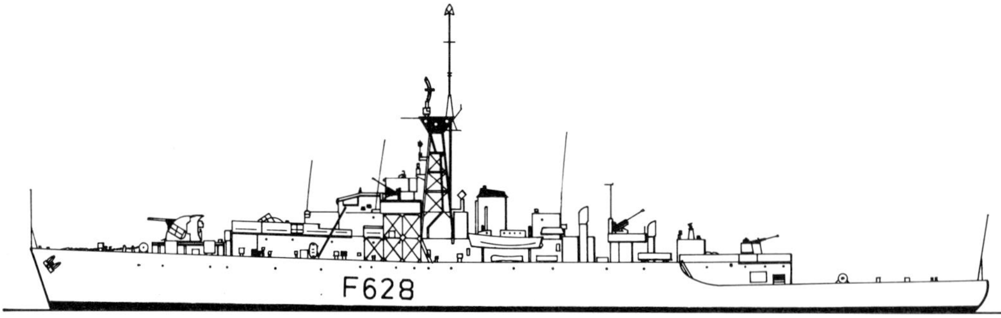

BUILDERS - Harland and Wolff, Belfast.
LAID DOWN - 28th DEC 1943.
LAUNCHED - 6th JUL 1944.
COMPLETED - 9th JUL 1945.

LENGTH - 307 ft. o.a.
BEAM - 38·5 ft.
DRAUGHT - 12 ft.
SPEED - 19·5 knots.

© LM 92

Loch Achanalt (Pukaki)	F424	Transferred 3/9/48. Broken up Hong Kong 1966.
Loch Achray (Kaniere)	F426	Transferred 7/7/48. Broken up Hong Kong 1967.
Loch Eck (Hawea)	F422	Transferred 1/10/48. Broken up Hong Kong 1966.
Loch Katrine (Rotoiti)	F625	Transferred 7/7/49. Broken up Hong Kong 1967.
Loch Morlich (Tutira)	F517	Transferred 11/4/49. Broken up Hong Kong 1962.
Loch Shin (Taupo)	F421	Transferred 3/9/48. Broken up Hong Kong 1962.

Hawea and *Taupo* served with the Mediterranean Fleet in 1950 on an exchange basis.

The start of the Korean War saw the reactivation of several ships from the reserve fleet, including nine 'Loch' class which were formed into two frigate squadrons. *Loch Craggie*, *Loch Dungevan*, *Loch Lomond*, *Loch More* and *Loch Scavaig* were recommissioned for service in the Mediterranean where they replaced the destroyers *Chaplet*, *Childers* and *Cheviot*. At home, *Loch Alvie*, *Loch Fyne*, *Loch Insh* and *Loch Killisport* displaced the destroyers *Barrossa*, *Alamein*, *Aisne* and *Jutland*. The new frigate squadrons remained active until 1952 when the ships were paid off, although seven were retained in service and were earmarked for a modernisation programme which commenced in 1953. Also in 1953, two vessels represented the class at the Spithead Coronation Review — *Loch Ruthven* and *Loch Veyatie*.

The modernisation programme referred to involved mainly changes in armament. The single 4in gun was replaced by a Mk XVI twin 4in mounting with its associated director positioned on the after end of the bridge. The previous mixed light AA armament was removed and replaced by a uniform battery of six 40mm guns consisting of a Mk V twin mounting in the position formerly occupied by the pom-poms, and four single mountings. The single guns were positioned in the bridge wings and on either beam abaft the funnel. The Type 277 radar was retained but improved communication equipment was fitted. The seven ships to undergo modernisation were *Loch Alvie*, *Loch Fada*, *Loch Fyne*, *Loch Insh*, *Loch Killisport*, *Loch Lomond* and *Loch Ruthven*.

The modernised ships saw extensive service, particularly in the Middle and Far East where their general handiness and adequate gun armament made them suitable for peacetime policing and patrolling, as well as the traditional showing-the-flag duties. To assist her in the discharge of these duties, a detachment of Royal Marines was embarked in *Loch Killisport* in July 1956. She thus became the first Royal Navy frigate to carry Royal Marines as part of her normal complement, a practice which was later applied to other frigate classes. The original detachment consisted of one officer, four NCOs and 17 marines.

While the modernised ships continued in service, other ships of the class were being paid off and scrapped. First to go were *Loch Glendhu* and *Loch Quioch* in 1957, followed by *Loch Scavaig* and *Loch Tarbert* in 1959. The other unmodernised ships were scrapped in the 1960s.

Of the modernised ships, *Loch Alvie*, *Loch Fyne*, *Loch Ruthven* and *Loch Insh* were withdrawn in 1960/61 and subsequently scrapped with the exception of *Loch Insh* which was sold to the Malaysian Navy in 1964 and saw several years useful service before being withdrawn from service in 1977. The three remaining ships (*Loch Lomond*, *Loch Fada* and *Loch Killisport*) underwent a major refit to suit them for service east of Suez. Work done included improvements to accommodation and air conditioning of some of the internal spaces. Following this refit the vessels continued in service for a few more years with *Loch Lomond* paying off in 1964, *Loch Killisport* in 1965, and finally *Loch Fada* in 1967. *Loch Fada* was the last of the wartime-built frigates in service with the Royal Navy and her passing finally severed the connection between the wartime frigate types and the entirely different postwar types.

Of the 28 'Loch' class vessels completed, three were transferred on completion to the South African Navy and later a further six were transferred to the New Zealand Navy. The fate of the remaining 19 vessels of the class is listed below:

Loch Alvie Broken up, in the Far East (possibly Singapore), 1965.

Loch Arkaig Sold to J. J. King and arrived Gateshead 28/1/60 for scrapping.

Loch Craggie Sold to Dantos Leal and arrived Lisbon 25/10/63 for scrapping.

Loch Dunvegan Sold to T. Ward and arrived Briton Ferry 25/8/60 for scrapping.

Loch Fada Sold to Shipbreaking Industries Ltd and arrived Faslane 1970 for scrapping.

Loch Fyne Sold to J. Cashmore and arrived Newport, Wales, for scrapping 6/8/70.

Loch Glendhu Sold to Clayton and Davie and arrived Dunston, Gateshead for scrapping 14/11/57.

Loch Gorm Sold to Kavounides Shipping Co, Greece in 1961 and converted to passenger ship. Scrapped Yugoslavia in 1966.

17

In the early 1960s HMS *Loch Killisport* was fitted with an experimental gunshield made of glassfibre reinforced products (GRP). This material was subsequently used in the Mk 8 4.5in gun turret installed in the Type 21 frigates and Type 42 destroyers. Note the saluting guns aft. *Fleet Photographic Unit*

18

HMS *Loch Fada* paid off in 1967, but in 1968 she was used for trials of a vertical launch version of the Seawolf missile then in an early state of development. The photograph shows one of these early rounds being launched from the after section of the ship. Despite the success of these trials, the Royal Navy adopted a conventional launcher system when the Seawolf finally entered service 10 years later. *British Aerospace*

Loch Insh Malaysian Navy *Hang Tuah* 1964. Withdrawn from service 1977, and scrapped.
Loch Killin Sold to J. Cashmore and arrived Newport 24/8/60 for scrapping.
Loch Killisport Sold to Hughes Bolckow and arrived Blyth 18/3/70 for scrapping
Loch Lomond Sold to Shipbreaking Industries and broken up at Faslane in 1968.
Inverkeithing 27/8/63 for scrapping.
Loch Quioch Sold to Clayton and Davie and arrived Dunston, Gateshead for scrapping 13/11/57.
Gateshead for scrapping 13/11/57.
Loch Ruthven Sold to Davies and Cann and broken up at Plymouth commencing November 1966.
Loch Scavaig Broken up by Italian shipbreaker at Genoa, arrived 5/9/59.
Loch Tarbert Sold to Italian shipbreaker and arrived Genoa 18/9/59 for scrapping.
Loch Tralaig Sold to P. and W. McLelland and arrived Bo'ness for scrapping 24/8/63.
Loch Veyatie Sold to W. H. Arnott Young and arrived Dalmuir 12/8/65 for scrapping.

Two other vessels, *Loch Assynt* and *Loch Torridon*, were completed in 1945 as Coastal Forces depot ships and were respectively renamed *Derby Haven* and *Woodbridge Haven*. In 1949 *Derby Haven* was reconverted to a frigate and was sold to Iran where she was renamed *Babr*. She served until 30 October 1969, when she was paid off and subsequently scrapped a few years later. *Woodbridge Haven* remained with the Royal Navy and was variously used as a training and target ship before being scrapped by Hughes Bolckow at Blyth, arriving there on 12 August 1965. Her final role before paying off was as a minesweeper support vessel.

Vessel	No	Builder	Laid Down	Launched	Completed
Loch Achanalt	F424 (K424)	H. Robb, Leith	14/9/43	23/3/44	11/8/44
Loch Achray	F426 (K426)	Smiths Dock, Middlesbrough	13/12/43	7/7/44	1/2/45
Loch Alvie	F428 (K428)	Barclay Curle, Whiteinch	31/8/43	14/4/44	21/8/44
Loch Arkaig	F603 (K603)	Caledon Shipbuilding Co, Dundee	1/11/44	7/6/45	17/11/45
Loch Assynt (Derby Haven)	K438	Swan Hunter and Wigham Richardson, Tyne	11/2/44	14/12/44	2/8/45
Loch Craggie	F609 (K609)	Harland and Wolff, Govan	28/12/43	23/5/44	23/10/44
Loch Dunvegan	F425 (K425)	Charles Hill and Sons, Bristol	29/9/43	25/3/44	30/6/44
Loch Eck	F422 (K422)	Smiths Dock, Middlesbrough	25/10/43	25/4/44	7/11/44
Loch Fada	F390 (K390)	J. Brown, Clydebank	8/6/43	14/12/43	10/4/44
Loch Fyne	F429 (K429)	Burntisland Shipbuilding Co	8/12/43	24/5/44	9/11/44
Loch Glendhu	F619 (K619)	Burntisland Shipbuilding Co	29/5/44	18/10/44	23/2/45
Loch Gorm	F620 (K620)	Harland and Wolff, Govan	28/12/43	8/6/44	18/12/44
Loch Insh	F433 (K433)	H. Robb, Leith	17/11/43	10/5/44	20/10/44
Loch Katrine	F625 (K625)	H. Robb, Leith	31/12/43	21/8/44	29/12/44
Loch Killin	F391 (K391)	Burntisland Shipbuilding Co	22/6/43	29/11/43	12/4/44
Loch Killisport	F628 (K628)	Harland and Wolff	28/12/43	6/7/44	9/7/45
Loch Lomond	F437 (K437)	Caledon Shipbuilding Co, Dundee	7/12/43	19/6/44	16/11/44
Loch More	F639 (K639)	Caledon Shipbuilding Co, Dundee	16/3/44	3/10/44	24/2/45
Loch Morlich	F517 (K517)	Swan Hunter and Wigham Richardson, Tyne	15/7/43	25/1/44	2/8/44
Loch Quoich	F434 (K434)	Blyth Shipbuilding Co	3/12/43	2/9/44	11/1/45
Loch Ruthven	F645 (K645)	Charles Hill and Sons, Bristol	4/1/44	3/6/44	6/10/44
Loch Scavaig	F648 (K648)	Charles Hill and Sons, Bristol	31/3/44	9/9/44	22/12/44
Loch Shin	F421 (K421)	Swan Hunter and Wigham Richardson, Tyne	6/9/43	23/2/44	10/10/44
Loch Tarbert	F431 (K431)	Ailsa Shipbuilding Co, Troon	30/11/43	19/10/44	22/2/45
Loch Torridon (Woodbridge Haven)	K654	Swan Hunter and Wigham Richardson, Tyne	2/5/44	13/1/45	19/10/45
Loch Tralaig	F665 (K665)	Caledon Shipbuilding Co, Dundee	26/6/44	12/2/45	4/7/45
Loch Veyatie	F658 (K658)	Ailsa Shipbuilding Co, Troon	30/3/44	8/10/45	13/7/46

Data: as modified
Displacement: 1,575 tons standard, 2,400 tons full load
Length: 307ft oa
Beam: $38\frac{1}{2}$ft
Draught: 12ft

Guns: 2×4in Mk XIV (1×2)
6×40mm AA (1×2, 4×1)
AS weapons: 2×Squid three-barrelled AS mortars
Machinery: 2×Admiralty three-drum boilers operating at 225lb/sq in. Four cylinder triple expansion reciprocating engines driving two shafts for total ihp of 5,500 tons (*Loch Arkaig* and *Loch Tralaig* had double reduction geared turbines giving 6,500ihp)
Speed: $19\frac{1}{2}$kts
Oil fuel: 735 tons
Complement: 124-140 (originally 103)

'Bay' Class AA Frigates

In 1944, as the emphasis of the war at sea moved from Europe and the North Atlantic to the Far East, a requirement arose for an escort vessel with a heavy AA firepower to accompany the British Pacific Fleet into Japanese waters. The simplest way to meet this requirement was to modify some of the 'Loch' class frigates then being built in large numbers. Accordingly plans were drawn up to modify 26 of the 'Loch' class to a new AA configuration: the new design to be designated the 'Bay' class.

The hull, machinery, superstructure and basic layout of the new class was the same as that for the 'Loch' class frigates, and the ships could be built by the same production centres. The main changes were in the armament, which consisted of two twin 4in AA mountings and two twin 40mm AA mountings. The 4in guns were carried in B position (replacing the two Squid mortars of the 'Loch' class) and 'X' position (replacing the multiple pom-pom) while the two 40mm mountings were carried on the upper deck just forward of the break in the forecastle. Fire control for the main armament was provided by a Mk V director equipped with Type 285 gunnery radar, and the 40mm guns were provided with a simple tachymetric director for each mounting. For anti-submarine use a Hedgehog mortar was situated on the forecastle in the position occupied by the 4in gun in the 'Loch' class, while aft were the usual depth charge rails and throwers.

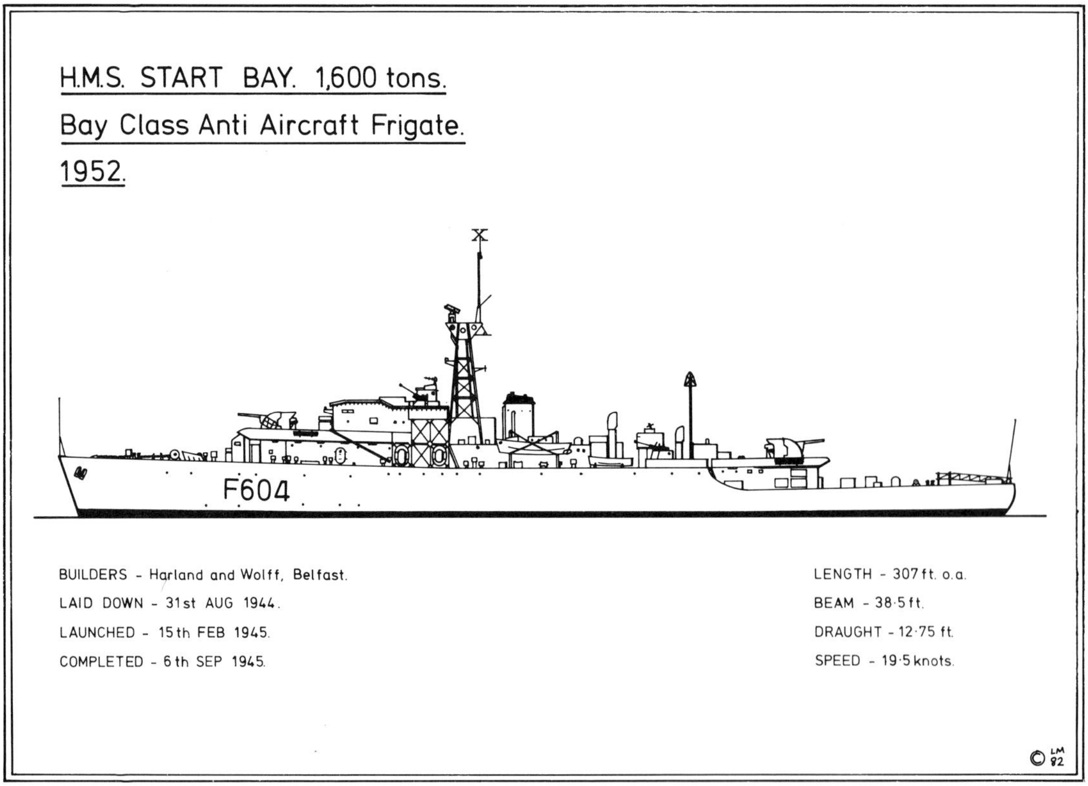

Other radars fitted included a Type 293 with its 'Cheese' aerial on a platform at the top of the lattice mast and a Type 291 with its aerial on a pole extension above the lattice mast platform. IFF transponders and interrogators were also carried, as was medium and high frequency DF equipment. The Type 291 acted as a general air warning radar while the Type 293 was used as a target indicating radar providing information for the Type 285 on the director to acquire the target. Altogether, the 'Bay' class frigates were effective AA platforms and were easily produced from the basic 'Loch' class design. The only serious problem to arise during the building programme was the provision of the twin 4in gun mountings, as production facilities were already fully stretched. In the event some vessels were equipped with mountings taken from other vessels which were being withdrawn from service or had been too badly damaged to be repaired.

The Admiralty originally planned to build 26 'Bay' class vessels but in fact only one was completed before VE-day and only another seven before VJ-Day. As most of the vessels were in an advanced stage of construction, only one was cancelled and 19 were completed as designed. A further six were completed to different designs, two as despatch vessels and four as surveying ships. Of the 19 completed as frigates, all were completed by the autumn of 1946 with the exception of *Morecombe Bay* and *Mounts Bay*. Launched by the builders, W. Pickersgill of Sunderland, in 1944 and 1945 respectively, they were not finally completed until 1949 by other shipbuilders. *Morcambe Bay* was completed by J. Samuel White at Cowes and *Mounts Bay* by J. I. Thornycroft at Woolston, Southampton.

Following the end of hostilities, several of the class were consigned to the Reserve Fleet, but others continued in commission, particularly in the Far East where their heavy gun armament made them ideal for peacetime patrol work. Their excellent seakeeping qualities were demonstrated on several occasions when they rode out the fierce typhoons which were a common hazard in that area.

In 1950 *Carnarvon Bay, Cawsand Bay, Enard Bay, Largo Bay, Padstow Bay, Porlock Bay, Start Bay, Widemouth Bay* and *Wigtown Bay* were in reserve, while *Tremadoc Bay* was being used for training purposes. The class was represented at the Coronation Review by *Burghead Bay, Enard Bay, Largo Bay, Start Bay* and *Widemouth Bay. Start Bay* was still part of the Reserve Fleet at this time and appeared at the rerview with her armament cocooned.

By the mid-1950s the usefulness of the class as front line warships was declining. The 4in guns and World War 2 fire control system were no match for the new generations of jet aircraft and the ships' relatively low speed and rudimentary AS equipment was of little effective use against modern submarines. The modernisation of the 'Loch' class had produced ships with adequate firepower for peacetime patrolling while at the same time their twin Squid mortars still retained a useful AS capability. In consequence it was no surprise when *St Austell Bay* and *Whitesand Bay* went to the breakers in early 1956 having seen only 10 years' service since their completion. The next year two more of the class, *Enards Bay* and *Widemouth Bay*, also went to the breakers. At the same time other vessels of the class were still active with, for example, *Burghead Bay* commissioned in May 1957 for service in the south Atlantic, *Mounts Bay* commissioning in October 1956 also for the south Atlantic, and *Cardigan Bay* commissioning at Singapore in November 1956 for further service in the Far East.

Several ships of the class were sold abroad. *Bigbury Bay* and *Burghead Bay* were transferred to the Portuguese Navy on 11 May 1959 and renamed *Pacheco Pereira* and *Alvares Cabral* respectively. Two years later, following a refit by J. I. Thornycroft, *Mounts Bay* and *Morecombe Bay* were also transferred to the Portuguese Navy and renamed *Vasco da Gama* and *Dom Francesco de Almeida.* In 1962 *Porlock Bay*, one of the last two remaining Royal Navy vessels, was transferred to the Finnish Navy and renamed *Matti Kurki.* The other vessel, *Cardigan Bay*, went to the scrapyard in 1962 as well.

As previously mentioned, several uncompleted hulls were adapted for other uses following the end of the war. Two of these, *Dundrum Bay* and *Gerrans Bay*, were completed as despatch vessels and renamed *Alert* and *Surprise.* As completed, the forward half of the ship was identical to the frigate, including the forward 4in gun mounting. Aft of the funnel all armament was deleted and extra accommodation was added on the quarterdeck. Above this the forecastle deck was extended to the stern giving a large open platform. Following their completion the two ships were allocated as commander-in-chief's yachts; *Alert* to the China Station and *Surprise* to the Mediterranean. In 1953, *Surprise* returned to the United Kingdom where she underwent modifications to act as Royal Yacht at the Fleet Coronation Review in 1953. Her forward gun mounting was removed and a special platform constructed in its place for Her Majesty to use as a reviewing stand. During the review she flew the Royal Standard as well as the flag of the Flag Officer, Royal Yachts, Vice-Adm E. M. C. Abel Smith CB, CVO. Following this occasion she reverted to her original configuration and returned to the Mediterranean. The open deck aft was useful for the ceremonial occasions associated with the presence of a commander-in-chief but, in later years, was used as a helicopter landing deck for transferring visitors and stores. Although not strictly frigates, the two vessels retained their frigate pendant numbers (F647 *Alert* and F436 *Surprise*) until their disposal in 1965 and 1971. By this time of course, the Royal Navy had shrunk to a size where luxuries such as commander-in-chief's yachts could not be justified or afforded.

Four other vessels (*Herne Bay*, *Luce Bay*, *Pegwell Bay*, *Thurso Bay*) were completed as survey ships and were renamed *Dampier*, *Dalrymple*, *Cook* and *Owen*. The conversion of the incomplete hulls was carried out by Chatham Dockyard in the case of *Dampier* and *Owen*, while the other two were completed by Devonport Dockyard. All four vessels were commissioned between 1948 and 1950.

The importance of the 'Loch/Bay' class to postwar frigate development lay not in their capabilities. Indeed, in the early 1950s they were officially classed as 'Second Rate Frigates' in recognition of the fact that they were eclipsed by the new postwar designs. Their unique feature was that they demonstrated that it was possible to produce by a dispersed organisation a range of specialised frigates based on a common hull and machinery produced to standard design criteria. The success of this concept, which was amply demonstrated by the wide variety of uses the standard hull was put to, resulted in a determined effort to produce a new range of bigger, faster and more capable frigates based again on a common hull. This was to lead to the 1945 frigate concept, to which reference will be made in the following chapters.

Name	Number	Builders	Laid Down	Launched	Completed	Remarks
Bigbury Bay	K606/F06	Hall Russell (Aberdeen)	30/5/44	16/11/44	10/7/45	Portuguese Navy 1959. Sold 6/7/70 and scrapped.
Burghead Bay	K622/F622	Charles Hill and Sons, Bristol	21/9/44	3/3/45	20/9/45	Portuguese Navy 1959. Sold 23/6/71 and scrapped.
Cardigan Bay	K630/F630	H. Robb, Leith	14/4/44	28/12/44	25/6/45	Sold West of Scotland Shipbreaking. Arrived Troon for scrapping 5/3/62.
Carnarvon Bay	K636/F636	H. Robb, Leith	8/6/44	15/3/45	20/9/45	Sold Italy. Arrived La Spezia 28/8/59 for scrap.
Cawsand Bay	K644/F644	Blyth Shipbuilding Co	24/4/44	26/2/45	13/11/45	Sold Italy. Arrived Genoa 5/9/59 for scrapping.
Enard Bay	K435/F35	Smiths Dock, Middlesbrough	27/5/44	31/10/44	4/1/46	Sold Shipbreaking Industries. Arrived Faslane 15/11/57 for scrapping.
Largo Bay	K423/F423	W. Pickersgill, Sunderland	8/2/44	3/10/44	26/1/46	Sold to T. W. Ward. Arrived Inverkeithing 11/7/58 for scrapping.
Morecombe Bay	K624/F624	W. Pickersgill, Sunderland	30/4/44	1/11/44	22/2/49	Portuguese Navy 1961. Sold 7/9/70 and scrapped.
Mounts Bay	K627/F627	W. Pickersgill, Sunderland	23/10/44	8/6/45	11/4/49	Portuguese Navy 1961. Sold 2/12/71 and scrapped.
Padstow Bay	K608/F608	H. Robb, Leith	25/9/44	24/8/45	11/3/46	Sold Italy. Arrived La Spezia 11/8/59 for scrap.
Porlock Bay	K650/F650	Charles Hill and Sons, Bristol	22/11/44	14/6/45	8/3/46	Finnish Navy 1962. Discarded 1975.
St Austell Bay	K634/F634	Harland and Wolff, Belfast	30/5/44	18/11/44	29/5/45	Sold Shipbreaking Industries. Arrived Charlestown 13/2/56 for scrap.
St Brides Bay	K600/F600	Harland and Wolff, Belfast	30/5/44	16/1/45	15/6/45	Sold Shipbreaking Industries. Arrived Faslane 3/9/62 for scrapping.
Start Bay	K604/F604	Harland and Wolff, Belfast	31/8/44	15/2/45	6/9/45	Sold J. Cashmore. Arrived Newport 7/58 for scrap.

19
HMS *Whitesand Bay* enters Portsmouth in September 1954, prior to paying off into reserve. She carries a Type 293 radar at the top of the lattice mast and a Type 285 on her gunnery director. The Type 291 originally carried at the masthead has been removed but extra 40mm guns are carried on the quarterdeck making a total of eight 40mm in all. *Wright and Logan*

20
The last 'Bay' class in service with the Royal Navy was HMS *Cardigan Bay* seen here steaming past HMS *Albion*. Note the HF/DF on the top of the foremast and that there are no 40mm guns on the quarterdeck. In the foreground can be seen two Sea Venom FAW Mk 22 fighters of No 894 Naval Air Squadron; photograph taken c1960. *Fleet Photographic Unit*

Name	Number	Builders	Laid Down	Launched	Completed	Remarks
Tremadoc Bay	K605/F605	Harland and Wolff, Belfast	31/8/44	29/3/45	11/10/45	Sold Italy. Arrived Genoa 18/9/59 for scrapping.
Veryan Bay	K651/F651	Charles Hill and Sons, Bristol	8/6/44	11/11/44	13/5/45	Sold Shipbreaking Industries. Arrived Charlestown 1/7/59 for scrapping.
Whitesand Bay	K633/F633	Harland and Wolff, Belfast	8/8/44	16/12/44	30/7/45	Sold Shipbreaking Industries. Arrived Charlestown 13/2/56 for scrapping.
Widemouth Bay	K615/F615	Harland and Wolff, Belfast	26/4/44	19/10/44	13/4/45	Sold Hughes Bolckow. Arrived Blyth 23/11/57 for scrapping.
Wigtown Bay	K616/F616	Harland and Wolff, Belfast	24/10/44	26/4/45	19/1/46	Sold Shipbreaking Industries. Arrived Faslane 4/59 for scrapping.
Alert	K647/F647	Blyth Shipbuilding Co	28/7/44	10/7/45	24/10/46	Sold T. W. Ward. Arrived Inverkeithing 31/10/71 for scrapping.
Surprise	K436/F436	Smiths Dock, Middlesbrough	21/4/44	14/3/45	9/9/46	Sold P. and W. McLellan, Arrived Bo'ness for scrapping 29/6/65

Data: As completed
Displacement: 1,600 tons standard; 2,530 tons full load
Length: 307ft oa
Beam: $38\frac{1}{2}$ft
Draught: $12\frac{3}{4}$ft
Guns: 4×4in (2×2) AA in Mk XVI mountings
6×40mm (2×2, 2×1) AA
Alert and *Surprise* had only 2×4in (1×2) and 2×40mm (2×1)
AS weapons: 1×Hedgehog multiple spigot mortar. Depth charge throwers and rails.
Machinery: 2×Admiralty three-drum boilers operating at 225lb/sq in
Four-cylinder triple expansion engines driving two shafts giving a total of 5,500ihp
Speed: $19\frac{1}{2}$kts
Oil fuel: 720 tons
Complement: 157

21
HMS *Start Bay* was one of the ships representing the Reserve Fleet at Spithead in 1953. She still carries her Type 291 radar at the very top of the foremast and HF/DF on a pole mast aft. *Skyfotos*

2 The Conversions

Type 15 (Full Conversion) Frigates

At the close of World War 2, the progress shown by German submarine design had come as a shock to the Allies. The Type XXI, for example, had an underwater speed of nearly 17kts and was equipped with a variety of torpedoes including acoustic homing weapons specifically intended for use against escort vessels. The peroxide-powered Type XXVI was even faster. Against this sort of opposition, the 19kts of the standard 'Loch' class escort was hopelessly inadequate. By 1950, the Soviet Navy had absorbed the lessons of captured German technology and was embarking on a massive production programme of the 'Whisky' class submarine which was, in effect, a straightforward copy of the German Type XXI.

With the end of hostilities in Europe, Allied naval intelligence staff were able to unfold the story of German submarine development and the Admiralty embarked on a programme designed to produce an AS vessel capable of meeting the threat posed by the new types of submarines. In the immediate postwar period the development of new weapon systems had little financial priority and consequently progress was slow. Events in the late 1940s, such as the imposition of the Churchillian-termed 'Iron Curtain', the Berlin Airlift and the start of the Korean War, led to the realisation that the world was not about to lapse into a period of utopian peace and that it was necessary to bring our armed forces up to date. Although modern frigate designs were being finalised, it would take many years before the first of these could be in service and a faster and less expensive method was needed to provide an immediate boost to our outdated AS forces.

The answer lay in the large numbers of wartime destroyers which were in service or reserve with the Royal Navy. Starting with the 'O' class, the first of which was laid down in 1940, 80 destroyers comprising the 'O', 'P', 'Q', 'R', 'S', 'T', 'U', 'V', 'W' and 'Z' classes were built to a basically standard design. Also built were a further 32 vessels of the 'Ca', 'Ch', 'Co' and 'Cr' classes to a similar standard design. There were several variations of layout, armament and equipment, but the hull and machinery was virtually identical in all classes. Although some were sunk during the war and others were sold to foreign and Commonwealth navies in the years immediately following the cessation of hostilities, by 1951 47 remained with the Royal Navy as well as 26 of the 'C' class vessels. Most of the remaining ships had seen relatively little war service and were consequently in very good condition.

Accordingly, plans were drawn up to convert the basic destroyer design to a fast AS frigate. The first pair of vessels to undergo reconstruction were *Relentless* at Portsmouth dockyard and *Rocket* at Devonport starting in 1949. All superstructure, masts and armament were removed and the hull was stripped of equipment and the machinery overhauled. The forecastle deck was then extended aft to leave only a small quarterdeck. Forward of the funnel, a new superstructure was constructed across the full width of the hull and extended forward to end in a bridge with a rounded front. The new superstructure housed a spacious operations room with new radar display and communications equipment. There was also a separate sonar room and the extended forecastle deck provided much improved and more spacious accommodation for the crew. One of the problems of wartime escort vessels had been the limited and cramped accommodation which, in bad weather, seriously affected the efficiency of the crew. With the new design, strenuous efforts were made to alleviate this by giving the sailors much improved living space as well as a modern catering system. The extended forecastle deck meant that the crew could move about the ship to their duty stations without being exposed to the weather. In fact, apart from the gun crews, the ship could be operated and fought with the crew entirely under cover. This was done not only for reasons of crew comfort but also to give the ship a limited capability to operate in zones of nuclear fallout, a factor which was to play an increasingly important part in postwar warship design.

Extensive use was made of aluminium in the reconstruction of the ships; this enabled extra superstructure areas to be added without affecting stability adversely. Many postwar designs, both British and foreign, featured aluminium superstructure sections but recently a note of caution has restricted the use of this material. This followed a serious fire on the USS *Belknap* in 1975 where, following a collision, the entire upper superstructure literally disappeared as the aluminium itself burnt away.

As befitted their new role as frigates, the ships were

given a completely new armament. The main gun armament consisted of two 4in guns in a Mk XIX twin mounting which was unusually positioned aft of the main superstructure and just forward of the quarterdeck. As such, the Type 15s became the first major British warships to have an aft-mounted main armament, a feature which gave rise to lively discussion at the time! The fire of the 4in guns was controlled by an MRS-1 director positioned just forward of the gun mounting and incorporating a Type 262 centimetric gunnery radar. Above and behind the bridge a twin 40mm Mk V (Utility) mounting was carried with fire control being provided by an STD (simple tachymetric director) mounted on a raised platform just abaft of the guns. The guns were intended mainly for AA use and in this respect the Type 15s were better off than the original destroyer design despite carrying fewer guns. The reason for this was that the original destroyer armament of four 4.5in guns had only a limited elevation, whereas the 4in Mk XIX was a true high angle mounting and was provided with a proper radar-equipped fire control system.

As frigates, the main function of these vessels was to attack submarines and to this end a heavy AS armament was carried. On the quarterdeck, just below the 4in gun mounting, were two Limbo AS three-barrelled mortars. Limbo was a development of the wartime Squid, but fired its projectile over a greater range and could be reloaded, aimed and fired by remote control. After firing the mounting was tilted on to its side so that the barrels were horizontal and in line with the loading apertures of the mortar handling rooms alongside the mountings. Hydraulic rams pushed new projectiles into the barrels which were then returned to the firing position. The Limbo was aimed and fired from the new operations room in the forward superstructure. As a weapons system, Limbo was very successful and remained in operational use for over 30 years.

As part of her conversion, *Relentless* was fitted with two single torpedo tubes on trainable mountings installed on the upper deck on either beam just abaft the mainmast. These tubes were intended to fire the then new Mk 20E torpedo which was an electrically powered acoustic homing weapon intended for anti-submarine use. As the torpedo was still under development, the tubes fitted on *Relentless* were probably intended for trials use only and they were subsequently removed when the ship was refitted in 1955/56. Unlike the Limbo system, the Mk 20E torpedo was a complete failure which was mainly due to the fact that it was too slow to catch fast moving submarines. Despite this, several vessels in later classes of postwar frigates were equipped to fire the torpedoes and the idea finally died out around 1960 when the tubes were removed from all vessels then so fitted.

The original tripod foremast was removed and a new lattice mast was stepped to carry new radar and communication equipment. Atop this was the ANS aerial for a Type 293Q 10cm radar which provided target information for the MRS-1 fire control system. Below this, on a small platform projecting forward of the lattice structure, was the Type 974 navigation radar aerial. Forward of the foremast and mounted atop a deckhouse was the distinctively shaped ANU aerial for the Type 277Q surface warning radar which, as its name implied, was used for the detection of surface targets including submarine snorkels or periscopes. A pole extension to the foremast carried the HF/DF aerial while both VHF and UHF communication aerials were carried on the foremast and on a short lattice mainmast stepped amidships. Several 'whip' aerials were mounted on the funnel sides and at various points around the superstructure. These aerials were to become a familiar feature of all postwar ships and replaced the previous wire aerials which were strung between the masts. They were much more resistant to blast and battle damage.

A total of 23 vessels was converted as described and, inevitably in such a large programme, there were several variations within the class. Three vessels (*Troubridge*, *Ulster*, *Zest*) were completed with a different bridge structure which was mounted a deck higher and further back than the round faced bridge of the other vessels. The new structure did not extend the full width of the ship and featured angled sides to give better all round visibility to the bridge staff. The new structure was almost identical to the bridge fitted to the subsequent Types 12, 14, 41, 61 and 81 frigates and for this reason became known as the 'frigate' bridge.

The new bridge displaced the twin 40mm mounting which was now positioned at the forward end of the superstructure in front of the bridge.

The type of AS weapon fitted was also subject to variation. As already related, *Relentless* and *Rocket* (the prototype conversions) were equipped with the Limbo AS mortar but the other two 'R' class converted (*Rapid* and *Roebuck*) had two Squid mortars installed in lieu. *Troubridge*, the only 'T' class to be converted to a Type 15 frigate, was Limbo-equipped as were all 'U' class conversions including *Grenville.* The nine 'V' and 'W' class vessels were given the Squid mounting and *Zest*, the only 'Z' class converted, was equipped with Limbo.

It had been envisaged that, following the trials aboard *Relentless*, the Type 15 frigates would carry an AS torpedo armament but in the event only *Ulster* was fully equipped. Eight tubes were carried in fixed single mountings installed on each beam abreast the mainmast. Each tube was angled to fire 45° forward of the

22
HMS *Ulster*, seen here as a destroyer in 1950, is representative of the 23 wartime standard destroyers converted to fast AS frigates. *Wright and Logan*

23
The first of the new Type 15 frigates was HMS *Relentless*, which gave her name to the class. She is seen here at Devonport in July 1951 just after the completion of her conversion. The AS torpedo tubes carried amidships were removed at her first refit.
Wright and Logan

24
HMS *Troubridge* was one of three Type 15 frigates fitted with the so called 'frigate' bridge which necessitated the moving of the twin 40mm mounting to a position forward of the bridge. *Wright and Logan*

HMS RELENTLESS. 2300 tons.

Type 15 (Full Conversion) Frigate.

1953.

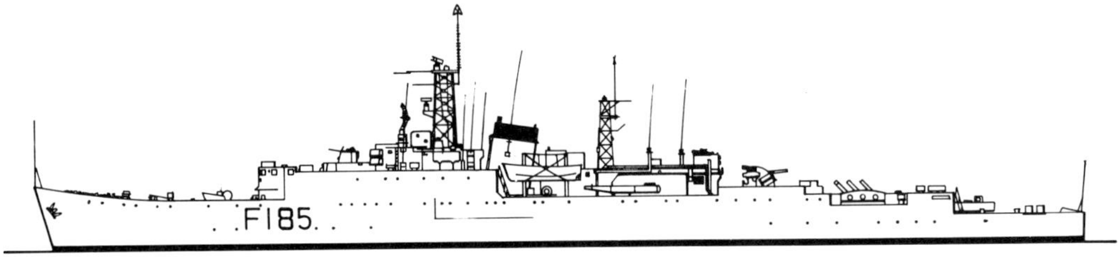

BUILDERS - J. BROWN and Co. Ltd.
LAID DOWN - 20th JUN 1941.
LAUNCHED - 15th JUL 1942.
COMPLETED - 30th NOV 1942.

Converted to Type 15 Frigate
at Portsmouth Dockyard
1949 to 1951.

LENGTH - 358 ft. o.a.
BEAM - 35·75 ft.
DRAUGHT - 14·5 ft.
SPEED - 31 knots.

©

beam on each side. The tubes were removed after a while (probably 1961) when the Mk 20E torpedo was finally abandoned. The only other ship of the class to carry any AS torpedo tubes was *Undaunted*, which in 1958 carried three fixed tubes on the starboard beam but these were subsequently removed.

Undaunted was also one of two Type 15's to be fitted with a helicopter landing platform built up over the stern. The other one so fitted was *Grenville* and the work was carried out in the period 1957/59. Using these flight decks, trials were carried out with three prototype Saunders Roe P531 turbine-powered light helicopters. These operations were the first occasion when a frigate carried and operated a helicopter and, following the successful conclusion of the trials, an uprated version of the P531 was ordered in quantity for the Royal Navy. The new version became the Westland Wasp and was operated by all subsequent helicopter-equipped frigates up to and including the Type 21. *Grenville's* flight deck was removed after a few years but *Undaunted* retained her's until the end of her career.

After conversion to Type 15 frigates, several vessels were further modified to act as training vessels and were mostly allocated to the Dartmouth Training Squadron where they were used to give sea experience to officer cadets. The modifications involved the removal of the twin 40mm mounting and the construction of an open bridge over the existing enclosed bridge. An additional deckhouse was constructed in the space previously occupied by the 40mm guns. Vessels so modified were *Venus* and *Vigilant* in 1955, followed by *Roebuck* and *Wakeful* in 1958/59. *Wakeful* subsequently had her 4in gun turret removed and extra deckhouses added aft.

Several vessels of the class were converted to act as trials and training vessels. Following the helicopter trials, *Grenville* went on to act as a trials ship for the Admiralty Surface Weapons Establishment at Portsmouth. Her 4in guns and AS mortars were removed and extra deckhouses erected aft. An extra mast was stepped in the position previously occupied by the 4in gun turret and this was used to mount experimental radio and radar equipment. Eventually the third mast was itself replaced by a massive lattice structure almost as tall as the foremast and on this was mounted the aerial of a long range surveillance radar. This was probably an early version of the Type 1022 radar now being fitted to the later Type 42 destroyers and to the new 'Invincible' class aircraft carriers. For the trials role *Grenville* was also fitted with the enlarged open bridge over the original bridge and a glazed observation tower just in front of the foremast. *Verulam* was also used as an AS trials vessel and had her 4in guns removed and additional deckhouses added. In 1966, following a refit when her damaged stern was replaced by a section taken from *Urchin, Ulster* was used as trials and training ship by ASWE. Her 40mm mount-

25
This view of HMS *Zest*, the only 'Z' class destroyer to be converted to a frigate, clearly shows the arrangement of the two Limbo AS mortars. The small dish aerial of the Type 262 radar can be seen on the MRS-1 fire control director mounted above the Mk XIX twin 4in mounting.
Fleet Photographic Unit

26
HMS *Virago* (foreground) and HMS *Venus* in 1962 when *Venus* was serving with the Dartmouth Training Squadron. Note the larger bridge fitted on *Venus* for training purposes compared with the standard layout of *Virago* which was serving with the 17th Frigate Squadron at the time this photograph was taken.
Fleet Photographic Unit

ing was removed but otherwise her appearance was unaltered.

Rapid was at one time used as the seagoing training ship for HMS *Caledonia* at Rosyth. This establishment was responsible for the training of engineroom artificers and consequently her machinery was in first class order although her armament had been removed. She enjoyed a brief moment of glory when she took part in a race against HMS *Cavalier* for the title of 'Fastest Ship in the Fleet'. The race took place in July 1971 off the Firth of Forth, with the object being to cover the greatest distance in two hours. Although leading for most of the time, a boiler safety valve lifting caused a loss of boiler pressure which allowed *Cavalier* to creep ahead and win by the slenderest of margins. *Rapid* was subsequently converted to a target ship in 1974 and ended her days in this role.

Commencing in 1949, the conversion programme continued until 1957 with *Troubridge* being the last to complete. Some vessels were converted at the naval dockyards, but many were contracted out to private companies. Dates and places of conversion, together with the fate of each vessel (where known) are set out below:

Rapid converted Alex Stephens and Sons, Glasgow, 1952/53. Expended as a target 1981.

Relentless converted Portsmouth Dockyard 1949/51. Broken up T. W. Ward, Inverkeithing, 1971.

Rocket converted Devonport Dockyard, 1949/51. Sold W. H. Arnott Young; arrived Dalmuir March 1967 for scrapping.

Roebuck converted Devonport Dockyard 1952/53. Sold T. W. Ward; arrived Inverkeithing 8/8/68 for scrapping.

Troubridge converted Portsmouth Dockyard/ J. Samuel White, Cowes 1955/57. Broken up J. Cashmore, Newport, 1970.

Ulster converted Chatham dockyard 1953/56. Training hulk HMS *Ralaigh*, Torpoint, 1977-80. Broken up T. W. Ward, Inverkeithing 1980/81.

Ulysses converted Devonport Dockyard 1952/53. Broken up Plymouth, 1970.

Grenville converted private yard 1953/54. Paid off Easter 1974. Laid up Portsmouth for disposal. Broken up 1983.

Undaunted converted J. Samuel White, Cowes, 1952/54. Sunk as target off Gibraltar by combined missile and torpedo attack from HMS *Norfolk* and HMS *Swiftsure* (SSN), 1978.

Undine converted J. I. Thornycroft, Woolston, 1954. Sold J. Cashmore, Newport; arrived for scrapping 14/11/65.

Urania converted Harland and Wolff, Liverpool, 1953/54. Broken up Shipbuilding Industries, Faslane, 1971.

Urchin converted Barclay Curle 1952/54. Stern section cut off in 1966 to repair *Ulster* (qv). Sold West of Scotland Shipbreaking; arrived Troon 6/8/67 for scrapping.

Ursa converted Palmer, 1953/54. Sold J. Cashmore, Newport; arrived for scrapping September 1957.

Venus converted 1952/54 Devonport Dockyard. Broken up Briton Ferry 1972.

Verulam converted Portsmouth Dockyard 1952. Broken up J. Cashmore, Newport, 1972.

Vigilant converted J. I. Thornycroft 1951/52. Sold Shipbreaking Industries, Faslane; arrived 4/6/65 for scrap.

Virago converted 1952/53 Chatham Dockyard. Sold Shipbreaking Industries, Faslane; arrived 4/6/65.

Volage converted J. Samuel White, Cowes, 1951/52. Broken up Portsmouth Shipbreakers, 1972.

Wakeful converted Scotts, Greenock, 1952/53. Broken up T. W. Ward, Inverkeithing, 1971.

Whirlwind converted Palmers. 1952/53. Expended as target. Sank at moorings October 1974.

Wizard converted Devonport Dockyard, 1954. Sold T. W. Ward, Inverkeithing; arrived 7/3/67 for scrapping.

Wrangler converted Harland and Wolff, Belfast 1951/52. Sold to South Africa 1957 and expended as a target, April 1976.

Zest converted Chatham Dockyard, 1954/56. Broken up W. H. Arnott Young, Dalmuir, 1970.

Several other conversions were carried out by Commonwealth navies on destroyers which had previously been transferred to them. *Quiberon, Quickmatch, Queenborough* and *Quadrant* had been transferred to the Royal Australian Navy in 1945 and were converted to Type 15 frigates in the period 1952-57. The first pair were converted at Williamstown and the other two at Cockatoo Island. The Australian conversions differed slightly from the British versions in that the bridge structure was a deck higher and set further back with the twin 40mm mounting positioned in front of it. Two conversions were carried out by the Royal Canadian Navy, which had two suitable vessels — the *Algonquin* (ex-HMS *Valentine* which transferred to the RCN on completion in 1944) and *Crescent*. Again there were minor differences from the British design: both vessels carried a twin 3in AA mounting instead of the 40mm mounting, with *Crescent* carrying the 4in mount forward and the 3in aft. Both vessels had enlarged bridges, two single 40mm guns and AS torpedo tubes. *Algonquin* was converted at Esquimault Dockyard in 1954 with *Crescent* following in 1956. *Crescent* was the only one of the 32 'C' class destroyers to undergo conversion to become a fast AS frigate.

As rebuilt, the new frigates were excellent AS

27
HMS *Undaunted* at speed in the English Channel in 1971. She was one of two Type 15 frigates fitted with a helicopter flight deck for early trials to test the viability of operating helicopters from warships. At the time of this photograph she was acting as leader of the 2nd Training Squadron and her after 4in gun mounting has been replaced by a deckhouse aft. Close inspection will reveal a Morris Mini parked on the deck just behind the mainmast. *Undaunted* must have been the only frigate to carry her own shoregoing transport! *Skyfotos*

28
Stripped of all armament except the Limbo AS mortars, HMS *Ulster* is seen here serving as a training vessel in 1971. The 'frigate' type bridge fitted to this ship (as well as *Troubridge* and *Zest*) can be clearly seen. It is interesting to compare this picture with the earlier photo showing *Ulster* as a destroyer. *Skyfotos*

29
HMS *Grenville* spent her last active years as a trials ship for the Admiralty Surface Weapons Establishment (ASWE). Already fitted with the larger bridge, she was further modified by the removal of her 4in guns and the addition of an after deckhouse and a weatherproof observation platform in front of the foremast. Although not shown in this photograph provision was made for a third mast to be erected in front of the after deckhouse to carry various pieces of trials equipment. *HMS Osprey*

vessels. The new design showed a thoughtful appreciation of the factors affecting AS warfare in the postwar period and they provided an effective boost for the Royal Navy's escort capability at a vital period in the Cold War of the 1950s and 1960s. There was perhaps some disappointment for traditionalists, both naval and civilian. Gone were the rakish destroyers bristling with guns and torpedo tubes, and in their place came ships looking like no other warships before them. Clean lines and few guns were the result of the changing face of naval warfare where detection and ranging equipment was almost more important than the weapons themselves. The Type 15 conversions set the scene for the development of the modern postwar frigate and subsequent designs built upon the lessons learnt with this class. The conversions represented excellent value for money and they gave a new lease of life to destroyer hulls which otherwise would probably have been discarded and scrapped much earlier. As it was, it was not until 1965 that the first of the class went to the breakers with many vessels continuing into the 1970s carrying out useful tasks as training and trials ships.

Name	No	Builders	Laid Down	Launched	Completed
Rapid	F138	Cammell Laird	16/6/41	16/7/42	20/2/43
Relentless	F185	J. Brown and Co Ltd	20/6/41	15/7/42	30/11/42
Rocket	F191	Scotts (Greenock)	14/3/41	28/10/42	4/8/43
Roebuck	F195	Scotts (Greenock)	19/6/41	10/12/42	10/6/43
Troubridge	F09	J. Brown and Co Ltd	10/11/41	23/9/42	8/3/43
Grenville	F197	Swan Hunter, Tyne	1/11/41	12/10/42	27/5/43
Ulster	F83	Swan Hunter, Tyne	12/11/41	9/11/42	30/6/43
Ulysses	F17	Cammell Laird	14/3/42	22/4/43	23/12/43
Undaunted	F53	Cammell Laird	8/9/42	19/7/43	3/3/44
Undine	F141	Thornycroft (Woolston)	18/3/42	1/6/43	23/12/43
Urania	F08	Vickers Armstrong, (Barrow)	18/6/42	19/5/43	18/1/44
Urchin	F196	Vickers Armstrong, (Barrow)	26/3/42	8/3/43	24/9/43
Ursa	F200	J. I. Thornycroft, (Woolston)	2/5/42	22/7/43	1/3/44
Venus	F50	Fairfield (Govan)	12/1/42	23/2/43	28/8/43
Verulam	F29	Fairfield (Govan)	26/1/42	22/4/43	10/12/43
Vigilant	F93	Swan Hunter, Tyne	31/1/42	22/12/42	10/9/43
Virago	F76	Swan Hunter, Tyne	16/2/42	4/2/43	5/11/43
Volage	F41	J. Samuel White, (Cowes)	31/12/42	15/12/43	26/5/44
Wakelful	F159	Fairfield (Govan)	3/6/42	30/6/43	17/2/44
Whirlwind	F187	Hawthorn Leslie Ltd	31/7/42	30/8/43	20/7/44
Wizard	F72	Vickers Armstrong, (Barrow)	14/9/42	29/9/43	30/3/44
Wrangler	F157	Vickers Armstrong, (Barrow)	23/9/42	30/12/43	14/7/44
Zest	F102	J. I. Thornycroft, (Woolston)	21/7/42	14/10/43	20/7/44

Data: 'R' class as destroyers
Displacement: 1,705 tons standard; 2,425 tons full load
Length: 358ft oa
Beam: 35$\frac{3}{4}$ft
Draught: 13$\frac{1}{2}$ft (max)
Guns: 4×4.7in Mk IX (4×1) on CP XVIII mounting
1×2pdr quadruple pom-pom AA
6×20mm AA
2×0.303 MG
Torpedoes: 8×21in tubes (2×4)
AS weapons: 4×depth charge throwers (4×1) and two stern ramps
70 depth charges carried
Machinery: 2×Admiralty three-drum boilers working at 300lb/sq in and 630°F, driving two shafts through Parsons single reduction turbines, giving a total of 40,000shp
Speed: 36kts (32kts at full load)
Complement: 176

Data: 'R' class Type 15 conversion
Displacement: 2,300 tons standard; 2,700 tons full load
Dimensions: As originally built except full load displacement increased to 14$\frac{1}{2}$ft
Guns: 2×4in guns (1×2) on Mk XIX mounting
2×40mm AA (1×2) on Mk V (Utility) mounting
AS weapons: Two Limbo or Two Squid AS mortars (see text for variations)
2×21in torpedo tubes (2×1) firing Mk 20E acoustic homing torpedoes (*Relentless* only)
Sonar: Types 170 and 174
Machinery: As originally fitted
Speed: 31kts full load
Complement: 174

Type 16 (Limited Conversion) Frigates

Following the trial conversion of *Relentless* and *Rocket* to Type 15 frigates, a major programme was put in hand in 1951 to convert a total of 44 wartime destroyers to 'Fast Anti-Submarine Frigates'. The original plan called for 24 Type 15 conversions (only 23 were actually carried out for the Royal Navy) but time and money did not permit the full reconstruction to be applied to the other 20. A scheme for a cheaper and less extensive conversion was therefore drawn up, and the ships rebuilt to this standard were designated Type 16 (Limited Conversion) frigates. In the event, only 10 destroyers were rebuilt as Type 16s. This was mainly for financial reasons as the Royal Navy was also involved at the time in a major new ship building programme. In view of their limited capabilities, compared with the Type 15 frigates and new constructions, the Type 16 conversions were given a relatively low financial priority and were intended very much as a stopgap measure until more modern vessels could be brought into service.

The work involved in the reconstruction was relatively straightforward. The original destroyer main armament of 4.7in guns (4in guns in *Paladin* and *Petard*) was removed as was the mixed collection of AA guns which included 20mm, 40mm and 2pdr weapons. All ships retained their after quadruple bank of 21in torpedo tubes but the forward set, where still fitted, was removed. All depth charge rails and throwers were also removed. The tripod foremast was removed and replaced by a lattice structure to carry new radar equipment; except for *Teazer*, *Tenacious*, *Termagent* and *Terpsichore* which had been originally completed with a lattice mast.

All ships retained their standard destroyer machinery and their performance was consequently unaltered. The standard open bridge was retained on all vessels except *Teazer, Tumult* and *Terpsichore*, which were given a fully enclosed frigate type bridge surmounted by an open searchlight platform. The enclosed bridge, which had been a standard feature of most American wartime destroyers, only began to appear in the Royal Navy at this time and was a significant factor in increasing crew efficiency in adverse weather conditions. The only argument in favour of open bridges was the much superior visibility but this was not so important in the postwar period when radar had virtually taken over as the only significant target detection system. In those Type 16s equipped with the enclosed bridge, a small operations room was installed immediately below, but this was nowhere near as large or comprehensively equipped as in the Type 15 conversions.

Forward of the bridge, in B position, a twin 4in Mk XIX mounting was installed. Fixed rails on the side of the turret were used for carrying and firing 2in rockets which were used for target illumination purposes. A rudimentary optical director mounted above the bridge provided the fire control system (compare with the radar-equipped MRS-1 fire control system installed in the Type 15 frigates). A light AA armament of seven 40mm AA guns was carried. A Mk V twin mounting with an associated STD was installed on the superstructure island which had separated the torpedo tubes, and five Mk IX single mountings were carried, one in each bridge wing, one right aft on the quarterdeck, and two on the after steering platform just abaft the funnel.

AS armament consisted of two Squid AS mortars installed on the after superstructure in the position previously occupied by X gun. A rectangular deckhouse aft of the Squids was the mortar handling room. Here mortar bombs were brought up by hoist from a magazine below, prepared for firing, and run out on rails to a position alongside the Squid mounting. The mounting was tilted on to its side and the mortar bomb rammed by hand into the mortar tube. This process must have been fraught with difficulty on a pitching and rolling deck in bad weather and it was for this reason that the Limbo system was developed where the loading process was carried out automatically with the handling crew under cover. The set of four 21in torpedo tubes was retained and fired the standard Mk 9 torpedoes intended for use against surface targets, although it was hoped that a suitable AS homing torpedo would be developed which could be fired from the tubes. In the event this did not happen, although in 1955/56 *Terpsichore* was fitted with two single trainable mountings, one on each boom. These were probably for trials with the Mk 20E torpedo which was later withdrawn from service.

The radar fit was modernised with a Type 293Q surface warning radar mounted at the top of the lattice foremast and a Type 974 navigational radar on a forward projecting platform below. IFF transponder and interrogator aerials were mounted on the foremast and an air warning radar on a short polemast erected on the after deckhouse. HF/DF was carried at the top of the foremast and UHF and VHF communication aerials were mounted on the foremast cross-trees. Several communication 'whip' aerials were mounted on the funnel sides and around the bridge. A comprehensive sonar fit included Type 146B search, Type 147P depth finder, Type 162 bottom target classifier and Type 174 mortar control.

H.M.S. TUMULT. 1,800 tons.

Type 16 (Limited Conversion) Frigate.

1956.

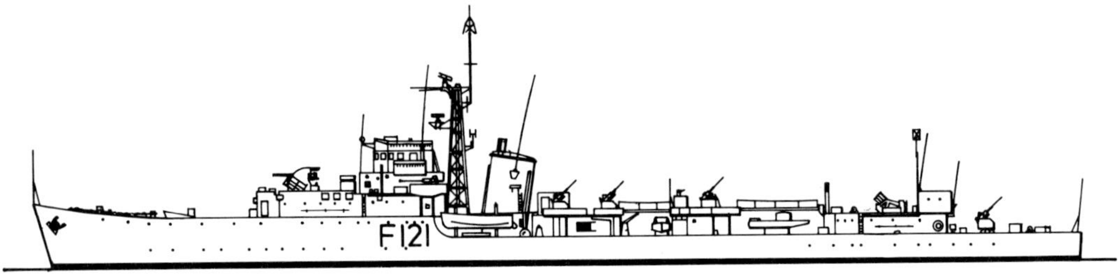

BUILDERS - J. Brown and Co. Ltd.
LAID DOWN - 16th Nov 1941.
LAUNCHED - 9th Nov 1942.
COMPLETED - 2nd Apr 1943.

Converted to Type 16
Frigate by Grayson
Rollo Ltd. 1952-53.

LENGTH - 363 ft. o.a.
BEAM - 35·75 ft.
DRAUGHT - 14·5 ft.
SPEED - 32 knots.

Altogether, the alterations produced a workmanlike AS vessel which was quickly and economically produced at a time when it was needed. The Type 16 was not, however, as sophisticated as the more extensively converted Type 15 and the ships had relatively short careers, being phased out of service as new construction frigates became available.

All 10 ships converted were completed in the period 1952 to 1956 with *Tuscan* being the first to commission. Details of the dates and places of the conversions together with the ships' eventual fate are listed below:

Orwell converted at Rosyth Dockyard 1952. Sold J. Cashmore and arrived Newport for scrapping 28/6/65.

Paladin converted Rosyth Dockyard 1952-54. Sold Clayton and Davie and arrived Dunston on Tyne 25/10/62 for scrapping.

Petard converted by Harland and Wolff, Belfast. Sold P. MacLellan, Bo'ness; arrived for scrapping June 1967.

Teazer converted by Mountstuart Dry Docks, Cardiff 1953-54. Sold W. H. Arnott Young; arrived Dalmuir 7/8/65 for scrapping.

Tenacious converted Rosyth Dockyard 1951-52. Sold to West of Scotland Shipbreaking, Troon; arrived for scrapping 29/6/65.

Termagant converted by Grayson Rollo, Birkenhead, 1952-53. Sold W. H. Arnott Young, Dalmuir; arrived for scrapping 5/11/65.

Terpsichore converted by J. I. Thornycroft, Woolston, 1953-54. Sold to West of Scotland Shipbreaking; arrived for scrapping 17/5/66.

Tumult converted by Grayson Rollo, Birkenhead, 1953-54. Sold W. H. Arnott Young, Dalmuir; arrived for scrapping 25/10/65.

Tuscan converted by Mountstuart Dry Docks, Cardiff, 1949-50. Sold P. MacLellan, Bo'ness and arrived 26/5/66 for scrapping.

Tyrian converted Harland and Wolff, Liverpool and Gordon Klison, Birkenhead, 1951-53. Sold West of Scotland Shipbreaking, Troon, and arrived for scrapping 9/3/65.

Two other vessels were converted to Type 16 frigates. They were the ex-British destroyers *Onslow* and *Onslaught* which had been sold to Pakistan in 1949 and renamed *Tippu Sultan* and *Tughril* respectively. In 1957 they returned to the UK and converted to Type 16 frigates, the work being completed in 1959.

In Royal Navy service, the ships were little altered following their reconstruction. In September 1957, *Paladin* was modified for minelaying duties with the removal of her torpedo tubes and the installation of

30
HMS *Paladin* was one of two 'P' class destroyers subsequently converted to frigates. Although designed to carry the standard prewar destroyer armament of four 4.7in guns, the 'P' class were equipped with five 4in guns due to shortages of the intended armament. The photograph shows *Paladin* in 1946 when she was serving as a target ship for the 3rd Submarine Flotilla and she only carries two 4in guns. *Wright and Logan*

31
This photo shows *Paladin* as converted to a Type 16 frigate and clearly shows the changes from the original destroyer layout. Less extensive than the Type 15 conversions, the main alterations were to the armament and radar equipment and the basic layout of the ship was unaltered. In 1957 *Paladin* was modified for minelaying and the equipment for this can be seen on the stern. *Wright and Logan*

32
HMS *Tyrian* in 1953, one of seven 'T' class destroyers converted to Type 16 frigates. Note the Type 293Q radar on the foremast with the HF/DF aerial above it. The Squid mortars and the mortar handling room can be seen right aft. She retains the original open destroyer bridge. *Wright and Logan*

mine carrying rails along either side of the upper deck. In this configuration she could carry 30 mines. *Orwell* was similarly modified.

With the introduction of the Type 15 and 16 conversions, as well as the later new construction frigates, the Admiralty looked to the past to find a term to classify the various frigate types. Consequently, for a time, the larger new frigates were known as First Rate escorts; the converted frigates and the Type 14 'Blackwood' class (qv) as Second Rate escorts, and the remaining World War 2 types such as the 'Loch' class were known as Third Rate escorts. The practice of giving ships a 'Rate' stemmed from the sailing navy where the ships of the line were classified according to the number of guns carried and rated accordingly. As the older frigates and conversions passed out of service the rate classification fell into disuse.

Name	No	Builders	Laid Down	Launched	Completed
Orwell	F98	J. I. Thornycroft, Woolston	16/5/40	2/4/42	7/10/42
Paladin	F169	J. Brown & Co Ltd, Clydebank	22/7/40	11/6/41	12/12/41
Petard	F56	Vickers Armstrong, Tyne	26/12/39	27/3/41	14/6/42
Teazer	F23	Cammell Laird	20/10/41	7/1/43	13/9/43
Tenacious	F44	Cammell Laird	3/12/41	24/3/43	30/10/43
Termagent	F189	W. Denny and Bros, Dumbarton	25/11/41	22/3/43	18/10/43
Terpsichore	F19	W. Denny and Bros, Dumbarton	25/11/41	17/6/43	20/1/44
Tumult	F121	J. Brown & Co, Clydebank	16/11/41	9/11/42	2/4/43
Tuscan	F156	Swan Hunter, Wallsend	9/9/41	28/5/42	11/3/43
Tyrian	F67	Swan Hunter, Wallsend	15/10/41	27/7/42	8/4/43

Data: 'T' class as destroyers
Displacement: 1,802 tons standard; 2,530 tons full load
Length: $362\frac{3}{4}$ft oa
Beam: $35\frac{3}{4}$ft
Draught: $14\frac{1}{2}$ft (max)
Guns: 4×DP 4.7in on Mk XXII mountings
2×40mm and 8×20mm AA guns (or 12×20mm and no 40mm)
Torpedoes: 8×21in tubes (2×4)
AS weapons: 4×depth charge throwers and two stern racks
70 depth charges carried
Machinery: 2×Admiralty three-drum boilers working at 300lb/sq in and 630°F, driving two shafts through Parsons single reduction turbines giving a total of 40,000shp
Speed: 36kts (32kts at full load)
Complement: 179

Data: As converted
Displacement: 1,800 tons standard; 2,300 tons full load
Dimensions: As built
Guns: 2×4in (1×2) on Mk XIX mounting
Two 40mm (1×2) on Mk V mounting
5×40mm (5×1) on Mk IX mountings
Torpedoes: 4×21in torpedo tubes (1×4)
AS weapons: 2×Squid three-barrelled AS mortars
Machinery: As built
Speed: As built
Complement: 175

33
HMS Teazer was one of three Type 16 conversions fitted with the enclosed 'frigate' bridge (the others were *Tumult* and *Terpsichore*). Despite their conversion, these ships still looked very much like traditional destroyers, an effect heightened by the retention of the torpedo tubes which can be seen just in front of the after deckhouse.
Wright and Logan

3 The 1951 Frigate Programme

'Salisbury' Class (Type 61) AD Frigates

The Type 15 and 16 conversions described in the last chapter were intended as a stopgap measure pending the introduction of new and purpose-built frigate designs. Work on new frigate designs had commenced as far back as 1944 when the Admiralty realised that the performance of the latest German U-boat designs would outstrip the then current frigate types. A study of the requirements for a new frigate led to the formulation of the '1945 Frigate Concept' which envisaged three separate types using a common hull and steam turbine machinery. A staff requirement called for a speed of at least 23kts at full load displacement, six months out of dry dock. It was envisaged that the ships would have to be constructed in a country possibly partly devastated by nuclear attack and therefore it was planned that the ships would be built of prefabricated sections which could be transported easily to a shipyard for assembly.

In 1947, as a result of further studies, it became apparent that provision of adequate sets of steam machinery would become problematic during wartime or emergencies. It was therefore decided to recast the designs around diesel engines as these would be easier to supply and install and also would not require such a high standard of engineroom personnel. The adoption of diesel propulsion for a large surface warship was a new departure for the Royal Navy and was probably influenced by the success of German wartime developments. They had always regarded the diesel as an eminently suitable plant for warship propulsion and by 1945 had brought it to a level of development far exceeding that of the Allies. A design existed for a German destroyer which would have achieved 37½kts together with a range of 16,000 miles at 19kts when powered by eight MAN diesels giving a power output of 76,000bhp through two shafts.

The success of the 'Loch/Bay' concept where a single hull with a standard propulsion system could be adapted for different tasks had led to the decision to attempt the same again with a more modern design. There were obvious economic benefits in this scheme which also held the advantage that production could be switched from one type to another as circumstances demanded. The three frigate types envisaged were: anti-submarine (Type 11), anti-aircraft (Type 41) and aircraft direction (Type 61). The first of these types to be laid down was a Type 61, HMS *Salisbury*, on 23 January 1951. This vessel was the first postwar design to be laid down and represented the beginning of a major programme to provide the Royal Navy with a force of ships capable of dealing with the air and underwater threats of the 'Atomic Age'. Although the other types represented a logical progression from the 'Loch/Bay' class, the Type 61 aircraft direction frigate was a new concept.

The postwar navy was structured around the complete ascendancy of air power. The aircraft carrier and its associated strike aircraft represented the main striking power of the Royal Navy: while the main threat came from land-based aircraft. The control of air battles at sea demanded powerful radar and communications equipment as well as the necessary organisation for the exploitation of such equipment. It was just not possible to fit all the electronic equipment and associated operations rooms into one warship and so the concept of a vessel whose primary function was the control and direction of aircraft was born. The concept had been tried in World War 2 using a variety of converted vessels such as tank landing ships. Although they proved very useful they were not able to combine with major task forces as they were too slow. The new frigate design provided a suitable hull in which to mount a wide variety of radar equipment and this meant that the new type would be able to combine in a tactical sense with other vessels of an escort group. It was intended that the new aircraft direction vessels would operate mainly as part of a convoy escort or as part of a small task force which did not include larger vessels which would normally carry out the aircraft direction role — such as aircraft carriers or cruisers. It is interesting to note that the first vessel of the postwar frigate programme was of the new type and this gives some idea of the importance attached to the concept.

The all-welded hull was of a novel design, having a raised forecastle deck to improve seaworthiness and being considerably larger than previous frigate designs. Power was provided by a total of 12

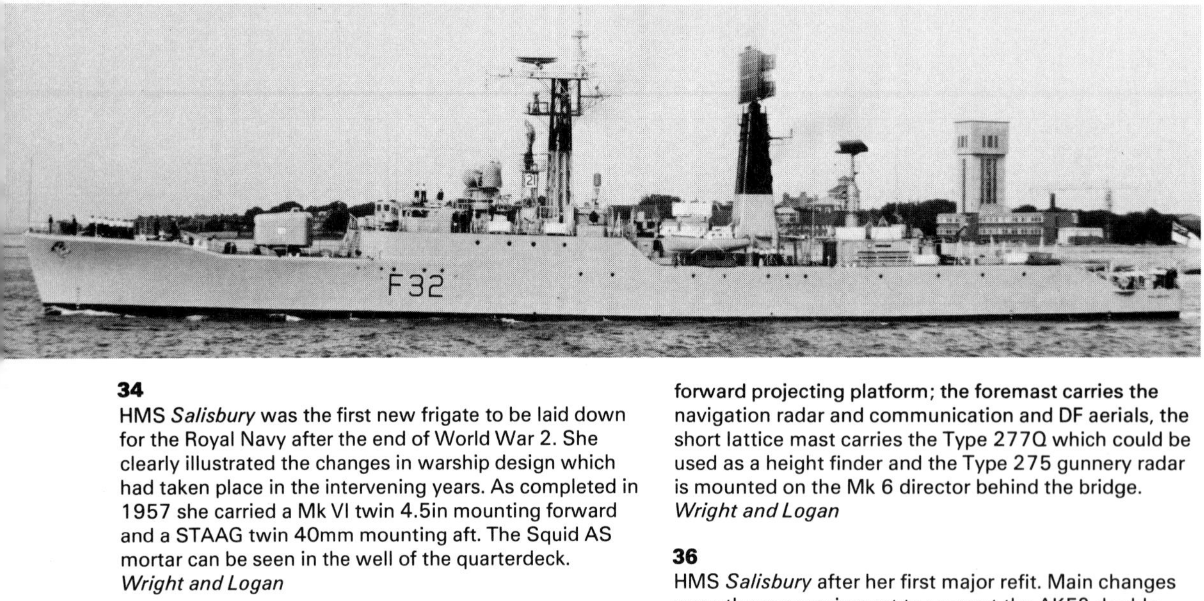

34
HMS *Salisbury* was the first new frigate to be laid down for the Royal Navy after the end of World War 2. She clearly illustrated the changes in warship design which had taken place in the intervening years. As completed in 1957 she carried a Mk VI twin 4.5in mounting forward and a STAAG twin 40mm mounting aft. The Squid AS mortar can be seen in the well of the quarterdeck.
Wright and Logan

35
This 1958 photograph of HMS *Llandaff* shows the radar equipment originally fitted. Right aft is the hayrake aerial of the Type 982 aircraft direction radar, atop the mainmast is the Type 960 long range radar with IFF interrogator below and a Type 293Q cheese aerial on the forward projecting platform; the foremast carries the navigation radar and communication and DF aerials, the short lattice mast carries the Type 277Q which could be used as a height finder and the Type 275 gunnery radar is mounted on the Mk 6 director behind the bridge.
Wright and Logan

36
HMS *Salisbury* after her first major refit. Main changes were the new mainmast to support the AKE2 double bedstead aerial of the Type 965 long range radar, which replaced the earlier Type 960. The Type 293Q has been moved to the top of the foremast and the STAAG mounting has been replaced by a Mk V twin 40mm. A taller mast supports the Type 982 aerial aft.
Mike Lennon

Admiralty Standard Range Mk 1 diesel engines arranged in three separate enginerooms. Four engines were connected to each of two shafts by means of fluid drive clutches and reduction gearboxes. The remaining four ASR1 units were not connected to the propulsion system but were used for the production of electrical power, each engine driving a 360kW alternator. In *Llandaff*, one of the diesel alternators was replaced by a 500kW gas turbine-powered alternator. It was necessary to have so many separate diesel units because a diesel engine produces its optimum power and efficiency within a very narrow rpm band and consequently it is better to produce extra power when required by coupling in extra engines rather than by excessive variation of engine speed. This arrangement gave the added bonus of increased survivability in the event of battle damage due to the dispersion of the power units. *Lincoln*, the last of the class to be completed, was fitted with controllable pitch propellers in a further attempt to increase propulsion efficiency and improve control response. Another advantage of diesels was that the ship could be got under way at much shorter notice than was required for steam-powered vessels.

The diesel fuel was stored in the hull's double bottom and as it was consumed it was replaced by seawater, thereby ensuring that the ship's stability remained reasonably constant even when most of the fuel had been used and the ship would otherwise be riding light. Finally, the diesel propulsion system gave the ships higher endurance than would have been the case with an equivalent steam-powered ship. One disadvantage of the multiple diesel arrangement was the amount of internal space occupied. The machinery in the Type 61 (and Type 41) took up just over 29% of the internal deck area compared with only 20% in the contemporary Type 12 design (qv) and 18.5% in the 'Leander' class laid down 10 years later.

The 'raison d'etre' of this class was, of course, its radar systems, and the outfit carried was of a diversity only seen previously on capital ships. Two lattice masts were provided to carry the majority of the electronic equipment and the exhaust trunking from the diesels was carried up through them. This gave rise to the then unusual sight of a large warship with no apparent funnels. The foremast carried the VHF/UHF communication aerials, DF equipment and a Type 268 navigation radar. Forward of this, a short lattice mast carried the ANU aerial of the Type 277Q combined air/surface warning radar with a height finding capability. Aft, a lattice mainmast supported a four-dipole aerial for the Type 960 long range (up to 150 miles) air warning radar and below this was the ANU 'cheese' aerial for the Type 293Q target designation

HMS SALISBURY
Type 61 Aircraft Direction Frigate
1972

BUILDERS - H.M. Dockyard Devonport.
LAID DOWN - 23rd JAN 1952
LAUNCHED - 25th JUN 1953
COMPLETED - 27th FEB 1957

LENGTH - 340ft. o.a.
BEAM - 40ft.
DRAUGHT - 15.5ft.
SPEED - 24 knots.

37
HMS *Chichester* in 1969 showing the configuration of the Type 61s after their second major refit. The foremast is now plated in and the Type 293Q radar has been replaced by a Type 993 and advanced ECM and ESM equipment is carried on the pole topmast. Corvus chaff launchers are fitted at the base of the foremast.
Wright and Logan

38
HMS *Salisbury* in her final operational guise. The Seacat missile system is installed aft and single 20mm guns have been fitted abreast the bridge. The ESM equipment at the masthead appears less comprehensive than that carried by *Llandaff*. *HMS Osprey*

39
HMS *Lincoln* on her final commission showing the layout of the GWS20 Seacat missile system. Note that the Squid mortar has been removed. *MoD (Navy)*

40
HMS *Chichester* was converted in 1972/73 to act as a guardship at Hong Kong. Stripped of most of her radar equipment she presents a sorry sight with the bare stump of the mainmast dominating the after part of the ship. Apart from the 4.5in guns, armament comprises a 40mm gun aft and two single 20mm guns abreast the foremast. *Wright and Logan*

radar. Finally, mounted atop a deckhouse aft was the distinctive 'hayrake' aerial for the Type 982 aircraft direction radar. A large operations room was provided between decks where the information from the various radars was presented to the team of aircraft and fighter controllers.

Despite the weight of electronic equipment, a normal frigate type armament was carried. This consisted of a twin Mk VI 4.5in gun turret forward and a twin 40mm STAAG mounting mounted aft. Also carried was a Squid AS mortar on the quarterdeck and Types 174 and 170 sonars were carried to provide a submarine detection and aiming system. These vessels were, therefore, able to provide a limited amount of firepower to assist in the close range defence of a convoy or task force. *Lincoln* was completed with a larger after deckhouse which was intended to carry a director for a Seacat missile system which would have replaced the 40mm AA guns. However the Seacat system was not fitted when the ship was completed; instead a single 40mm gun was mounted in the same position as the twin 40mm STAAG of the other ships of the class.

In 1962 *Salisbury* completed a 16-month refit which included the removal of the original lattice mainmast and its replacement by a wider, plated mast or 'mack' which housed the diesel exhausts. The new mast supported a large AKE2 'bedstead' aerial for the new Type 965 long range radar which replaced the previous Type 960. The type 293Q aerial was repositioned atop the foremast on a newly constructed platform which also supported a pole topmast carrying new ESM equipment. The other ships of the class were subsequently altered to conform with this layout. In the late 1960s the whole class underwent a further major refit which involved more alterations. The foremast was plated in to match the mainmast and *Salisbury* and *Lincoln* were fitted with the Seacat missile system, *Salisbury's* after superstructure being built up to match that already on *Lincoln*. The STAAG mountings were removed from all four and, in *Llandaff* and *Chichester*, replaced by a standard Mk V twin 40mm mounting and its associated simple tachymetric director (STD). *Lincoln* and *Salisbury* were also later equipped with two single 20mm guns mounted one on either beam abreast the bridge. All four received the multiple 3in rocket launchers for the Knebworth/Corvus chaff decoy system, which were mounted abreast the foremast.

In 1973, *Chichester* was converted to act as a guardship at Hong Kong. All radars were removed except for the Type 993 (which had replaced the Type 293Q on all ships) and the navigation radar. The 4.5in main armament was retained, a single 40mm replaced the twin mounting and the single 20mm guns in the bridge wings were retained. Thus equipped she presented a sorry sight with the stump of her unused mainmast giving the ship a very unbalanced and spartan appearance. She returned to the UK in 1976 and was laid up in reserve, being scrapped at Queenborough in 1981.

Llandaff served until December 1976, when she was transferred to the Bangladesh Navy under the new name of *Oomar Farooq*. She was the first ship to be operated by this new navy and her pendant number became F16, a reversal of her original F61.

Lincoln, the only member of the class not equipped with stabilisers, was temporarily fitted with wooden bow sheathing to enable her to rough it with the gunboats of the Icelandic Navy during the 1976 Cod War but subsequently paid off into reserve and is presently listed for disposal. She had seen action in the Indonesian Confrontation of the early 1960s, the Biera patrol, and two cod wars — which demonstrates the variety of tasks carried out by frigates in the Royal Navy even in so called peacetime.

Salisbury, the lead ship of the class, paid off into reserve in June 1978. During that year she was to be sold to Egypt and actually sailed as far as Gibraltar on her delivery voyage before the deal was cancelled and she returned to the UK. In 1980 she was designated as a static sea training ship for HMS *Raleigh*, a training establishment at Torpoint, Cornwall, where she still serves in that role. It is interesting to note that, at the time of her withdrawal from service in 1978, she was the last Royal Navy ship to carry the Squid AS mortar.

The class has had a long and useful career with the Royal Navy but after the first four of the class had been laid down, the trend to general purpose designs together with the conversion of eight 'Battle' and 'Weapon' class destroyers to aircraft direction ships led to the cancellation of three further vessels of this type. The cancelled vessels would have been named *Exeter*, *Gloucester* and *Coventry*, names which were later allocated to Type 42 destroyers. The cancelled contracts were replaced with orders for other frigate types.

Name	**No**	**Builders**	**Laid Down**	**Launched**	**Completed**
Salisbury	F32	HM Dockyard, Devonport	23/1/52	25/6/53	27/2/57
Chichester	F59	Fairfield Shipbuilding and Engineering, Govan	26/6/53	21/4/55	16/5/58
Llandaff	F61	Hawthorn Leslie Ltd	27/8/53	30/11/55	11/4/58
Lincoln	F99	Fairfield Shipbuilding and Engineering, Govan	1/6/55	6/4/59	7/7/60

Data: As built
Displacement: 2,170 tons standard; 2,400 tons full load
Length: 340ft oa
Beam: 40ft
Draught: $15\frac{1}{2}$ft
Guns: 2×4.5in DP (1×2) in Mk VI mounting
2×40mm AA (1×2) on STAAG mounting (1×40mm on *Lincoln*)
AS weapons: 1×Squid
Sonar: Types 170, 174
Machinery: 8×Admiralty Standard Range (ASR1) diesels driving two shafts, giving a total of 12,400shp
Speed: 24kts
Oil fuel: 230 tons
Complement: 207 (later 237)

'Leopard' Class (Type 41) AA Frigates

The genesis of this class has been described in the previous section relating to the Type 61 frigates. The Type 41s employed the same hull and propulsion units and differed only in their armament and equipment. As AA escort vessels they were the successors of the wartime 'Bay' class and employed the same philosophy of carrying the heaviest gun armament possible. This consisted of four 4.5in guns in two Mk VI turrets mounted fore and aft. A Mk 6M director, incorporating the Type 275 gunnery radar, controlled the guns for both surface and air target engagement. Mounted just forward of the after 4.5in turret was a close range blind fire director (CRBFD) which was equipped with a Type 262 gunnery radar and this acted as a standby director for use against aircraft if the main director was out of action. Alternatively, the CRBFD could be used to control the after turret whilst the Mk 6M controlled the fore turret. Also fitted, just abaft the mainmast was a twin 40mm STAAG mounting again carrying the Type 262 radar. Thus equipped, the ship was capable of firing against three separate aircraft targets simultaneously. The heavy gun armament was on a par with virtually all previous British destroyer designs (except the 'Darings' which mounted six 4.5in guns) and consequently the Type 41s were capable of carrying out several functions — such as shore bombardment — normally performed by destroyers. To complete the armament a Squid AS mortar was mounted on the quarterdeck with fire control provided by sonar Types 170 and 174, as in the Type 61s.

Radars fitted included a Type 960 (long range air warning) mounted atop the mainmast, and a Type 293Q target designation radar on the foremast. HF/DF and a navigation radar were also carried. All the ships of the class were equipped with stabilisers which helped to maintain a steady platform for AA gunnery. *Jaguar*, as with the Type 61 *Lincoln*, was fitted with controllable pitch propellers.

Of the five ships laid down for the Royal Navy, one, *Panther*, was purchased while under construction by the Indian Navy and renamed *Bramaputra*. India subsequently order two more of this class and these were named *Beas* and *Betwa*. Both were completed in 1960 and differed slightly from RN vessels in that they carried a Mk V utility twin 40mm mounting instead of the more complex and less reliable STAAG mounting. Internal accommodation was also altered to suit local requirements.

When completed, the Royal Navy vessels were allocated mainly to the South American station where their impressive appearance and long range made them ideal for the traditional peacetime task of showing the flag. For this purpose they constituted the 7th Frigate Squadron and replaced the 'Bay' class frigates previously deployed to this area. Later the ships served all over the world — including participation in the 'Cod Wars' with Iceland as well as commissions in the Indian Ocean and Persian Gulf. In 1963 *Lynx* and *Puma* underwent a modernisation refit which involved the replacement of the Type 960 radar by the new Type 965. The AKE1 aerial of the type 965 was larger and heavier than the aerial of the earlier radar and so the lattice mainmast was replaced by a new plated structure. The Type 293Q radar previously mounted on the foremast was replaced by the newer Type 993 radar. The troublesome and erratic STAAG mounting was removed and replaced by a single 40mm gun. New ESM and ECCM equipment was carried on an extended fore topmast. *Leopard* was similarly refitted between October 1964 and February 1966 with *Jaguar* following suit. It was intended that all ships of the class would be equipped with Seacat missiles to replace the 40mm gun but this was never done, mainly for economic reasons.

By the early 1970s the lack of any missile armament made them obsolescent in their designed role. Large scale modernisation was impracticable because of their age and the expense, and because their relatively low speed meant that they could not act as task force

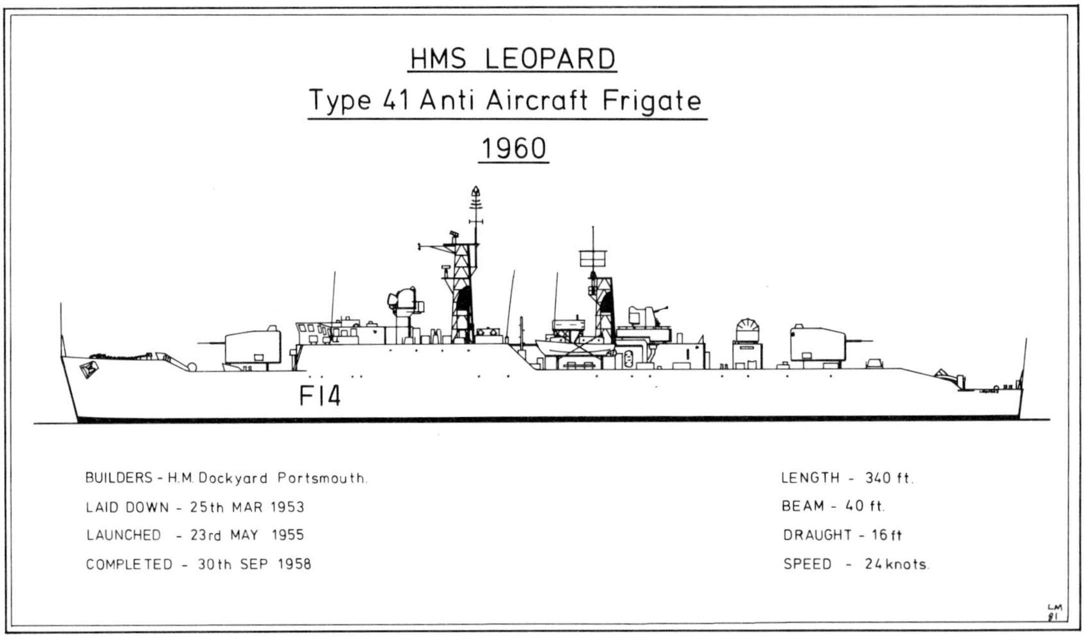

escorts. Consequently they were gradually withdrawn from service and laid up in reserve. *Puma*, withdrawn from service in 1974, was sold for scrap in 1976 and *Leopard* followed suit in 1978. After service with the 5th Frigate Squadron including a deployment to Iceland during the 1973 Cod War, *Jaguar* was assigned to the Standby Squadron, but, in 1976, she was recommissioned for further service in Icelandic waters. During this period she was fitted with a heavy wood sheathing to cover the bows and protect the ship from damage caused by the aggressive manoeuvring of the Icelandic gunboats. Following this she returned to reserve until sold to Bangladesh in 1978 and was renamed *Ali Hyper*. *Lynx*, last ship of the class in Royal Navy service, spent several years in reserve before also being sold to Bangladesh. She was handed over to her new owners on 12 March 1982 at Portsmouth and was renamed *Abu Baka*. She sailed for the Far East a week later, on 19 March.

In retrospect, it is unfortunate that these ships could not have been modernised with the Seacat missile system as, although their slow speed meant they could not act as escorts for a major carrier task force, they would have been ideal for use in the recent Falklands operation where they could have provided some air defence for the merchant ships and heavy ship-to-shore bombardment firepower. Their slow speed would have been no drawback in these operations and their long range on the diesel engines would have stood them in good stead.

Name	**No**	**Builders**	**Laid Down**	**Launched**	**Completed**
Jaguar	F37	W. Denny and Bros	2/11/53	20/7/57	12/12/59
Leopard	F14	HM Dockyard, Portsmouth	25/3/53	23/5/55	30/9/58
Lynx	F27	J. Brown and Co Ltd	13/8/53	12/1/55	14/3/57
Puma	F34	Scotts Shipbuilding and Eng Co, Greenock	16/11/53	30/6/54	27/4/57
Panther	F31	J. Brown and Co Ltd	20/10/55	15/3/57	31/3/58

Data: As built
Displacement: 2,300 tons standard; 2,520 tons full load
Length: 340ft oa
Beam: 40ft
Draught: 16ft
Guns: 4×4.5in DP (2×2) in Mk VI mountings
2×40mm AA (1×2) on Mk V Utility mounting
AS weapons: 1×Squid
Sonar: Types 170, 174
Machinery: 8×Admiralty Standard Range (ASR1) diesels driving two shafts giving a total of 12,400shp
Speed: 24kts
Oil fuel: 220 tons
Complement: 205 (later 235)

41

HMS *Lynx* in 1957 just after her completion. The CRBFD with a Type 262 radar mounted on it could control the after 4.5in turret independently of the main director if required. Note the clear arcs of fire afforded to the STAAG mounting carried high up behind the mainmast. *Wright and Logan*

42

Serving with the 7th Frigate Squadron was HMS *Jaguar*. At the top of the lattice foremast is the Type 293Q radar with ECM and HF/DF aerials above it. The Type 960 long range air warning radar is carried on the mainmast and the twin dishes of the Type 275 can be seen on the Mk 6 director behind the bridge. *HMS Osprey*

'Whitby'/'Rothesay' Class (Type 12) AS Frigates

Although provision was made in the 1951 Frigate Programme for specialised air defence frigates (Types 41 and 61), the main thrust of the construction programme was for AS vessels. The hull and diesel propulsion system of the other types was only good for a speed of 25kts and this was not considered enough to combat submarines such as the German Type XXI (16kts underwater) and Type XXVI (22kts underwater). It was assumed that the Soviet Navy, having captured examples of these submarines at the end of the war, would have built improved versions of both. The projected AS version of the Type 41/61 was designated Type 11, but was abandoned in favour of a steam turbine-powered design which produced enough power to give a speed of 30kts. The steam plant required a larger hull than the other frigates (the extra length helping in the attainment of higher speeds) and the addition of a funnel, with the result that the final design bore little more than a passing family resemblance to the other types. The return to steam and increased dimensions meant that the new ships were considerably more expensive than the other diesel-powered vessels and were not so suitable for fast large-scale production. This apart, the Type 12 proved to be an excellent basic design with unrivalled seakeeping qualities and it emerged as the basic Royal Navy AS vessel for the next 20 years.

The hull was of a then unusual form, having a raised forcastle deck which sloped down to weather deck level just forward of the gun turret. The bow showed considerable flare and, coupled with the generally fine lines of the hull, this meant that — except in the worst conditions — spray was thrown well clear of the deck and superstructure. This was most important, especially in the North Atlantic and Arctic areas where these ships could expect to spend much of their time, as it helped to prevent an excessive build up of ice on the ship. One of the problems encountered during World War 2 had been the difficulties caused by ice building up on the superstructure of warships. This caused weapons to become unusable, froze radar aerials solid, affected stability

HMS EASTBOURNE

Type 12 Whitby Class Frigate

1965

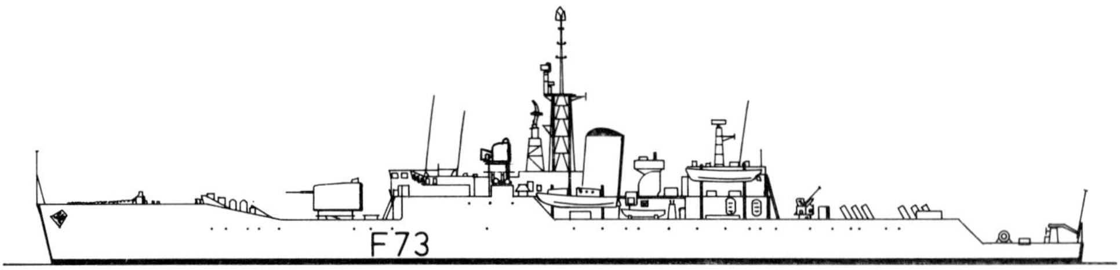

BUILDERS - Vickers Armstrong, Tyne.
LAID DOWN - 13th. JAN 1954
LAUNCHED - 29th DEC 1955
COMPLETED - 9th JAN 1958

LENGTH - 369.8 ft.
BEAM - 41 ft.
DRAUGHT - 17ft.
SPEED - 31 knots.

LM 81

and in some cases put ships in danger of capsizing due to the weight of ice on the deck and upperworks. Considerable thought was directed to alleviating this problem. As well as the improved hull form already mentioned, the deck edges were radiused (instead of having the normal sharp angle between the plane of the deck and the side of the hull). This allowed water to flow more easily off the deck and the smoother surface made ice formation more difficult. The anchors were recessed into the sides of the bow which removed another cause of ice forming spray.

The main AS weapon was the Mk 10 Limbo mortar, which was a development of the Squid system, and two of these were carried in a sheltered well in the after quarter of the ship. In this position the mortars could be loaded and fired in any weather conditions. The three-barrelled mounting fired a 400lb streamlined projectile at ranges up to 1,000yd in any desired direction (including straight ahead when the projectiles were fired over the forward superstructure). For its time, the Limbo was an extremely effective weapon and it is still in service today on some Royal Navy frigates although it is generally being superseded by homing torpedoes and helicopter-launched weapons.

For submarine detection and attack information a comprehensive sonar outfit was carried. Type 174 (search) and Type 162 (bottomed target classification) sonars provided the initial detection data and a Type 170 (a pencil beam attack sonar) was carried to give the accurate bearing and depth information needed for effective use of the Limbo's capabilities. Also fitted were 12 21in torpedo tubes which were arranged on the upper deck amidships with four single fixed mountings and one twin trainable mounting on each beam. The fixed tubes were angled out at 45° to fire forward of the beam and were mounted forward of the trainable tubes. In fact not all the 'Whitby' class was so fitted on completion. *Scarborough* was the first to carry the torpedo tubes and the earlier ships were given the mountings during routine refits in the late 1950s. Although intended to fire AS homing torpedoes rather than the standard surface torpedo, the installation was not a success because of the failure to develop an effective weapon. The Mk 20E homing torpedo used aboard these ships (and other contemporary frigates) proved to be too slow against the then current generation of high underwater speed submarines, and no suitable British replacement was developed until the Stingray lightweight homing torpedo was accepted for use in the fleet in the early 1980s. By 1963 the AS torpedo tubes had been removed from all ships of the class.

Gun armament consisted of a Mk VI twin 4.5in mounting forward and a STAAG twin 40mm AA mounting aft. The Mk VI mounting was identical to the installation in the 'Daring' class destroyers and the contemporary Type 41 and 61 frigates. A Mk 6M director, incorporating a Type 275 gunnery radar with its distinctive twin aerial dishes, provided the fire control for the dual purpose 4.5in guns. The STAAG was one of the electronic and mechanical marvels of the age. The mounting incorporated its own Type 262 gunnery radar, the aerial of which consisted of a small parabolic dish. This was rotated mechanically to give a conical scan covering an arc of 30° and when a target was detected within a range of 5,000yd, the radar would lock on to it and cause the mounting to track the target. The rate of change of the angular bearing of the target in elevation and azimuth, coupled with range information derived from the Type 262 radar, allowed an automatic computation of the target's future position and the guns were automatically aligned with the predictor. The whole outfit (guns, radar, predictor) was carried on a fully stabilised mounting and with so many separate systems, all subject to the ravages of the weather and severe vibration when the guns fired, maintenance absorbed a disproportionate amount of time and effort. Although installed in Type 61 and 41 frigates as well as the Type 12, the difficulties associated with keeping the STAAG working eventually proved too much and it was progressively removed from all ships. In the 'Whitby' class it was replaced by a single 40mm gun.

Radar equipment included a Type 293Q, with its distinctive 'cheese' aerial carried at the top of the lattice foremast, while a Type 277Q was mounted on a short lattice structure between the gunnery director and the foremast. Other electronic equipment carried included a navigation radar and also HF/DF and ECM devices mounted on a pole extension to the foremast.

The first of the class, *Whitby*, was laid down in September 1952 and a further five were laid down in the following two years. The other ships of the class were *Torquay, Tenby, Scarborough, Eastbourne* and *Blackpool*. As completed, these ships were fitted with a rather short and upright funnel but problems with smoke and fumes, as well as boiler draughting, led to a taller raked funnel with a domed top being fitted to all ships. The later ships were completed with the new funnel design and the others modified at a later date, although *Scarborough* retained her original funnel for most of her active life. As already mentioned, the deck-mounted AS torpedo tubes were removed and the extra deck space used to expand the after superstructure and increase accommodation space.

The 'Whitby' class continued in service until the early 1970s when the ships age, and the ever-continuing defence economies, led to their gradual withdrawal. *Tenby* and *Scarborough* were sold to Pakistan in 1974, but plans to have them modernised before delivery were abandoned and they were subsequently scrapped without ever sailing under the flag of their new owners. *Blackpool* served with the Royal New Zealand Navy from 1966 to 1971 and on return to the UK she was placed in reserve with her 4.5in gun turret removed. Later she ended her days as a target for Rosyth-based ships before being sold to J. A. White (a Forth-based shipbreaker) in September 1980. *Whitby* was discarded in 1975 and was eventually broken up at Queenborough in 1979. *Eastbourne* was stripped of her armament in 1973 and became a seagoing training ship for engineroom trainees from HMS *Caledonia*, Rosyth. In 1979, she was relegated to the status of harbour training hulk and is no longer seaworthy. The sole seagoing survivor of the class is HMS *Torquay* which is employed as a navigation training and trials ship based at Portsmouth. In this role she has lost her after 40mm gun and one of her AS mortars and has a large deckhouse constructed aft. She carries what was the first CAAIS (Computer Assisted Action Information System) to go to sea and after carrying out trials with this equipment, it was retained for training purposes. *Torquay* was one of the ships listed for eventual disposal in the sweeping 1981 defence review although she remains in service at the time of writing.

Naval planning in the mid-1950s envisaged future task forces consisting of aircraft carriers protected by an inner screen of missile-armed destroyers and an outer screen of smaller fleet escorts. This outer escort was seen as a 3,000-ton vessel with a speed of 30kts or more. The guided missile destroyer requirement led eventually to the 'County' class destroyers in the mid-1960s but the smaller escort was never built. Instead, the Type 12 frigates (which had originally been designed to escort convoys and amphibious forces) were selected for the job as their speed and seaworthiness characteristics made them suitable for such employment. In order to meet this requirement and to take advantage of improvements in armament and other equipment, the Type 12 design underwent some modification and a period of two years passed between the laying down of the last of the 'Whitby' class and the first of the altered design, HMS *Rothesay*, in November 1956.

Taking their name from the lead ship, the new group of frigates was known as the 'Rothsay' class and a total of nine was built, the last being laid down July 1958. The main external difference when compared with the previous 'Whitby' class was in the enlarged after superstructure which replaced the smaller deckhouse and twin 40mm mounting of the earlier vessels. It was intended to mount a Seacat missile launcher and its associated director in this position

HMS YARMOUTH. 2,380 tons.
Type 12 Rothesay Class Frigate.
1970.

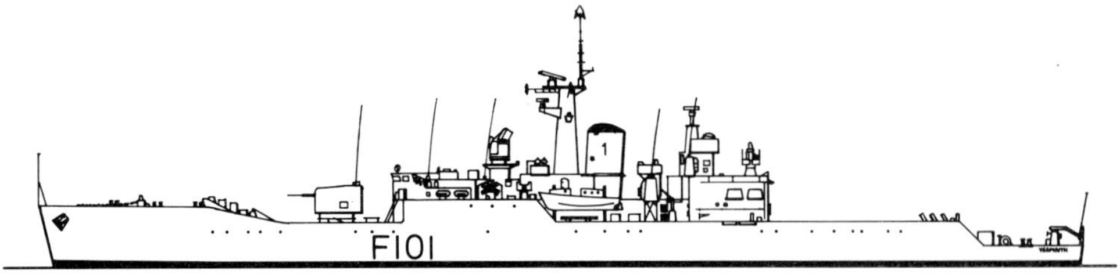

BUILDERS - J. BROWN and Co.
LAID DOWN - 29th NOV 1957
LAUNCHED - 23rd MAR 1959
COMPLETED - 26th MAR 1960

LENGTH - 370 ft.
BEAM - 41 ft.
DRAUGHT - 17 ft.
SPEED - 30 knots

43

Type 41 HMS *Lynx* in April 1972 showing alterations made after a major refit. An AKE1 aerial for a Type 965 radar replaces the previous Type 960 on the mainmast which is now of plated construction while the Type 293Q on the foremast has been replaced by a Type 993 'cheese' aerial. The STAAG mounting, which was a nightmare to keep serviceable, has been replaced by a single 40mm gun and the MRS1/CRBFD has been removed. Corvus chaff launchers are carried abreast the foremast.
Wright and Logan

44

The Type 12 AS frigate represented a great step forward in ASW capability and was undoubtedly one of the most successful designs to see service with the Royal Navy. HMS *Whitby*, lead ship of the class, is shown here shortly after completion in 1956. Note the short, upright, funnel and the STAAG twin 40mm gun mounting aft.
Fleet Photographic Unit

45

The upright funnel of the original Type 12 design was not successful and later ships had a taller raked funnel with a domed top and the earlier ships were altered to conform. HMS *Tenby* here displays the revised funnel design and the platform at the top of the mast carrying the Type 293Q radar has been lowered slightly. While still carrying the STAAG mounting aft, she is also equipped with AS torpedo tubes along either side of the upper deck; photograph taken 1960. *Wright and Logan*

but, as this weapon was not available when the vessels were completing, a single 40mm gun was carried instead. The design again had provision for AS torpedo tubes but the disposition was altered. The trainable twin mounting was fitted forward of the fixed mounts which were angled to fire at 45° aft of the beam, this arrangement being the reverse of the arrangement in the 'Whitby' class.

Propulsion machinery was the same Y-100 plant as installed in the previous vessels and this gave a total of 30,000shp. Electrical power was provided by two 400kW turbo generators and two 300kW diesel generators which compared with the 350kW and 200kW output for the respective installation of the 'Whitby' class. The uptakes from the boilers were carried up to the raked funnel which had been retrospectively fitted on the other ships. Internally, improved accommodation was provided for the crew with partial bunk sleeping and air conditioning in some sections of the ship.

The performance of the Type 174 sonar and the later Type 177 (first fitted in the 'Tribal' class frigates laid down 1958-60) meant that submarine targets could be located and tracked while still outside the range of the Limbo mortars. To get over this problem the Royal Navy adopted the MATCH (MAnned Torpedo Carrying Helicopter) system and this was first introduced in the 'Tribal' class. The success of the helicopter in this role led to the decision to modify some existing vessels to carry one. Accordingly, starting with *Rothesay*, all the 'Rothesay' class was modified between 1966 and 1972. The existing after superstructure was removed as well as the forward Limbo mounting (the AS torpedo tubes had already been removed from all ships of the class), and a new structure erected which incorporated a hangar capable of housing a Wasp HAS1 helicopter and its supplies and stores. The space left by removing the Limbo was plated over to form a small flightdeck. A quadruple Seacat launcher and its associated GWS20 director was mounted atop the hangar while an MRS3 fire control system replaced the original Mk 6M director. The Type 293Q radar on the foremast was replaced by the improved Type 993 whilst the Type 277Q was made redundant by the Type 903 incorporated in the MRS3 system. Two single 20mm cannon were carried on either side of the bridge and also mounted were the multi-barrelled launchers for the chaff-carrying rockets of the Knebworth/Corvus system. These were intended to provide a passive defence against radar-guided anti-ship missiles by throwing up a group of radar decoys in the path of the missile and thus deflect it away from the target. When *Rothesay* completed her modernisation refit in 1968, she was one of the first operational ships in the fleet to carry this system. Other changes included the replacement of the lattice foremast with a taller plated structure and an increase in funnel height to carry the smoke and fumes from the boilers clear of the after superstructure and flightdeck.

Due to their extensive modernisation the 'Rothesay' class was almost comparable to the later 'Leander' class (qv) and consequently it continued in service well after the demise of the 'Whitby' class from operational duties. At the end of 1975 *Londonderry* was taken in hand for a major refit and conversion to a trials vessel and when this was completed in October 1979, she presented a radically altered profile. All armament was removed and mounted on the after superstructure was a very tall mast with another equally tall mast sprouting from the quarter deck. The after mast was in fact a portable affair and could be removed at short notice if required. Both masts were to be used for mounting aerials of equipment under trial and the ship was also used for evaluating various items of onboard equipment such as JTIDS (Joint Tactical Information Distribution System) and various navigation aids. The ship was also fitted with what is described as a 'Pump Jet Propulsion System' although the exact nature and details of this have not been officially released. In her last commission she carried an experimental gun mounting carrying a naval version of the 30mm Rarden cannon fitted to the Army's Scorpion light tank. This gun was probably intended as a replacement for the 20mm and 40mm light AA guns presently carried by most RN warships, but adoption of a new light AA gun has been rather overtaken by events in the Falklands and it remains to be seen if the 30mm gun will be used. Following completion of her trials programme, *Londonderry* arrived in Portsmouth on 31 March 1982 for paying off. *Lowestoft*, another 'Rothesay' class ship, has also been used for trials in recent years mainly in connection with sonar equipment. Other than a small structure on the quarterdeck, she shows no external variation from her sister ships.

At the beginning of 1982, several 'Rothesay' class ships had been relegated to the Standby Squadron and, following on from the 1981 defence review, were under consideration for disposal. Among these were *Berwick*, *Brighton* and *Falmouth*. In the ordinary course of events it would not have been long before the rest of the class was laid up and scrapped, as most of them had seen more than 20 years service. The Argentine invasion of the Falkland Islands in April 1982 changed all that and one ship in particular found herself hitting the headlines in a way her crew could not possibly have foreseen. The ship concerned, HMS *Plymouth*, probably played one of the most active roles of any of the ships comprising the task force sent to recapture the islands. Sailing with the first group of Task Force ships she was involved in the operations to regain South Georgia, following which the commander of the Argentinian forces on the island, Capt Alfredo Astiz, signed the surrender documents aboard the ship. Following her success, *Plymouth* then set sail for the Falklands where she accompanied the landings at

46

Following a refit completed in 1972, HMS *Torquay* was used for training and for trials with CAAIS. A large deckhouse was erected aft which necessitated the removal of the 40mm guns and one of the Limbo mortars. A new plated foremast replaced the lattice mast and the funnel was increased in height. HMS *Torquay* is still in service and carries the last Mk 6 director in the Royal Navy. The photograph was taken in 1974.
Skyfotos

47

HMS *Eastbourne* in 1973 following her conversion to a seagoing training ship. All armament has been removed and an additional, open, bridge has been constructed above the original enclosed bridge. *C. and S. Taylor*

48

HMS *Brighton* on builder's trials in 1961. She was the second 'Rothesay' class frigate to be completed and show the enlarged after deckhouse designed to accommodate the Seacat missile system, although a single 40mm gun was actually installed.
Yarrow (Shipbuilders) Ltd

49
HMS *Rothesay*, name ship of the second Type 12 batch, is shown here in her original configuration. Note that the fixed AS torpedo tubes are angled to fire aft compared to the forward facing tubes of the 'Whitby' class as shown in the photograph of HMS *Tenby*. *Rothesay* is also equipped with a Mk V twin 40mm mounting and associated director instead of the single 40mm carried by the rest of the class. *Fleet Photographic Unit*

50
HMS *Rothesay* after her modernisation refit completed in 1968. One of the Limbo AS mortars has been removed and a hangar and flight deck constructed to enable the ship to operate a Wasp helicopter. Atop the hangar is a GWS20 Seacat missile system and a new plated mast carries a Type 993 radar as well as HF/DF and ECM equipment. The Mk 6M director has been replaced by an MRS3 fire control system and Corvus chaff launchers and single 20mm guns have been fitted abreast the bridge. *HMS Osprey*

San Carlos and then acted as one of the ships providing the landings with cover against air attack. She was engaged on this duty for longer than any other ship in the task force and during this phase she fired nine Seacat missiles and claimed five enemy aircraft destroyed. On 8 June she was subjected to fierce air attack and was hit by four bombs. Luckily none of them exploded on board the ship but one of them caused depth charges to explode on the flight deck, blowing a hole in the ship's side and starting a fire. Another bomb destroyed the Limbo AS mortar and left one of the projectiles in a dangerous state. A bomb disposal specialist was called in to defuse the mortar bomb which could have blown off the stern of the ship and in the meantime the crew was mustered on the forecastle. Once the mortar bomb was rendered safe and the fire put out, the crew was able to effect essential repairs and the ship returned to operational readiness. With the cessation of hostilities, *Plymouth* returned home, via Gibraltar, and reached Rosyth on 14 July, proudly bearing the scars of her actions. Despite the weight of metal thrown at her she suffered only five wounded and none of her crew was killed.

Plymouth was not the only 'Rothesay' class vessel to see action in the Falklands. Playing an equally important role was HMS *Yarmouth*, which had also sailed as part of the initial task force. Although not involved in the South Georgia action she was present when the *Sheffield* was hit by an Exocet missile and assisted the Type 21 frigate, HMS *Arrow*, to rescue survivors from the burning destroyer. Later, in company with *Plymouth* and other ships, she escorted the landing force into San Carlos water and for the next 10 days she took part in the fierce actions to defend the force against the relentless attacks of the Argentine Air Force. Once again she found herself engaged in the melancholy task of rescuing survivors when she assisted the *Ardent* in the last few hours before she sank after being hit by several bombs. Following her stint in 'Bomb Alley' she transferred to the naval gunfire support force, which was engaged in bombardment operations around Port Stanley, as part of the final operations to regain the Falklands. When the Argentine forces finally surrendered, *Yarmouth* was dispatched to South Thule in company with the ice patrol ship, HMS *Endurance*, to evict a party of Argentine military personnel who had been occupying the island since 1976, although their presence had been tacitly ignored at the time. Following a demonstration bombardment by *Yarmouth*, the Argentine forces surrendered without firing a shot and the island was returned to British sovereignty. *Yarmouth* was then finally able to set sail for home.

Although not directly involved in the Falklands campaign, several ships of the class were affected by events in the South Atlantic. *Falmouth* and *Berwick* were withdrawn from reserve at the start of the crisis and given rapid refits to prepare them for service. *Lowestoft*, which had been serving as a sonar trials ship, was taken in hand at Portsmouth to prepare for active service. HMS *Rhyl* was also similarly prepared and both ships were ready by mid-June when the Argentinian forces surrendered. *Lowestoft* then proceeded to Gibraltar where she was to act as guardship, replacing another ship which had been detached to the Falklands. All ships prepared for the Falklands were painted grey overall, losing the distinctive black tops to the funnels and masts and having their pendant numbers painted out. The ship's name, normally carried in stainless steel letters on either side of the stern, was also removed so that the ship could not be identified readily. In some cases, extra 20mm guns were fitted.

The ships now in commission will probably remain in service until those ships damaged in the Falklands are returned to service. However, these vessels are now all over 20 years old and, given the current economic climate, their days must now be numbered. The 'Rothesay' and preceding 'Whitby' class frigates have proved to be a successful and durable design and their conventional and sturdy construction has stood them in good stead. The later 'Leander' class was a straightforward development of the Type 12 design with little modification to hull and machinery with in itself is a tribute to the fact that the original design was ideal for the job.

As with most RN frigates of the period, several Type 12 frigates were ordered by Commonwealth navies. Two 'Whitby' class were built for India and named *Talwar* and *Trishul*. They differed slightly from RN vessels in that they carried an extra two single 40mm guns. Two 'Rothesay' type were built in the UK for the Royal New Zealand Navy and these were named *Otago* and *Taranaki*. They were similar to Royal Navy vessels except for some revised crew accommodation to suit the Royal New Zealand Navy's local conditions. Both were fitted with 21in AS torpedo tubes and retained these for some years after they were removed from RN vessels. Four ships based on the Type 12 design were also built in Australia to a modified design to suit RN requirements. Finally three ships (*President Kruger*, *President Pretorious* and *President Steyn*) were completed for the South African Navy. One of these, *President Kruger*, was sunk in early 1982 following a collision with a fleet tanker while refuelling under way. Most of her crew were saved but 13 men were reported missing.

Name	No	Builders	Laid Down	Launched	Completed
Whitby	F36	Cammell Laird	30/9/52	2/7/54	10/7/56
Torquay	F43	Harland and Wolff	11/3/53	1/7/54	10/5/56

51
The Seacat missile considerably enhanced the close range AA capabilities of the 'Rothesay' class frigates. One of these missiles is seen leaving a quadruple launcher aboard an unidentified Type 12. Note the bright flare on the trailing edge of one of the tail fins which enables the aimer to visually track the missile in flight.
Shorts Brothers Ltd

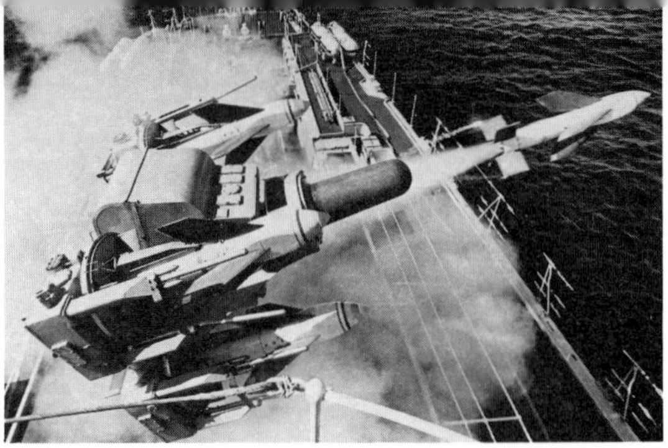

52
The Mk 10 Limbo AS mortar viewed aboard HMS *Brighton* in 1981. The mortars need to be laid over in the horizontal position during helicopter operations so that they do not project above the level of the flightdeck.
Author

53
HMS *Brighton* at Newcastle in 1981. This close up view shows the MRS3 director carrying the dish of the Type 903 radar while the Type 978 navigation radar is on the platform projecting forward from the mast. On top of the bridge is the DF loop aerial, and the Corvus chaff launchers and single 20mm guns are visible behind the white liferaft containers. Note the ship's crest above the bridge and repeated on the cover of the Type 903 radar dish. *Author*

54

In 1979, HMS *Londonderry* completed conversion to a trials ship. Apart from the Royal Yacht, she became the only three masted ship in the Navy. All armament has been removed and two new masts, intended to carry equipment under test, have been stepped aft. The after mast is a temporary structure which could be easily removed if required. *C. and S. Taylor*

55

Dramatic picture showing HMS *Yarmouth* alongside the stricken HMS *Ardent*. As *Ardent* lists heavily to starboard, her survivors are transferred slowly to the other frigate. *Yarmouth* was the oldest operational warship to take part in the Falklands War (with the sole exception of the carrier *Hermes*) having been first commissioned in 1960. *Central Office of Information*

Name	Number	Builders	Laid Down	Launched	Completed
Tenby	F65	Cammell Laird	23/6/53	4/10/55	18/12/57
Scarborough	F63	Vickers Armstrong (Tyne)	11/9/53	4/4/55	10/5/57
Eastbourne	F73	Vickers Armstrong (Tyne); Completed Barrow	13/1/54	29/12/55	9/1/58
Blackpool	F77	Harland and Woolf	20/12/54	14/2/57	14/8/58
Rothesay	F107	Yarrow, Scotstoun	6/11/56	9/12/57	23/4/60
Londonderry	F108	J. Samuel White, Cowes	15/11/56	20/5/58	18/10/61
Brighton	F106	Yarrow Scotstoun	23/7/57	30/10/59	28/9/61
Yarmouth	F101	J. Brown and Co	29/11/57	23/3/59	26/3/60
Falmouth	F113	Swan Hunter	23/11/57	15/12/59	25/7/61
Rhyl	F129	HM Dockyard Portsmouth	29/1/58	23/4/59	31/10/60
Lowestoft	F103	Alex Stephens and Sons	19/6/58	23/6/60	26/9/61
Berwick	F115	Harland and Woolf	16/6/58	15/12/59	1/6/61
Plymouth	F126	HM Dockyard Devonport	1/7/58	20/7/59	11/5/61

Data: As built
Displacement: 2,150 tons standard (modified 'Rothesay' 2,380); 2,560 tons full load (modified 'Rothesay' 2,800)
Length: 370ft oa
Beam: 41ft
Draught: 17.3ft
Guns: 2×4.5in DP (1×2) on Mk VI mounting 2×40mm (1×2) on STAAG mounting (1×40mm in 'Rothesay' class)
Torpedoes: 12×21in AS torpedo tubes (8×1 fixed, 2×2 trainable)
AS weapons: 2×Limbo mortars
Sonar: Types 162, 170, 174
Machinery: 2×Babcock and Wilcox boilers operating at 550lb/sq in and 850°F. English Electric geared turbines, two shafts giving a total of 30,000shp
Speed: 30kts
Oil fuel: 400 tons
Complement: Originally 152; later 225 (235 in modified 'Rothesay')

'Blackwood' Class (Type 14) Utility AS Frigates

Although the Type 12s ('Whitby' class) had excellent qualities as AS vessels, they were comparatively expensive to build and were not capable of rapid construction in times of emergency. The original policy of the postwar frigate programme had been to provide a single hull which could be fitted out for a variety of roles, but the Type 12 represented a departure from this policy and a further design became necessary in order to provide a cheap, easily-built and effective anti-submarine vessel. Accordingly, a new design which represented the Admiralty's idea of a minimum AS frigate was drawn up and given the designation Type 14 (Utility). To allow for rapid construction the ship was to be built up from prefabricated welded sections which could be constructed away from the main shipyard and transported by road for final assembly. This dispersion of effort was intended to allow assembly of the ships to continue in wartime even if some of the shipyards had been put out of action by enemy bombing.

Conventional steam turbines were selected as the propulsion system but, as World War 2 experience had shown that the manufacture of large numbers of turbine units was difficult in wartime conditions, it was decided that the Type 14 would be designed as a single shaft vessel to reduce demand for these vital components. A single screw, of course, meant that a vessel was more likely to be put out of action as a result of mechanical defects or by battle damage but this was deemed acceptable as it was anticipated that the large number of such ships available in time of war would provide a degree of cover. The steam plant fitted was, in fact, half of the two-shaft installation of the Type 12 with the exception that two smaller boilers were used to provide steam for the Y-100 turbine set instead of the single larger boiler of the original installation. With an output of 15,000shp, the machinery drove the ship at a speed of almost 28kts (a considerable improvement over the wartime frigates of a similar size).

56
Several 'Rothesay' class frigates were prepared for service in the Falklands but hostilities ended before any could be sent to replace *Yarmouth* and *Plymouth* which had played such important parts in the recapture of the islands. HMS *Lowestoft* is shown here at Portsmouth in June 1982 following a short period in dockyard hands to prepare her for service in the South Atlantic. Note the overall grey colour scheme, and the lack of pendant number and nameplate on the stern. An additional 20mm gun is carried on either side of the hangar.
Mike Lennon

57
The Clyde-built HMS *Hardy* was the first Type 14 frigate to be completed; this photograph shows her shortly after being handed over to the RN in December 1955.
Yarrow Shipbuilders Ltd

The hull was comparatively narrow for its length of 310ft and its length/beam ratio was similar to that of previous destroyer types. It featured the raised forecastle deck which had characterised the other frigate designs and a raised bulwark enclosed the forward portion of this section. Although the ships were very manoeuvrable and the hull shape had excellent seagoing characteristics, it was discovered when the ships entered service that the forward hull was too lightly constructed to cope with the stresses imposed by high speeds and rough seas and the whole class was progressively strengthened in 1958-59.

The main armament, in keeping with the specialised AS role of the ships, comprised two Mk 10 Limbo mortars mounted on the quarterdeck together with their associated mortar handling rooms. Sonar Types 174, 170 and 162 provided the detection and aiming systems. This was the same outfit as carried by the 'Whitby' class and, indeed, the Type 14 design was little inferior to the larger Type 12 in terms of AS capabilities. As with the Type 12, the smaller vessels were designed to carry AS homing torpedoes to be fired from twin trainable mountings on either beam abreast the funnel. In the event, the torpedo tubes were only mounted in *Blackwood*, *Duncan*, *Exmouth*, *Malcolm* and *Palliser* but as with the other frigate designs they were removed in the early 1960s.

The only other armament consisted of three single 40mm AA guns mounted on either side of the bridge and on the quarterdeck right aft. This light gun armament was a direct result of fitting the advanced AS equipment of the larger frigates into a relatively small hull which left no room for any other significant armament. It was presumably envisaged that the Type 14s would operate in conjunction with larger ships as they would be incapable of dealing with a gun-equipped, surfaced submarine by themselves. The lack of a medium calibre gun led to much criticism of the design and certainly limited the usefulness of the class. The only radar fitted was the Type 974 which was basically a navigation set although it could provide a short range surface surveillance element.

In view of their limited capabilities, the whole class found themselves employed on the many peacetime duties which are the lot of the Royal Navy but which do not require a full size major warship. Fishery protection was one such task and *Russell, Palliser, Duncan* and *Malcolm* were allocated to the Fishery Protection Squadron in 1958-59 replacing six 'Algerine' class minesweepers. Several ships of the class were employed in the various 'Cod Wars' with Iceland where there seakeeping qualities were taxed to the utmost in the extreme weather conditions of the area. Following her service as leader of the Fishery Protection Squadron,

HMS PELLEW

Type 14 Utility Frigate

1959

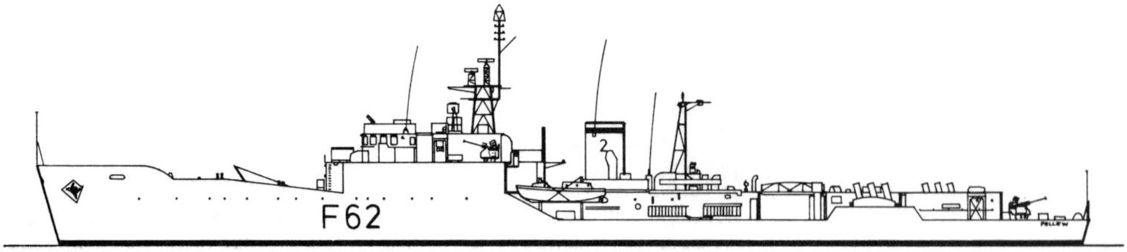

BUILDERS - Swan Hunters and Wigham Richardson.
LAID DOWN - 5th NOV 1953
LAUNCHED - 29th SEP 1954
COMPLETED - 26th JUL 1956

LENGTH - 310 ft.
BEAM - 33 ft.
DRAUGHT - 15 ft.
SPEED - 27·7 knots.

LM 81

58
Although not the first of the class, the Type 14s were known as the 'Blackwood' class after the ship of that name, which is seen here entering Portsmouth with a Rear Admiral's flag at the masthead. HMS *Blackwood* was one of the few Type 14 frigates fitted with AS torpedo tubes which can be seen on the upper deck just below the funnel. *Fleet Photographic Unit*

59
HMS *Exmouth* leads two other Type 14s into Portland harbour. The extensive ducting and new funnel, occasioned by the installation of gas turbine propulsion, can be seen to take up virtually all the space between the foremast and the AS mortars. Otherwise the ship carries the same armament and equipment as a standard Type 14. *HMS Osprey*

Duncan was transferred to the Portland-based 2nd Training Squadron in 1965. Other Type 14s to serve with this unit included *Dundas*, *Exmouth*, *Hardy* and *Murray*. During their operational lives the ships were very little altered. As already mentioned those equipped with AS torpedo tubes had them removed while all vessels had their after 40mm gun removed. Most, with the exception of *Duncan* and *Palliser*, were equipped with the more up to date Type 978 navigation radar to augment the Type 974 fitted originally.

The one vessel to undergo major reconstruction was the *Exmouth* which, in 1966, was taken in hand at Chatham Dockyard where she was converted to become the Royal Navy's first major warship to be powered entirely by gas turbines. The original steam plant was removed and replaced by a 15,000shp Olympus and two Proteus (total 6,500shp) turbines. The Olympus fitted in this ship was considerably derated in order to avoid over-stressing the hull which was only designed to absorb 15,000shp and was not further strengthened for higher speeds whilst being refitted for gas turbine operation. For the same reason, and for the sake of simplicity, the installation was of the COGOG type which meant that the ship could be powered by either the Olympus or the two Proteus but not both types together. The external appearance of the ship was altered by the installation of a large streamlined funnel set further aft than the original (which was removed) and by prominent intakes and filters for the gas turbines. The original armament of two Limbo mortars and two single 40mm guns was retained and the conversion was completed on 20 July 1968. She subsequently played an important part in the development of gas gurbine expertise in the Royal Navy and lessons learnt in her operation were incorporated in later designs. After various tests and trials she served with the 2nd Training Squadron until being laid up in reserve in December 1976. She was subsequently sold for scrapping and arrived at Briton Ferry for breaking up in February 1979.

In a contracting navy it was not considered that any effective modernisation could be carried out on this class due to its relatively small size and consequently the vessels gained the dubious distinction of being the first postwar frigates to be scrapped. *Murray* was the first to be disposed of in 1970 with *Pellew* and *Grafton* following the next year. *Blackwood* and *Malcolm* went in 1976 and 1978 respectively after being laid up for several years. *Keppel* was broken up at Sittingbourne in 1979, the same year that *Exmouth* went to the breakers. Several of the class survive as accommodation or static training ships including *Hardy* which was the last operational ship, paying off in April 1978 into reserve at Portsmouth

HMS EXMOUTH. 1,180 tons.

Type 14 Frigate (Gas Turbine Conversion)

1973

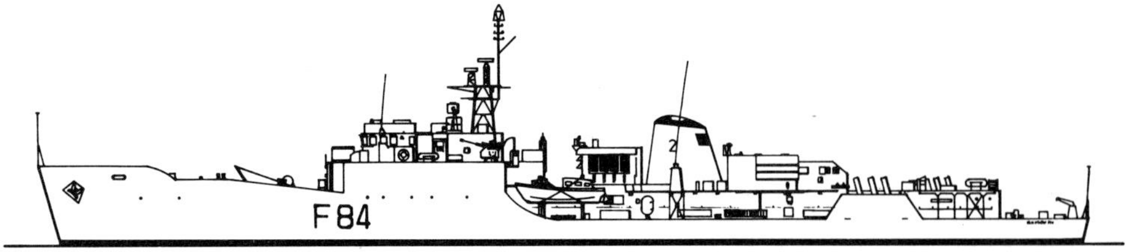

BUILDERS - J. Samuel White and Co. Ltd.
LAID DOWN - 24th MAR 1954.
LAUNCHED - 16th NOV 1955.
COMPLETED - 20th DEC 1957.

Conversion to Gas Turbine propulsion completed by Chatham Dockyard, 20th July 1968.

LENGTH - 310 ft o.a.
BEAM - 33 ft.
DRAUGHT - 15·5 ft.
SPEED - 28 knots.

© LM 82

where she was subsequently used as a stores and accommodation ship for the naval base. Also lying at Portsmouth are *Russell and Palliser*, the former acting as a static training ship for the engineering apprentices at HMS *Sultan*, while the latter is listed for disposal. North of the border, *Duncan* lies at Rosyth where she acts as an immobile tender for the training establishment HMS *Caledonia*

In retrospect it can be seen that while the Type 14 could play a useful role in a traditional World War 2 type convoy action, they were otherwise limited by their small size and specialised armament and this led to their early demise in a period when the Royal Navy was undergoing a steady decline in terms of ship numbers. An interesting comparison can be made with the contemporary French 'Le Normand' class of fast escorts which, on a similar displacement to the Type 14, mounted up to six 57mm AA guns as well as AS torpedo tubes and a Bofors AS mortar.

Ships of the Type 14 ('Blackwood') class were named after famous frigate captains of the Napoleonic period and students of warship names will be interested to note that two of the ships, *Exmouth* and *Pellew*, are named after the same man — Capt Pellew took the title of Lord Exmouth when he was raised to the peerage as a reward for his valorous escapades.

Name	No	Builders	Laid Down	Launched	Completed
Blackwood	F78	J. I. Thornycroft Co Ltd	14/9/53	4/10/55	22/8/57
Duncan	F80	J. I. Thornycroft Co Ltd	17/12/53	30/5/57	21/10/58
Dundas	F48	J. Samuel White, Cowes	17/10/52	25/9/53	9/3/56
Exmouth	F84	J. Samuel White, Cowes	24/3/54	16/11/55	20/12/57
Grafton	F51	J. Samuel White, Cowes	25/2/53	13/9/54	11/1/57
Hardy	F54	Yarrow, Scotstoun	4/2/53	25/11/53	15/12/55
Keppel	F85	Yarrow, Scotstoun	27/3/53	31/8/54	6/7/56
Malcolm	F88	Yarrow, Scotstoun	1/2/54	18/10/55	12/12/57
Murray	F91	Alex Stephens and Sons	30/11/53	25/2/55	5/6/56
Palliser	F94	Alex Stephens and Sons	15/3/55	10/5/56	13/12/57
Pellew	F62	Swan Hunter, Tyne	5/11/53	29/9/54	26/7/56
Russell	F97	Swan Hunter, Tyne	11/11/53	10/12/54	7/2/57

Data: As built
Displacement: 1,180 tons standard; 1,456 full load
Length: 310ft oa
Beam: 33ft
Draught: 15ft
Guns: 3×40mm (3×1)
Torpedoes: 4×21in AS (2×2)
AS weapons: 2×Limbo
Machinery: 2×Babcock and Wilcox boilers operating at 550lb/sq in and 850°F. English Electric geared turbines on one shaft giving a total of 15,000shp
Speed: $27\frac{3}{4}$kts ($24\frac{1}{2}$ full load)
Complement: 112

60
HMS *Dundas* had the distinction of being the first frigate of the postwar construction programme to be launched, in September 1953. Seen here in later life with the 2nd Training Squadron she also has had her after 40mm gun removed. The amount of space taken up by the two Limbo mortars can be gauged from this photo.
C. and S. Taylor

4 General Purpose Frigates

'Tribal' Class (Type 81) GP Frigates

By 1954 the wisdom of building specialised frigate types was being questioned, particularly on cost grounds, although the operational problems of grouping the right ships together at the right time and in the right place were also an important factor. Consequently design work began in that year on a frigate which could carry out most of the specialist functions of the previous separate Types 12, 41 and 61 designs. The outcome of this work was the 'Tribal' class of general purpose frigates (designated Type 81) and the first of the new class was ordered in February 1956 although, in fact, the design was not finalised until February 1957 and the first keel not laid until January 1958.

The most interesting feature of the design was the introduction, for the first time in a major Royal Navy warship, of gas turbines as part of the main propulsion system. The system adopted was COSAG (combined steam and gas turbine) and was developed both for the Type 81 frigates and the contemporary 'County' class guided missile destroyers. The main propulsion was provided by a conventional 12,000hp steam turbine which alone could drive the ship at over 20kts while further power was available from the G-6 gas turbine (7,500shp) to boost the speed to 28kts. Used on its own the gas turbine was capable of moving the ship at 21kts. The advantages of this system were that the main steam turbine could be designed to give optimum fuel efficiency at normal cruising and operational speeds and the gas turbine would provide extra power on demand when required. This in turn means that less boiler capacity was required (only one boiler was installed) with appropriate savings in space and manpower. Also, in an emergency, or when the steam system was cold, the ship could be got under way and manoeuvred at only a few minutes' notice. One disadvantage of the system as installed in the 'Tribal' class, was that a second funnel was required to carry the exhaust of the gas turbine and took up deck space which would not have been lost in a conventional steam turbine installation as in the previous Type 12 design. In fact the Type 81 was the only frigate design ever to feature two prominent funnels (the Type 41/61 designs had two separate uptakes for the diesel exhausts but these were contained in the mast structures and did not appear as separate funnels). Of course the operational flexibility gained with the new system outweighed any disadvantages and the Royal Navy was able to gain valuable experience in the operation of gas turbines in service under a wide variety of conditions. Experience was to show that the gas turbine was reliable enough to be run continuously for long periods rather than just as a boost engine. This fact was to lead to improved gas turbines being used as the sole form of propulsion in later designs (see Appendix 3 for details of gas turbine development).

A second major feature of the final design was the provision, for the first time in a British frigate design, of guided missiles as part of the main armament. Space was provided on each beam for a quadruple Seacat launcher and its associated GWS21 guidance and control system. The launchers were positioned abreast the foremast while the directors were mounted on platforms positioned on either side of the second funnel. Compared to later missile designs the Seacat was a relatively straightforward system. The missile was steered by radio command guidance, the signals being generated from a joystick control used by the missile aimer in the director. The target could be tracked either visually or by the Type 262 radar incorporated in the director. Due to delays in the development and procurement of the Seacat system, all the Type 81 frigates were completed with a single 40mm gun in place of each missile launcher and the GWS21 director was not fitted. The exception to this was *Zulu* which was completed with the Seacats installed as designed. The other vessels of the class were refitted with the Seacat system at a later date as the equipment became available.

A third innovation was the provision of facilities for the carriage and operation of a helicopter as an integral part of the ship's equipment. The provision of a hangar and flight deck meant that only one Limbo mortar could be carried as against the two fitted in the Type 12 and 14 designs, but this loss was more than outweighed by the greater flexibility and range of the helicopter.

Apart from the specific innovations mentioned above, the 'Tribal' class frigates differed from earlier frigates and destroyers by having a completely flush deck with considerable sheer. Forward of the midships point a superstructure block extended the full width of the ship and supported the bridge and mainmast. The two funnels were set well aft and raked back with the fore funnel

61
HMS *Ashanti*, the first of the 'Tribal' class, just after her completion in 1961. As with all of the class except *Zulu*, she carries single 40mm guns abreast the mast instead of the designed Seacat missile system.
Fleet Photographic Unit

62
HMS *Gurkha* running trials in 1963. The AKE1 aerial of the Type 965 radar is at the masthead and a Type 293Q is mounted on a short lattice structure abaft the bridge. Behind the after funnel is a secondary director which could control the after 4.5in gun independently of the MRS3 main director mounted on the bridge.
Fleet Photographic Unit

63
HMS *Mohawk* shortly after commissioning for service as leader of the Persian Gulf Squadron and whose badge is attatched to the funnel. Note the deck identification letter (M) painted on the flight deck. As more frigates were equipped with helicopter flight decks it became necessary to introduce a two letter code for the identification letters; thus *Mohawk's* letters become MO. *Fleet Photographic Unit*

HMS. ASHANTI. 2,300 tons.

Type 81 General Purpose Frigate.

1971.

BUILDERS - Yarrow and Co., Scotstoun.
LAID DOWN - 15th JAN 1958.
LAUNCHED - 9th MAR 1959.
COMPLETED - 23rd NOV 1961.

LENGTH - 360 ft. o.a.
BEAM - 42·3 ft.
DRAUGHT - 17·5 ft.
SPEED - 28 knots.

© LM 82

taller than the other. Further aft was set a small superstructure which incorporated the hangar with the flight deck on its roof.

The main gun armament comprised two single 4-5in guns in Mk V mountings positioned just forward of the bridge and on the quarterdeck. These mountings had come from scrapped 'C' group destroyers and were modified to improve the sighting and loading arrangements before being fitted. The use of these was mainly dictated by financial considerations as well as their ready availability. They fired a 25kg shell to a maximum range of 19km with a maximum rate of fire of nearly 14 rounds per minute, although the sustained rate would be nearer eight rounds per minute. The mounting allowed a maximum elevation of 50° which gave only limited effectiveness against aircraft and they were mainly intended for use against surface and shore targets. Fire control was provided by an MRS3 director mounted above and behind the bridge and incorporating a Type 903 radar for target tracking. The gun mountings featured remote power control (RPC) and were normally aimed and controlled by the director, but local fire control was possible. The forward 4.5in turret carried three 2in rocket flare launchers on either side and these were used for illuminating targets at night. This arrangement had featured on the 4in guns of the wartime frigate designs but had not appeared on other postwar designs.

The Seacat system already mentioned provided a simple and effective close range air defence system and was subsequently widely fitted to almost all British and several foreign warships. Two four-round launchers were fitted on each beam and the maximum range was approximately 4,750m.

Anti-submarine weapons consisted of a single Limbo mounting and a Wasp helicopter. The original design also included six single fixed AS torpedo tubes. These were to have been carried amidships angled out at 45°, three on each side, but were never fitted. A comprehensive outfit of sonars was carried including Types 177, 170 and 162. As these had a range well in excess of the Limbo mortar (approximately 1,000m), the Wasp helicopter was able to extend the ship's effective range considerably as an AS system by carrying depth charges and homing torpedoes to attack any detected target.

To fulfil the general purpose concept, it was necessary for the ship to carry a comprehensive radar outfit including a long range surveillance radar to enable aircraft direction tasks to be carried out. A Type 965 radar was fitted with its large AKE1 'bedstead' aerial carried on tall lattice foremast constructed of tubular alloy to reduce weight. Forward of this a small lattice structure carried the 'cheese' aerial of a Type 993 medium range radar used for target indicating purposes. Finally a Type 978 navigation radar was carried on a small platform projecting forward from the foremast. The whole outfit of radar and other sensors and weapons was controlled from a spacious operations room immediately abaft and below the bridge. This was air conditioned and, at the time of building, incorporated some of the most up to date equipment available.

The helicopter hangar aft was decidedly cramped and the flight deck was barely large enough for its purpose. After landing, the helicopter's main rotor blades were folded and the tail rotor boom also folded. The helicopter was then manoeuvred on to the lift and struck down into the hangar where the lift then formed part of the hangar floor. A folding canvas hatch cover was rigged over the lift well to provide a roof to the hangar. These arrangements were difficult to operate and consequently the helicopter was only struck below when weather conditions demanded; normally it was merely lashed down on the flightdeck, although this then restricted the field of fire of the Limbo mortar. It is possible that the ship was originally designed to carry two Limbo mortars and that later one mortar was deleted to make space for a hangar and flightdeck. In any event, later designs featured considerably improved facilities for the helicopter.

As far as the crew was concerned, these ships were a major step forward as regards comfort. They were the first frigates to be designed with cafeteria messing and bunk sleeping. Full air conditioning was provided for all accommodation, operational and working spaces which meant that the ships were suitable for employment in any climatic conditions. Previously ships had required modifications to operate in areas featuring extremes of climate such as the Persian Gulf or the Arctic. As part of the crew, a detachment of Royal Marines was carried complete with their weapons and equipment. This idea had first been tried out in HMS *Loch Killisport* and the success of the concept led to its adoption in the 'Tribal' class and later in all other frigates as well.

The class was, of course, named after the famous flotilla of 'Tribal' class destroyers which had a most distinguished war record. At the time of their inception, the destroyers represented a complete change of design philosophy when compared with previous designs and it was fitting that the Type 81 frigates, with their numerous innovations and new general purpose role, should perpetuate the famous names of their forebears. *Ashanti* was the lead ship of the class and was commissioned in late 1961, following which she was the subject of intensive trials to test the viability of her new propulsion system. Following the successful completion of these trials she was then engaged in further trials with the prototype Saunders Roe P531 helicopters to evolve suitable techniques for the operation of light helicopters from frigate flightdecks, although she did not receive her permanent Wasp helicopter until 1964.

The last vessel to complete was *Zulu* in April 1964. The whole class was employed worldwide on normal frigate duties but saw considerable service in the Middle East, Persian Gulf and West Indies where their high standards of accommodation and extensive air conditioning made them ideal for tropical service. In 1969 *Nubian* acted as a mid-Atlantic guardship for the trans-Atlantic air race organised to commemorate the 50th anniversary of the first direct aerial crossing of the ocean by Alcock and Brown. The long range of her Type 965 radar enabled here to track and control the Victor airborne tanker aircraft and steer them to a mid-ocean rendezvous with the participating military aircraft including a Royal Navy Phantom and an RAF Harrier.

Modifications were limited. In the late 1960s and early 1970s, those vessels not already equipped with Seacats were so fitted and the 40mm guns removed. At the same time, all ships were equipped with two single 20mm guns mounted on either beam just forward of the bridge. These were intended for use on peacetime police and patrol duties where the use of a larger gun or a guided missile was too expensive and inappropriate. This lesson had been learnt in the Indonesian Confrontation (1962/63) when it was found that patrolling frigates had no suitable weapons for engaging small craft such as junks and fishing boats which were being used for gun running and other anti-social activities.

Another piece of equipment to be fitted to all vessels of the class from 1970 onwards was the Knebworth/Corvus multiple rocket launcher system which was designed to provide decoys for the radar guidance system of attacking missiles. The multi-barrelled launchers were fitted on either beam abreast the bridge.

Ashanti and *Ghurka*, in 1968 and 1969 respectively, were fitted with the new Type 199 variable depth sonar (VDS). The equipment for this was installed on the quarterdeck and consisted of a winch and a controllable boom operating through a well cut in the stern.

Although a useful class for peacetime patrol and showing the flag duties, the relatively low speed and limited armament made the vessels unsuitable to combine with the fleet in the formation of task forces. They were employed almost exclusively on detached duties and with the introduction of new frigate types, coupled with a general run down in naval strength, they were relegated in rapid succession first to the Standby Squadron and then listed for disposal. *Ashanti* was the first to be laid up in 1979 and the last operational ship of the class, *Tartar*, decommissioned in December 1980 when she also paid off into the Standby Squadron. Following the defence review of 1981 all seven vessels were listed for disposal in August 1981, although none was sold.

As a postscript, it is interesting to note a scheme pro-

64
HMS *Ashanti* was one of two Type 81 frigates to be equipped with the Type 199 VDS when she was refitted in 1968. At the same time she was re-equipped with Seacat missiles on either beam and the Type 293Q radar was replaced by a Type 993. 20mm guns were mounted on either beam just forward of the bridge and these, and the other modifications, are apparent in this view of *Ashanti* as leader of the 6th Frigate Squadron in 1971. Note the canvas cover over the opening in the flight-deck caused by lowering the lift to strike down the Wasp helicopter. *Skyfotos*

65
HMS *Eskimo* enters Portsmouth in the mid-1970s. The 'Tribals' were equipped with the GWS21 Seacat system and the directors for this, mounted on either beam abreast the after funnel, were based on the MRS1 fire control system which had featured in earlier frigates and utilised the same Type 262 radar. *C. and S. Taylor*

66
HMS *Gurkha* was one of three Type 81 frigates reactivated as a result of the Falklands crisis and is shown here in October 1982, in the all grey finish applied to RN operational ships following experience in the campaign. She carried a later version of the MRS3 director (compare with the version carried by *Eskimo* in the preceding photograph). *Mike Lennon*

posed by Vosper Ship Repairers to modernise the ships with a view to selling them to foreign navies. The modernisation involved the removal of the two 4.5in guns and their replacement with a single automatic 76mm gun mounted forward. Aft, the Mk 10 mortar, hangar and flightdeck were to be removed and a new hangar installed serving a conventional flightdeck extending to the stern so that the ship would be capable of operating a Lynx helicopter. A large streamlined funnel replaced the previous two separate funnels and a modern lightweight fire control system was to be installed. At one time it was reported that Venezuela was interested in purchasing some of the class, but whether they would have been modernised as part of the deal was not made clear. It seems a pity that the proposed modernisation could not have been applied to the class as a whole with all ships being retained in Royal Navy service as most of them had been relegated to the disposal list well before reaching what would normally be considered the end of their useful lives.

As it happened, the Falklands crisis brought a reprieve for some of the 'Tribal' class. In order to replace losses and to cover for ships undergoing repairs and refits as a result of damage sustained, it was decided to recommission three Type 81 frigates. Following a rapid refit to bring her up to operational standard, *Tartar* was commissioned at Devonport on 17 July 1982, followed by *Ghurka* at Rosyth on 24 July and *Zulu* at Chatham on 9 August. At present it is unlikely that any other of the 'Tribals' will see further service and, technically, they are still available for disposal. It is likely that when ships of other classes, damaged in the Falklands, return to service then the three activated ships will return at least to the Standby Squadron. However, the exercise has shown the value of having ships available in reserve and it would be a mistake to sell off ships such as these when they can be brought into service to back up front line ships at relatively short notice. It would take four or five years to build a replacement frigate but *Zulu* was refitted and commissioned within a period of only 50 days.

Name	No	Builders	Laid Down	Launched	Completed
Ashanti	F117	Yarrow and Co, Scotstoun	15/1/58	9/3/59	23/11/61
Eskimo	F119	J. Samuel White and Co, Cowes	22/10/58	20/3/60	21/2/63
Ghurka	F122	J. I. Thornycroft and Co Ltd, Woolston	3/11/58	11/7/60	13/2/63
Mohawk	F125	Vickers Armstrong Ltd, Barrow	23/12/60	5/4/62	29/11/63
Nubian	F131	HM Dockyard, Portsmouth	7/9/59	6/9/60	9/10/62
Tartar	F133	HM Dockyard, Devonport	22/10/59	19/9/60	26/2/62
Zulu	F124	Alex Stephens and Sons, Govan	13/12/60	3/7/62	17/4/64

Data: As built
Displacement: 2,300 tons standard; 2,700 tons full load
Length: 360ft
Beam: 42.3ft
Draught: 17.5ft
Guns: 2×4.5in (2×1) on Mk V mounting
2×40mm (2×1) AA (not *Zulu*)
Missiles: 8×Seacat (2×4) with GWS21 fire control (*Zulu* only)
AS weapons: 1×three-barrelled Limbo Mk 10
Aircraft: 1×Westland Wasp HAS1
Machinery: COSAG. Metrovick steam turbine 12,500shp; Metrovick G6 gas turbine 7,500shp
Speed: 28kts (20kts steam turbine only)
Complement: 253

'Leander' Class (Type 12M) GP Frigates

The 1951 frigate construction programme had resulted in 26 ships of four distinct classes (six 'Whitby' class, 12 'Blackwood' class, four 'Salisbury' class, four 'Leopard' class). Follow on orders produced the nine ships of the 'Rothesay' class while three more 'Salisbury' class and three further 'Rothesay' class were planned although orders for these six ships were cancelled and replaced by other contracts. Although the Royal Navy was thus given a reasonable number of escort vessels of modern design, the policy of building ships specialising in a particular role was not entirely satisfactory. From a financial point of view, it was obviously very expensive to design and build four different vessel types and the resultant lack of standardisation meant that routine operation and maintenance was more expensive than would be the case if only a single frigate type was being

67
The name ship of the largest class of frigates to be built for the Royal Navy since the end of World War 2, HMS *Leander* is shown here in her original configuration with two single 40mm guns on the hangar roof instead of the intended Seacat missiles. Although a straight development of the earlier 'Whitby/Rothesay' class, the 'Leanders' were a considerable improvement on the earlier vessels. An extensive rearrangement of internal spaces left more room for extra equipment and improved accommodation. *Fleet Photographic Unit*

68
HMS *Galatea* in 1968. She has the standard radar outfit consisting of a Type 903 on the MRS3 gunnery director, a Type 993 at the top of the foremast and a Type 965 on the mainmast. A navigation radar is carried on a small platform projecting forward of the foremast and ECM equipment is mounted on the side of the foremast. *Skyfotos*

69
HMS *Juno* in 1974. The director of the GWS22 Seacat system was based on the MRS3 gunnery director and can be seen offset to starboard on the hangar roof. The platform carrying the navigation radar is now angled out to port half way up the foremast. Note the high angle of elevation on the 4.5in guns. *Skyfotos*

70

HMS *Hermione* was one of the first Batch 3 Broad Beam 'Leanders' and was one of only four of this batch to carry VDS. Apart from the extra beam, the last batch of 'Leanders' featured several internal improvements over the first batches. Generating capacity was improved from 1,600kW in the first batch to 2,500kW, and propulsion machinery had been progressively modified so that it could now be remotely operated from a machinery control room. *Mike Lennon*

71

An aerial view of HMS *Achilles* just after completion in 1970. The Limbo mortar can be seen tilted on its side on the well aft of the flightdeck. In this position the mortar bombs are pushed into the barrels by hydraulic rams. Note that, although the ship has a well aft, the VDS is not fitted. *Yarrow (Shipbuilders) Ltd*

used. From an operational point of view there were problems in arranging suitable deployments so that the right vessels were available in the correct combinations for a particular task.

With the design and development of the 'Tribal' class, a move had been made away from the specialised types. They were, however, mainly designed for detached service on foreign stations and their speed and armament did not fit them for a role as major fleet escorts. Consequently it was decided to take the successful Type 12 design ('Whitby'/'Rothesay' class) as a basis for the development of a general purpose frigate. The basic hull and machinery of the Type 12 was retained (the Y-100 steam plant also used in the Type 14), the major difference being the elimination of the stepped quarterdeck which resulted in a completely flush deck apart from the raised forecastle section. The superstructure was completely redesigned into a single block positioned along the midships third of the hull. At the fore end of this was a new enclosed bridge giving a much improved view, especially aft. A tapered upright funnel with a domed top was mounted between two streamlined masts and a hangar for a Wasp helicopter was incorporated into the after end of the superstructure. Almost all the internal space was air conditioned which considerably improved working and living conditions although, perversely enough, many sailors preferred the older 'Whitby' class as it still retained the scuttles which allowed natural daylight into the messdecks. Despite this, the introduction of air conditioning and the resultant elimination of many openings to the outside atmosphere meant that effective measures could be taken against nuclear fallout and chemical agents.

The new design was referred to as the Modified Type 12 and, reflecting the growing importance of the frigate type, the units were named after characters from classical mythology; names which had previously been borne by cruiser type vessels. In all, 26 ships of the class were to be built for the Royal Navy making them by far the largest class of major warships to be built in this country since the end of World War 2.

A balanced armament was carried to allow the class to carry out a wide variety of tasks. The main gun armament featured two 4.5in guns in the ubiquitous Mk VI dual purpose mounting but the Mk 6M director previously used with this gun mounting was replaced by the new MRS3 fire control system utilising the Type 903 radar. The MRS3 director, with its distinctive dish aerial, was smaller and lighter than the Mk 6M and was mounted immediately abaft the bridge. For short range air defence two single 40mm AA guns were carried on the hangar roof although the designed armament was a

HMS AJAX. 2,450 tons.
Type 12 (modified). Leander Class Frigate.
1969

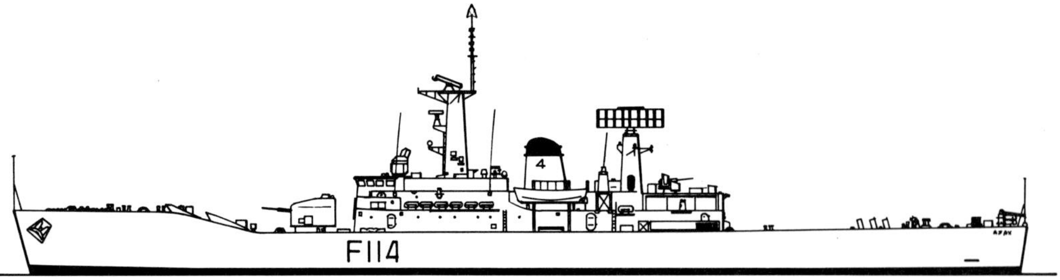

BUILDERS - Cammell Laird and Co. Ltd.
LAID DOWN - 12th OCTOBER 1959.
LAUNCHED - 16th AUGUST 1962.
COMPLETED - 10th DECEMBER 1963.

LENGTH - 372 ft.
BEAM - 41 ft.
DRAUGHT - 18 ft.
SPEED - 30 knots.

quadruple Seacat launcher with its associated director. The 40mm guns were only fitted on the first seven vessels (*Leander*, *Dido*, *Penelope*, *Ajax*, *Aurora*, *Galatea* and *Euryalus*) and subsequent vessels mounted the Seacats as intended. The earlier vessels were eventually refitted with the Seacats and the 40mm guns removed. In the late 1960s, those vessels carrying Seacats were equipped with two single 20mm guns mounted abreast the foremast on the upper superstructure. In the same period Knebworth/Corvus chaff dispensers were fitted abreast the mainmast as defence against air- and surface-launched anti-ship missiles. All Seacat-equipped ships mounted the GWS22 (Guided Weapon System Mk 22) director which closely resembled the MRS3 director and utilised a similar radar for target acquisition and ranging. The GWS22 director was offset to the starboard side of the hangar roof while the Seacat launcher was on the port side and further aft to give a reasonable field of fire. The single exception to this arrangement was *Naiad* which was the sole example equipped with the GWS20 system. This was a much simpler system where the director was moved manually to the target bearing by matching pointers displaying information from the ship's weapon direction system. This system was fitted for the Seacat installation in the 'Rothesay' class, *Salisbury* and *Lincoln* (qv) and the assault ships *Fearless* and *Intrepid*.

Anti-submarine weapons consisted of a Mk 10 three-barrelled Limbo mortar mounted in a recessed well aft of the flightdeck and a Westland Wasp helicopter (MATCH system). With its comparatively spacious hangar and adequate flightdeck, the helicopter could be operated much more effectively than was possible with the cramped arrangement of the preceding 'Tribal' class. Maintenance could be carried out in more convenient circumstances and a greater variety of stores and spares could be carried. A wide variety of sonars was fitted including the Type 177 (or Type 184 on later vessels), Type 170B attack sonar, Type 162 bottomed target sonar, and Type 199 variable depth sonar (in some vessels only — see below). The variable depth sonar was intended to be fitted in a well situated in the extreme stern of the ship. All vessels in the class (except the last five — *Scylla*, *Achilles*, *Diomede*, *Apollo* and *Ariadne*) had the VDS well but only *Leander*, *Dido*, *Aurora*, *Naiad*, *Arethusa*, *Cleopatra*, *Charybdis*, *Hermione*, *Jupiter* and *Bacchante* were actually equipped with the sonar gear. Variable depth sonar was a method of overcoming the fact that sonar rays can be refracted by layers of water of differing temperatures which meant that sonar signals from a surface vessel could be prevented from ever reaching a deep submarine. By lowering a sonar transmitter and receiver through some of the surface layers of water meant that the effective range of the sonar could be substantially increased. However, the resulting equipment was difficult to handle and operate, and was not of much use in areas of relatively shallow water such as the North Sea and British coastal waters. For these reasons the equipment was not fitted to all of the class.

The main radar was the Type 965 with an AKE1 aerial surmounted by an IFF interrogator. This was the same as that fitted to the 'Tribal' class and was used for air surveillance and aircraft direction. The aerial array was mounted on the short mainmast. For general air and surface warning a Type 993 was carried with its distinctive 'cheese' aerial mounted on a forward extension at the top of the foremast. A polelike extension to the foremast carried HF/DF and ECM equipment whilst a Type 975 or 978 navigation radar was carried on a small platform situated half way up the foremast structure.

The resulting ships had a handsome and balanced profile and with the large number built they formed the backbone of the Royal Navy's escort force throughout the 1970s and into the 1980s. The class was actually laid down in three distinct sub-groups or batches. The first batch of 10 ships were all built to the original design whilst the second batch of six had a revised engineroom layout featuring improved machinery designated Y-136 (the first group's machinery was designated Y-100). The third group of 10 ships had their beam increased to 43ft which improved stability as well as providing extra internal volume. These were referred to as the 'Broad Beam Leanders', and again detail improvements to the propulsion machinery gave rise to a new designation, Y160. Several vessels in the first group were built instead of cancelled vessels from the earlier programmes. *Leander*, *Ajax* and *Dido* were originally laid down as 'Rothesay' class vessels where their original names would have been *Weymouth*, *Fowey* and *Hastings*. *Penelope* was originally ordered as a Type 61 named *Coventry*.

The obvious qualities of the design were not lost on foreign navies and several were built for export while others were built to the basic design in overseas yards. Two were laid down in UK yards for the Royal New Zealand Navy in 1964 and 1969, whilst a further pair were laid down in 1971 and 1972 for the Chilean Navy. The latter pair featured four Exocet launchers on the quarterdeck. The Indian, Australian and Dutch navies ordered three, two and six vessels respectively; the vessels being built in the respective countries' own yards. The Dutch vessels carried Dutch radar equipment and had two quadruple Seacat launchers on the hangar roof.

At the beginning of the 1970s, the vessels of the first batch were approaching their mid-life refit and consideration was given to the incorporation of new weapons and electronic systems into the existing hulls. The Royal Australian Navy had developed the Ikara AS system which consisted of a rocket-propelled missile which carried a homing torpedo out to the computed position of a target submarine. The torpedo made a parachute-retarded descent into the target area and then eventually homed on to the target. The system had the great advantage of a sharply reduced reaction time as compared to the MATCH system and could also be used in all weathers. The original application of the Australian weapon system was in the Type 82 destroyers of which three were cancelled, leaving only HMS *Bristol* to complete. Subsequently it was decided to install the system in the Batch 1 'Leanders' as they became due for their major refits and *Leander*, the nameship of the class, was the first to undergo the lengthy process in the newly built Frigate Complex at Devonport Dockyard. Emerging in December 1972, her appearance was in marked contrast to the previous balanced outline of the class.

The installation of the Ikara system entailed major changes to the ships' armament and electronic systems. Forward, the 4.5in gun turret was removed and in its place a deckhouse extended forward of the bridge to a circular zareba mounted over the break in the forecastle deck. Inside the zareba was the actual missile launcher which could be covered by a folding 'pram hood' when not in use. The deckhouse contained the missile handling room where the missile could be assembled prior to being moved forward on to the launcher. The missile was in effect a small aeroplane with a span of 5ft (1.53m) and a length of 11ft 4in (3.43m) and was stored in the space previously occupied by the gun ammunition hoists and magazines. Whilst in store, the missile was complete with torpedo, but to save space the wings and fins were detached. When required for action the missile was moved to the missile handling room where the assembly was completed and a serviceability check carried out.

Once on the launcher, the operation of the missile was controlled by the ADAWS5 (Action Data Automation Weapon System). The ADAWS5 system fitted to the Ikara-equipped 'Leanders' was a reduced version of the ADAWS3 fitted to the Type 82, and subsequent Type 42, destroyers. Utilising a Ferranti FM1600 and a single display central equipment, the ADAWS5 provided fire control and weapon systems management. The new equipment naturally made demands on internal space and the operations room was enlarged and redisgned to provide room for two conferance radar displays as well as four labelled plan displays and two tote displays showing alphanumeric information.

In place of the MRS3 director fitted to the gun-equipped 'Leanders' a missile tracking radar was mounted atop the bridge, while just abaft of the bridge there was a smaller aerial on a short pole mast. This is the aerial for the command guidance system. The firing sequence of the Ikara missile commences when a submarine target is detected and identified within range. The ADAWS5 system calculates the correct angle of firing for the missile and moves the launcher to the appropriate bearing and angle of elevation. The computer will

HMS ARETHUSA. 2450 tons.
Leander Class Frigate (Ikara Conversion).
1978

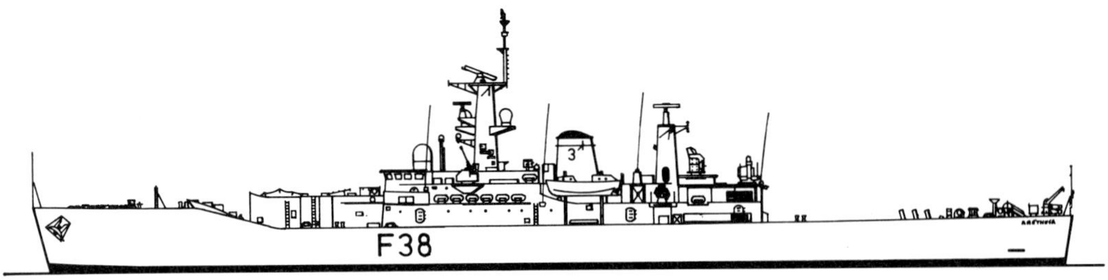

BUILDERS - J. Samuel White and Co. Ltd.
LAID DOWN - 7th SEPTEMBER 1962.
LAUNCHED - 5th NOVEMBER 1963.
COMPLETED - 24th NOVEMBER 1965.

IKARA conversion carried out at H.M. Dockyard Portsmouth. Completed in NOVEMBER 1976.

LENGTH - 372 ft.
BEAM - 41 ft.
DRAUGHT - 18 ft.
SPEED - 30 knots.

© LM 81

72
HMS *Ajax* was the second Batch 1 ship to be converted to carry the Ikara AS missile. Immediately in front of the bridge is the deckhouse containing the missile assembly area and forward of that is the covered zareba enclosing the missile launcher. *MoD (Navy)*

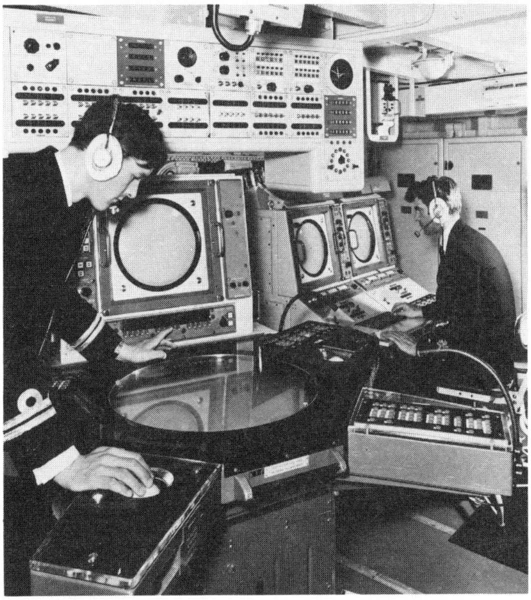

73
Part of HMS *Leander's* operations room after conversion. In the foreground is the 'conference' display for the principal warfare officer and his assistants. On this would be displayed synthetic data derived from radar and sonar information. The smaller vertical display would show alphanumeric data giving details of weapon states, hostile and friendly aircraft identifications, ship dispositions and any other information required. This data would be available from the computers installed as part of the ADAWS5 system. *Plessey Radar Ltd*

74
The bridge of *Euryalus* showing the missile tracking radar under the large dome and the smaller aerial for the missile command guidance system on the short mast behind. Also visible is one of the two 40mm guns carried by these ships on specially constructed platforms abaft the bridge. *Author*

identify the correct moment to launch and once airborne the missile is located and tracked by the tracking radar. The positions of the missile and target are continuously monitored by the computer and any necessary alterations of course are signalled to the missile by a coded radio link transmitted from the command aerial. The lightweight torpedo carried by the missile is released by radio command at a point calculated by the computer, descends into the sea by parachute, and homes acoustically on to the target. The missile body flies clear of the engagement area before ditching in the sea.

The Limbo AS mortar was retained as was the Wasp helicopter which could still be used for the dropping of homing torpedoes and other AS weapons. The converted 'Leanders' were thus equipped with no less than three separate methods of attacking submarines!

The Type 965 radar and its associated AKE1 aerial were removed as it was not required in the ships' new AS role. The internal space thus saved could be used for the installation of the new ADAWS equipment. A Cossor 1010 IFF interrogator was installed with its small aerial on the mainmast. The radar fit on the foremast was basically unchanged with the Type 993 radar remaining. New additions included SCOT (satellite communications terminal) aerials mounted on platforms projecting forward to starboard and aft to port of the foremast. The HF/DF equipment previously fitted at the peak of the foremast was replaced by a small stabilised 'headlamp' aerial having an ECCM function.

At the time of their conversion, most of the Batch 1 vessels had been equipped with a Seacat launcher on the hangar roof, offset to port. The converted vessels were fitted with two quadruple launchers mounted on the after corners of the hangar. A GWS22B fire control director was mounted on an elevated platform immediately abaft the mainmast. The new arrangement increased the number of missiles available to engage aerial targets but the positioning of the director meant that it was impossible to engage targets forward of the beam. Two single 40mm on electronically powered Mk 9 mountings were installed on the upper superstructure abeam the foremast, but these were only intended to give the ship some light firepower for the peacetime policing role and were of limited effectiveness against aerial targets.

Finally all the converted ships not already so equipped, were fitted with variable depth sonar.

The sum of all these modifications was a highly specialised, but very effective, AS frigate which was totally removed from the general purpose concept which had led to the inception of the 'Leander' class. Carrying a comprehensive selection of AS weapons and sonar devices, the Ikara-equipped 'Leanders' were probably the most effective vessels of their type in the world at the time of their conversion. However, their almost total lack of any self-defence capability against air or surface attack meant that they would normally only be able to operate as part of a larger force whose composition included vessels able to provide the necessary cover.

Of the 10 vessels comprising Batch 1, all were converted to carry the Ikara system except for *Penelope* which was acting as the trials ship for the Seawolf missile system, and *Cleopatra*. Dates and place of conversion are as below:

Name	**Completed**	**Place**
Leander	December 1972	Devonport
Ajax	September 1973	Devonport
Galetea	September 1974	Devonport
Naiad	July 1975	Devonport
Euryalus	March 1976	Devonport
Aurora	March 1976	Chatham
Arethusa	April 1977	Portsmouth
Dido	October 1978	Devonport

Although all in service at the time of writing, the defence review announced by the Conservative government in 1981 cast doubts on the future employment of these ships and it is likely that most of them will be placed in reserve with one or two of the oldest being sold or scrapped.

As the introduction of the Ikara missile to the Royal Navy led to the conversion of the earlier 'Leanders', so the introduction of the French-designed Exocet surface-to-surface missile led to the redesign and modification of the second or Batch 2 group of 'Leanders'. Exocet was a French-developed anti-ship missile powered by a two-stage solid fuel rocket motor with a maximum range of about 25 nautical miles (45km). Following successful trials aboard HMS *Norfolk* ('County' class guided missile destroyer) in May and June 1974, the missile was ordered in large quantities to be installed aboard several types of Royal Navy vessels. The demise of carrier-borne air power and the lack of large calibre guns in the fleet had meant that the Royal Navy lacked any effective method of attacking the ever growing Russian surface fleet, and it was for this reason that some of the 'Leander' class were selected to be equipped with the new missile.

Again, fitting the new weapon system gave rise to a radical change of appearance to the well known 'Leander' class silhouette. Forward of the bridge, the twin 4.5in gun turret was removed and replaced by a low superstructure carrying four Exocet canister launchers mounted in two pairs. The Exocet launcher consists of a sealed container holding one missile. After all four missiles have been fired it is necessary to return to a shore base for the empty containers to be removed and reloads to be mounted. The container system means that the missiles are constantly ready for firing and require no maintenance while the ship is at sea. The main drawback is the lack of reloads at sea which means that the ship's commander has to be very prudent in his use of the limited stock of missiles. One advantage of the Exocet missile is that, once it is launched, it is completely independent of

HMS CLEOPATRA. 2450 tons.

Leander Class Frigate (Exocet Conversion).

1978

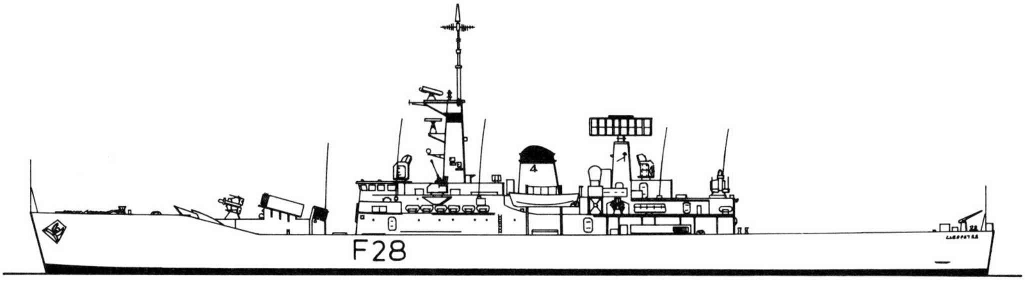

BUILDERS - H.M. Dockyard Devonport.
LAID DOWN - 19th JUNE 1963.
LAUNCHED - 25th MARCH 1964.
COMPLETED - 4th JANUARY 1966.

Exocet conversion carried out at H.M. Dockyard Devonport. Completed on 28th. November 1975.

LENGTH - 372 ft.
BEAM - 41 ft.
DRAUGHT - 18 ft.
SPEED - 30 knots.

the ship and requires no guidance link. This feature makes it very difficult for a potential enemy to jam or counter the missile. When a target is detected by the ship's Type 993 radar, the co-ordinates of its position are fed into the missile's inertial guidance system and constantly updated until the point of firing. Once launched, the missile speeds on its way to the computed target position skimming only a few feet above the surface of the sea (height is maintained by means of signals generated by the missile's radio altimeter). Between 12 and 15km from the target, the missile's own radar activates to provide the final guidance. The low level of approach and late activation of the radar means that effective countermeasures are difficult to mount (although British forces in the Falklands found Chaff quite effective). The fact that the missile launchers were lighter than the gun turret which they replaced, coupled with the fact that no extra radar or guidance systems needed to be installed, meant that for once no topweight or stability problems were caused by the new installation. This in turn meant that a margin was available for other equipment.

The VDS well aft was plated in and the faithful Limbo system removed, the resultant gap also being plated over. These alterations provided increased accommodation below the quarterdeck and resulted in a considerable increase in the area of the flightdeck. This was to enable the ships to operate the new Lynx helicopter which in itself was a major technological advance over the previously carried Wasp. The Lynx was faster, had a greater range and endurance, and could carry a heavier load than the Wasp. In 1981, Lynx flights were equipped with the Sea Skua missile which was particularly effective against fast surface targets and replaced the previous AS12 wire-guided missiles carried by the Wasp and Lynx. To accommodate the Lynx, which was much bigger than the Wasp, the hangar was extended several feet aft.

A quadruple Seacat launcher was mounted on each after corner of the enlarged hangar with a GWS 22D director on a built up section of superstructure just abaft the mainmast. Another quadruple launcher was situated on the forecastle, just forward of the Exocet launchers, and this was controlled by a GWS22D director mounted above the bridge and replacing the MRS3 director associated with the 4.5in guns. The arrangement allowed a 360° defence against aircraft with two separate control systems, and was a great improvement on the layout adopted on the Ikara conversions. The only guns carried were two Mk 9 single Bofors mountings on the upper superstructure abreast the foremast as in the earlier conversions.

Radar equipment remained basically unaltered but

improved ESM and ECCM equipment was mounted on the pole foremast which was now surmounted by a distinctive 'dunce's cap' aerial. On platforms winged out port and starboard just forward of the mainmast were the bulbous covers for the SCOT aerials.

To counteract the removal of the Limbo AS mortar, the Plessey STWS-1 (Ship's Torpedo Weapon System) was fitted. This consisted of two sets of triple torpedo tubes mounted on a platform at boat deck level either side of the hangar. The tubes could be operated by remote control and fired the American Mk 32 homing torpedo. This had a diameter of 324mm (roughly 12.75in) and was the ship-launched version of the Mk 46 air-dropped torpedo which was already carried by the Wasp and Lynx helicopters.

All in all, the Exocet-equipped 'Leanders' retained more of a general purpose capability than the Ikara conversions. Their main drawback was probably the limited number of Exocets carried, but the simplicity of the installation meant that space was available to carry other equipment such as the extra Seacat launcher and the Lynx helicopter.

All the ships of Batch 2 were converted together with the Batch 1 ships *Cleopatra* and *Penelope*. Dates and places of conversion are as follows:

Name	Completed	Date
Cleopatra	November 1975	Devonport
Phoebe	April 1977	Devonport
Sirius	October 1977	Devonport
Minerva	March 1979	Chatham
Argonaut	March 1980	Devonport
Danae	September 1980	Devonport
Penelope	March 1981	Devonport
Juno	Due 1983	Portsmouth

It will be noticed that the majority of the extensive conversion programme involving 'Leander' class frigates was carried out at Devonport Dockyard. This was because of the specially built facilities provided by the dockyard's Frigate Complex. Here, three enormous covered dry docks were available. Each dock, housed in the largest buildings of their type in Europe, was provided with full workshop and crane facilities so that work could proceed all year round without regard to weather conditions.

Penelope, one of the Batch 1 vessels which was subsequently given the Exocet conversion, had had a chequered history. Shortly after completion in 1963 she was withdrawn from normal duties to act as a sonar trials vessel and later the Type 965 radar was removed. Following this she was selected as the trials ship for the new Seawolf and its associated GWS25 guidance and control system. After a lengthy refit, she emerged in 1973 with a considerably altered appearance. Gone was the forward gun turret, the after 40mm guns and the Limbo mortar. To house the new radar systems and the associated operators and trials staff, two large interconnected deckhouses were constructed on the flight deck. The hangar space was also converted to provide further accommodation and no helicopter was carried. On top of the after deckhouse was the aerial of the Type 910 missile tracking radar with two dish aerials of the command link transmitters on the same mounting. The mainmast was heightened and at the top was a new cylindrical aerial housing which carried the aerials for a Type 967 L-band air surveillance radar and a Type 968 S-band surface target radar in a back-to-back arrangement. The foremast radar fit remained unaltered and the MRS3 fire control system, although redundant, was not removed. Possibly it was utilised for target tracking and ranging during the Seawolf trials. The Seawolf trials were extremely successful and the missile first went to sea on an operational ship when the first Type 22 frigate, HMS *Broadsword*, commissioned in 1979. During trials the Seawolf on one occasion demonstrated its ability to intercept a 4.5in shell in flight. The United States Navy was most impressed with the system and, at their request, *Penelope* visited America in order to demonstrate the missile to them. With her trials role completed, *Penelope* was taken in hand for conversion to an Exocet carrying 'Leander' and this work was nearing completion in late 1981.

With the conversion programme for the Batch 2 vessels well under way, attention turned to the Batch 3 (broad beam) vessels. The first vessel to undergo the metamorphosis, *Andromeda*, paid off at Devonport in January 1978. When she emerged three years later her appearance was even more completely altered than had been the case with the Exocet and Ikara ships. Indeed she was barely recognisable as a 'Leander' at all! At the start of the refit all the previous main armament systems (4.5in gun turret, Seacat missiles, Limbo mortar) were removed together with their associated control systems (MRS3 and GWS22 directors). Much of the upper superstructure was lightened, particularly aft of the funnel where deckhouses around the base of the mainmast were removed as were various platforms and support structures from the hangar sides. All existing radar systems were also removed.

Mounted on a platform at the break of the forecastle was a sextuple launcher for the Seawolf missile which, as described, had previously been tested aboard HMS *Penelope*. Immediately abaft the bridge was the Type 910 tracking radar and associated command aerial dishes, the whole system comprising the GWS25 missile system. The Seawolf was a much more effective self-defence system than the Seacat carried by previous 'Leanders' and could be used against anti-ship missiles as well as aircraft.

In the well of the forecastle were four Exocet container launchers which were mounted in pairs and angled out to

75
An aft view of HMS *Naiad* after conversion showing the VDS gear aft and the two quadruple Seacat launchers atop the hangar. The platforms projecting either side of the foremast are intended to carry the SCOT satellite communication system which was not fitted at the time this photograph was taken. *HMS Osprey*

76
HMS *Cleopatra* was the first of the class to be converted to carry Exocet missiles and these can be seen mounted on the foredeck replacing the 4.5in gun turret. Also on the forecastle is a Seacat missile launcher and its associated GWS22 director replacing the MRS3 gunnery director above the bridge. The AS torpedo tubes can just be seen at boat deck level abreast the hangar although *Cleopatra* and *Phoebe* were the only ships to carry them in this position. *HMS Osprey*

HMS ANDROMEDA. 2,600 tons.
Leander Class Frigate (Seawolf Conversion).
1981.

BUILDERS - H.M. Dockyard, Portsmouth.
LAID DOWN - 25 MAY 1966.
LAUNCHED - 24 th MAY 1967.
COMPLETED - 2nd DEC 1968.

Seawolf conversion carried out at H.M. Dockyard Portsmouth. Completed in April, 1981.

LENGTH - 372 ft. o.a.
BEAM - 43 ft.
DRAUGHT - 18·5 ft.
SPEED - 28 knots.

port and starboard — a different arrangement to the Batch 2 vessels where the launchers were aligned fore and aft. The launchers were also mounted directly on the forecastle deck rather than on a raised platform and the new arrangement meant that the Seawolf launcher had a much improved field of fire compared with the forward Seacat launcher mounted on the Batch 2 conversions.

Looking aft, the Limbo and VDS wells were plated over to provide extra accommodation and a larger flightdeck area, thus allowing room for a Lynx helicopter. To this end, the hangar was lengthened aft. The quarterdeck was cut away in the port after corner in order to provide space for the small hydraulic crane which had previously been mounted at the after end of the flightdeck where it presented something of a hazard to flying operations. It was now mounted at main deck level below the flight deck. This crane was used for streaming AS decoys, sonar listening devices and other items. On either side of the hangar on the upper deck were mounted the Plessey STWS-1 triple torpedo tubes firing AS torpedoes.

Amidships, the most striking change was to the funnel where the distinctive domed top, which was almost a 'Leander' 'trademark', was removed leaving a rather ungraceful flat top. This was one of many moves to reduce topweight. Abaft the funnel, on the starboard side, was a platform for a Gemini inflatable craft and a small boat which had previously been carried aft on the quarterdeck. A new crane was fitted to handle the boats and the appearance of this was very similar to the cranes carried by World War 2 German light cruisers. On the port side abeam the funnel was space for a seaboat and its davits, but this was not carried by *Andromeda* when she commenced trials in April 1981, following completion of the refit.

The foremast was altered in profile to give a broad platform at the top to carry the new radar equipment. This consisted of ESM equipment mounted around a thick conical structure which carried a further circular platform on which was mounted a fully stabilised radar aerial housing. Contained in this was the back-to-back arrangement of the Type 967 and 968 radar antennae as previously fitted on HMS *Penelope*. The weight of this double system, coupled with the height at which it was mounted, meant that great efforts had to be made in other directions to reduce topweight so that stability would remain within acceptable limits and this led to the rather 'bare' look of these conversions. The usual UHF communication aerials were fitted on crosstrees at the top of the foremast and a Type 975 navigation radar was mounted on a platform halfway up the mast and projecting forward and to port.

77
HMS *Sirius* at speed, with the flightdeck crew in the hangar awaiting the arrival of the ship's Lynx helicopter. The flightdeck area has been increased by deletion of the AS mortar in order that the ship could operate the Lynx which was considerably bigger than the Wasp. Note the AS torpedo tubes at the forward end of the flightdeck angled to port and starboard for flying stations.
HMS Osprey

78
HMS *Danae* in 1981. The lengthening of the hangar to take a Lynx helicopter gave more room for the twin Seacat launchers and their GWS22 director on the hangar roof. *HMS Osprey*

The original mainmast was removed and replaced by a taller, thinner and lighter structure surmounted by a pole aerial (possibly an improved TACAN system). Abreast the mainmast, to port and starboard, lightweight structures supported small circular platforms for the SCOT system aerials which were not fitted originally in *Andromeda* at the commencement of her post-refit trials. The 20mm guns, previously mounted just behind the enclosed bridge, were moved aft to a point abeam the foremast and lowered to boat deck level. The Knebworth/Corvus launchers remained on their platforms at boat deck level either side of the mainmast.

Not immediately obvious were alterations to the sonar and electronic equipment. The previous sonar types were replaced by the new Type 2016 which was a modern advanced capability sonar. The Seawolf GWS25 system employs two FM1600b computers and the ships are also fitted with ADAWS, probably similar to the ADAWS5 fitted to the Ikara conversions. The increased use of automation has had the effect of reducing the manning requirement and the complement of this version is only 214, which compares favourably with the 250 or more of the standard 'Leander'. Also, of course, the accommodation space for the lower number of men is improved. As converted, the Batch 3 'Leanders' have an AS capability matched only by the later Type 22 frigates (qv) and their self-defence measures are on balance better than those of the other conversions. At present *Andromeda* and *Charybdis* are in service with *Hermione*, *Jupiter* and *Scylla* nearing completion of their rebuilding.

The 'Leander' programme represented the largest class of major warships built for the Royal Navy since the end of World War 2. There were many benefits to be gained from such a long running programme of a standard design in terms of building costs and operating economies. It is perhaps surprising that the programme was continued to the planned 26 ships in a period where continuous defence cuts and reviews were the order of the day although even so the period of construction spanned 14 years which meant that the last ships were nearing completion while the earlier ships were being extensively altered to take advantage of new weapons. The graceful outline of the 'Leander' class frigate came to be almost synonymous with the Royal Navy throughout the 1960s and 1970s. Perhaps the best known ship of the class, as far as the general public was concerned, was HMS *Phoebe* which starred in a popular TV series entitled 'Warship'. In this series about life in the modern Royal Navy she was known as HMS *Hero* although she was displaced in later series of the programme by HMS *Jupiter* which had her pendant number repainted so that the casual observer would not notice the substitution.

Of course, Royal Navy frigates have more important things to do than embark on a career in show business and, although it is not possible to trace the career of all 26 ships, it is interesting to look at the travels of one ship of the class in order to gain an insight into the work life of a typical frigate.

HMS *Bacchante* was the 20th ship of the class to be laid down and was launched in February 1968 by Lady Twiss, wife of then Second Sea Lord, Adm Sir Frank Twiss. *Bacchante* was commissioned in October 1969 and after sea trials and working up, she was allocated to the Standing Naval Force Atlantic (STANAVFORLANT) which is a multi-national squadron made up of frigates and destroyers from various NATO navies. Remaining with STANAVFORLANT from April 1970 until July 1972 she then paid off into dockyard hands at Chatham for a refit during which her boilers were modified to burn diesel oil instead of the conventional heavy bunker oil. This was part of Royal Navy policy at the time of having all operational ships using the same type of fuel in order to alleviate supply and distribution problems. This refit was completed in February 1973 and later that year the ship was deployed to the West Indies as a guardship where she remained until April 1974 when she passed through the Panama Canal on her way to a showing the flag visit along the west coast of South America. *Bacchante* returned to Chatham for docking in June of the same year and then carried out weapon training at Portland the next month. The new year, 1975, saw her back with STANAVFORLANT for nearly two years until September 1976, after which there was a short deployment to the Middle East from which she returned in time to take part in the winter 'Cod War' with the Icelandic gunboats. Another refit commenced in January 1977 and this lasted until well into 1978 when she recommissioned for service with the 1st Frigate Squadron based at Devonport. During that year *Bacchante* had another short spell with STANAVFORLANT as well as a period in the Mediterranean and at Gibraltar. 1979 found her back in home waters until in August of that year she was assigned yet again to STANAVFORLANT (she must have been one of their most regular customers!) and travelled to the United States, Canada, Iceland and Norway. Early in 1980 *Bacchante* joined the 5th Frigate Squadron at Devonport and remained mainly in home waters carrying out fishery protection patrols and exercises as well as visiting various European ports. In March 1981 she left Plymouth to take part in the annual 'Springtrain' exercise and on completion of that she passed through the Mediterranean to the Middle East where she was assigned to the Gulf Patrol off the Straits of Hormuz at the mouth of the Persian

79

The first Batch 3 Seawolf conversion was HMS *Andromeda*, seen here in 1981 on completion of her modernisation. Exocet missiles and SCOT aerials have not yet been fitted. The removal of the domed top to the funnel and the general lightening of the upperworks has completely altered the character of these ships. The back-to-back aerial for the Types 967/968 radars is carried on a stabilised mounting at the top of the foremast. *MoD (Navy)*

80

HMS *Argonaut* makes a triumphant entry into Plymouth Sound on her return from the Falklands on 26 June 1982, when she was one of the first ships home from the conflict. A rectangular plate has been welded on the side of the hull just forward of the bridge to cover the hole made by the bomb which lodged in the forward magazine. *Western Morning News*

81

A few weeks before, the crew of *Argonaut* must have wondered if they were destined to see Plymouth again. In San Carlos Water the ship is engulfed in smoke as a fire spreads following the bomb hits. A Sea King helicopter hovers over the stern to deliver extra firefighting equipment. *HMS Fearless*

Gulf. She returned to Plymouth in August 1981 but, in the previous month, it had been announced that as part of Mr Nott's defence review she was to be paid off into reserve along with *Achilles*, *Diomede*, *Naiad* and *Dido*. It was later announced that *Bacchante*, along with *Dido* (an Ikara conversion), was to be sold to New Zealand. She was to pay off in September 1982 and it was expected that she would be transferred to the RNZN the following month. It was also announced that, apart from the five Batch 3 vessels already programmed, no more would be converted to carry Seawolf as the cost of these rebuildings (quoted as £70 million each) was too expensive.

Several 'Leander' class frigates were, as might be expected, involved in the operations to retake the Falkland Islands. The only Seawolf-equipped ship in commission at the time was *Andromeda* which returned from a deployment in the Western Atlantic on 23 April 1982, and after a quick turnround sailed for the South Atlantic where she was mainly employed as a close escort for the carrier *Invincible*. In this role her quick reaction Seawolf system was invaluable as a last ditch defence against air and missile attack. On completion of the hostilities she was one of the ships which escorted the *Canberra* into Port Stanley harbour.

Argonaut caught the public's attention when she was hit by two bombs while stationed in San Carlos Water. One penetrated the forward magazine and the other lodged in a boiler room. Both failed to explode, otherwise the ship would most certainly have been lost. As it was it took two days to make safe and remove the bomb in the boiler room while another four days were needed to do the same to the bomb in the forward magazine. At one stage during the efforts to remove the bombs, a team of welders took cover from one of the unceasing air attacks but the heat from their equipment ignited a fire which rapidly spread and threatened to engulf the ship. Luckily the strenuous efforts of her own and other ships' crews brought the fire under control and the ship was eventually operational again. Altogether *Argonaut* was attacked 15 times and claimed at least one aircraft shot down. After effecting further repairs alongside the repair ship *Stena Seaspread* (one of the requisitioned merchant ships which formed a large part of the task force) it was a very relieved crew which set sail for Plymouth where the ship arrived on 26 June 1982.

Minerva, an Exocet-armed 'Leander', was another of the class to see action in the Falklands. After leaving Plymouth on 10 May, 1982, she entered the Total Exclusion Zone on the 26th and arrived in San Carlos Water on the 29th where she was employed as an AA picket, relieving the battered *Argonaut*. Here she stayed for 13 days and although attacked many times she was not hit, although her Lynx helicopter was narrowly missed by a ground-launched Argentine Blowpipe missile. On one occasion the *Minerva* acted as controlling ship for a Sea Harrier which was vectored on to an Argentine Air Force C-130 Hercules which it promptly shot down — the only one of its type to be lost by the Argentines. *Minerva* returned to Plymouth on 3 August in company with the Type 21 frigate, HMS *Active*.

Penelope, the ship which had carried out the trials programme for the Seawolf missile which was to prove so successful in the Falklands, was also involved in the later stages of the campaign. Sailing from Plymouth in May she arrived in time to take part in the closing stages of the operations to retake the islands. Indeed she laid claim to be the last ship to be attacked during the course of the Falklands action. Employed as an escort for forces transferring by sea from the San Carlos anchorage to other points on the islands, she was one of the ships to remain in the area after the Argentine surrender. Another 'Leander' class ship to see service in the conflict was *Diomede*, an unmodified Batch 3 ship, which acted as an escort for the carrier task force. In the period following the war the carrier *Invincible*, which had remained on station after the *Hermes* had left for home, was eventually relieved by the newly commissioned *Illustrious*. Among the ships escorting *Illustrious* was the Type 22 frigate HMS *Battleaxe* and also HMS *Danae*, an Exocet-armed 'Leander'.

In relation to their numbers, 'Leander' class frigates would not have appeared to have played a significant role in the Falklands campaign. However it should be noted that a large proportion of the operational naval strength was dispatched to the South Atlantic including most of the Type 21 and Type 22 frigates so it was essential that some forces should be retained in home waters to meet the Royal Navy's NATO commitments and this was the duty that befell the majority of the 'Leander' class ships.

An interesting development occurred in June 1982 when HMS *Phoebe*, a Batch 2 ship whose conversion had been completed in April 1977, emerged from her latest refit showing a revised configuration for this type of ship. The forward Seacat launcher has been removed together with its associated director which had been mounted abaft the bridge. The four Exocet launchers have been lowered and mounted in the same manner as on the Batch 3 Seawolf conversions. Also removed is the AKE1 aerial of the Type 965 radar which was previously carried atop the mainmast. The SCOT aerials are now carried on pole structures on either beam, again in a manner similar to the converted Batch 3 ships. Other visible changes include the addition of a single 20mm gun on top of the bridge and another 20mm mounted on the extreme stern. It is possible that the ship has been modified to carry the modern Type 2016 panoramic sonar. The equipment

82

HMS *Andromeda* passes Fort Picklecombe as she enters Plymouth Sound, home at last from the Falklands. She seems to have acquired an advanced modification to her Seawolf launcher! Despite her involvement in the war, she has still not received her SCOT equipment.
Mike Lennon

83

HMS *Charybdis* slips out of Plymouth at the end of August 1982 shortly after commissioning following her Batch 3 modernisation. As a result of experience in the South Atlantic, the Royal Navy has started a programme to increase the close range firepower of its warships and to that end an Oerlikon GAM-BO1 20mm gun can be seen on the extreme stern of the ship. Otherwise she shows the standard features of the class including Type 910 radar — as part of the GWS25 Seawolf system — mounted above the bridge, Type 1006 navigation radar halfway up the foremast and ESM equipment below the main 967/968 aerial. Note the lightweight derricks for handling the inflatable boats which have replaced the traditional seaboats. *Mike Lennon*

for this sonar takes up a lot of internal space and may account in part for the removal of the Type 965 radar. The changes to this ship give the impression of a determined effort to reduce topweight; as appears to have been done with the Batch 3 conversions. It may be that the 'Leanders' are reaching the limit as far as the capacity of their hulls to accept new weapons and equipment is concerned, although in this respect they have shown themselves better able to absorb major reconstructions than the later and more critically designed Type 21 frigates. In *Phoebe*, the 40mm guns previously carried high up abreast the foremast have been replaced by lighter single 20mm mountings. Thus the ship now carries a light armament of four 20mm guns instead of the previous two 40mm. Whether this change is a direct result of experience in the Falklands is difficult to tell as the ship would have been undergoing refit for many months before the start of the crisis.

Other modifications to some ships of the class are as a direct result of the events in the Falklands. A major programme is underway to improve the close range defence of RN ships by the provision of more and better light automatic anti-aircraft guns (AAA or Triple A as they are sometimes termed). A number of 'Leander' class ships have recently been fitted with additional guns as a result of this policy. *Charybdis*, a Batch 3 ship which completed its conversion to a Seawolf equipped escort, has been given an Oerlikon GAM-BO1 20mm gun mounted on a bandstand structure at the after end of the quarterdeck. The GAM-BO1 is manufactured under licence in this country by the British Manufacture and Research Co Ltd and is a much more sophisticated weapon than the simple World War 2 design of the standard 20mm gun. It has a much greater rate of fire (1,000 rounds/minute) and an effective range of up to 2,000m. It can fire fuzed high explosive or semi-armour piercing ammunition and a large box magazine holds 200 rounds fed by belt to the gun. The mounting can be equipped with night and image intensifying sights making it a flexible weapon for use against air and surface targets. HMS *Ariadne*, an unmodified Batch 3 ship, has also been equipped with this weapon and it is likely that most other 'Leanders' will be so equipped.

Dido and *Bacchante* have already been sold to the RNZN and *Naiad*, *Achilles* and *Diomede* were due to have paid off into the Standby Squadron during 1982, although these plans were disrupted by the Falklands crisis. However, as the plans to reduce naval strength announced in the 1981 White Paper have still not been officially revised, it seems likely that a planned withdrawal of 'Leander' class ships from service will proceed steadily over the next few years. The Batch 1 Ikara ships will probably be the first to go as they are the oldest hulls and suffer from being over specialised as a result of their conversions. Only five of the 10 Batch 3 ships have been approved for modernisation and so a question mark lies over the future of the other ships which will not be converted. Nevertheless it is likely that the 'Leanders' will remain the largest single class of ships in the Navy for several years to come and it will probably be well into the 1990s before the last one pays off.

Name	**No**	**Builders**	**Laid Down**	**Launched**	**Completed**
BATCH 1					
Leander	F109	Harland and Wolff Ltd, Belfast	10/4/59	28/6/61	27/3/63
Ajax	F114	Cammell Laird and Co Ltd, Birkenhead	12/10/59	16/8/62	10/12/63
Dido	F104	Yarrow, Scotstoun	2/12/59	22/12/61	18/9/63
Penelope	F127	Vickers Armstrong, Tyne	14/3/61	17/8/62	31/10/63
Aurora	F10	John Brown & Co	1/6/61	28/11/62	9/4/64
Euryalus	F15	Scotts Shipbuilding & Engineering Co	2/11/61	6/6/63	16/9/64
Galatea	F18	Swan Hunter & Wigham Richardson, Tyne	29/12/61	23/5/63	25/4/64
Arethusa	F38	J. Samuel White & Co Ltd, Cowes	7/9/62	5/11/63	24/11/65
Naiad	F39	Yarrow, Scotstoun	30/10/62	4/11/63	15/3/65
Cleopatra	F28	HM Dockyard, Devonport	19/6/63	25/3/64	4/1/66
BATCH 2					
Minerva	F45	Alex Stephens & Sons, Glasgow	3/6/63	8/7/64	15/4/66
Phoebe	F42	Vickers Armstrong, Tyne	25/7/63	19/12/64	14/5/66
Sirius	F40	HM Dockyard, Portsmouth	9/8/63	22/9/64	15/6/66
Juno	F52	J. Thornycroft Ltd, Woolston	16/7/64	24/11/65	18/7/67
Argonaut	F56	Hawthorn Leslie Ltd, Hebburn on Tyne	27/11/64	8/2/66	17/8/67
Danae	F47	HM Dockyard, Devonport	16/12/64	31/10/65	7/9/67
BATCH 3 (Broad Beam)					
Hermione	F58	Alex Stephens & Sons, Glasgow	6/12/65	26/4/67	11/7/69

84
Latest in the line of modified 'Leanders' is HMS *Phoebe*, which had been converted to carry Exocet in 1977 and is seen here following another major refit in July 1982. The forward Seacat launcher and director have been removed and the Exocet launchers lowered. The Type 965 radar has been removed and a smaller mainmast stepped, seaboats have been replaced by inflatables and an extra 20mm gun is mounted above the bridge with a similar mounting just visible on the stern beneath the ensign.
Mike Lennon

85
HMS *Mermaid* shortly after her acceptance by the Royal Navy in 1973. Although a smart looking ship, her standard of weapons and equipment did not suit her for operational deployments in the NATO area. Note the Plessey AWS1 radar at the top of the foremast.
Yarrow (Shipbuilders) Ltd.

Name	Number	Builders	Laid Down	Launched	Completed
Andromeda	F57	HM Dockyard, Portsmouth	25/5/66	24/5/67	2/12/68
Jupiter	F60	Yarrow, Scotstoun	3/10/66	4/9/67	9/8/69
Bacchante	F69	Vickers Armstrong, Tyne	27/10/66	29/2/68	17/10/69
Charybdis	F75	Harland & Wolff Ltd, Belfast	27/1/67	28/2/68	2/6/69
Scylla	F71	HM Dockyard, Devonport	17/5/67	8/8/68	12/2/70
Achilles	F12	Yarrow, Scotstoun	1/12/67	21/11/68	9/7/70
Diomede	F16	Yarrow, Scotstoun	30/1/68	15/4/69	2/4/71
Apollo	F70	Yarrow, Scotstoun	1/5/69	15/10/70	28/5/72
Ariadne	F72	Yarrow, Scotstoun	1/11/69	10/9/71	10/2/73

Data: As designed
Displacement: 2,450 tons standard; 2,860 full load
Length: 372ft oa
Beam: 41ft
Draught: 18ft
Guns: 2×4.5in DP (1×2) in a Mk VI mounting
2×40mm AA (2×1)
AS weapons: 1×Limbo
Aircraft: 1×Westland Wasp helicopter
Machinery: 2×Babcock and Wilcox boilers operating at 550lb/sq in and 860°F. English Electric geared turbines, two shafts, 30,000shp
Speed: 30kts
Oil fuel: 460 tons
Complement: 251
Note: Broad beamed 'Leanders' displaced 2,500 tons (standard)/2,962 tons (full load). Beam was 43ft. All originally fitted with Seacat missiles instead of 40mm guns (see text)

Data: Ikara conversions
Displacement, Dimensions, Machinery, Speed: As standard 'Leander'
Guns: 2×40mm Mk 9 (2×1) AA
AS weapons: 1×Limbo
1×Ikara missile system
Missiles: 8×Seacat (2×4)

Data: Exocet conversions. Basic details as for standard 'Leanders' except:
Guns: 2×40mm (2×1) Mk 9 AA
AS weapons: 6×Mk 32 AS torpedo tubes (2×3)
Missiles: 4×MM38 Exocet missile launchers (4×1)
12×Seacat AA (3×4)
Aircraft: 1×Westland Lynx Mk 2 helicopter

Data: Batch 3 Exocet Conversion. Basic details as for standard broad beamed 'Leander' except for:
Displacement: 3,200 tons full load
Guns: 2×20mm (2×1)
AS weapons: 6×Mk 32 AS torpedo tubes (2×3)
Missiles: 4×MM38 Exocet missile launchers
6×Seawolf (1×6)
Aircraft: 1×Westland Lynx Mk 2 helicopter
Speed: 28kts
Complement: 214

HMS Mermaid

Serving only five years with the Royal Navy, this vessel had a most unusual background. She was originally ordered by the Republic of Ghana and was intended to be the flagship of their navy as well as acting as a presidential yacht for the state ruler, President Nkrumah. The ship was to be named *Black Star* and, at the time of her construction, was the largest warship to be ordered by any black African state. Her estimated cost was in the region of £5million which was far more than this developing third world country could justifiably afford. When President Nkrumah was deposed following a coup d'etat in Ghana in 1966, the new government took immediate steps to reduce the lavish expenditure of the previous ruler and the extravagant frigate being built in the United Kingdom was cancelled. The builders, Yarrow Shipbuilders and Co Ltd, were therefore left with the problem of what to do with the partially completed ship. It was decided that the best course of action was to complete the vessel with the hope that another customer could be found. Accordingly, work continued and the vessel was launched without ceremony on 29 December 1966, and after completion in June 1968 was laid up in the Firth of Clyde to await a buyer.

The design of the ship was based upon the Royal Navy Type 41/61 hull and machinery, modified to meet the requirements of the Ghanaian Navy. The hull was flush-decked and the diesel exhausts were trunked into a streamlined single funnel. A large superstructure block housed extra accommodation including staterooms and a dining/conference room appropriate to the presidential yacht role. Armament was kept fairly simple, partly to keep the cost down, and partly

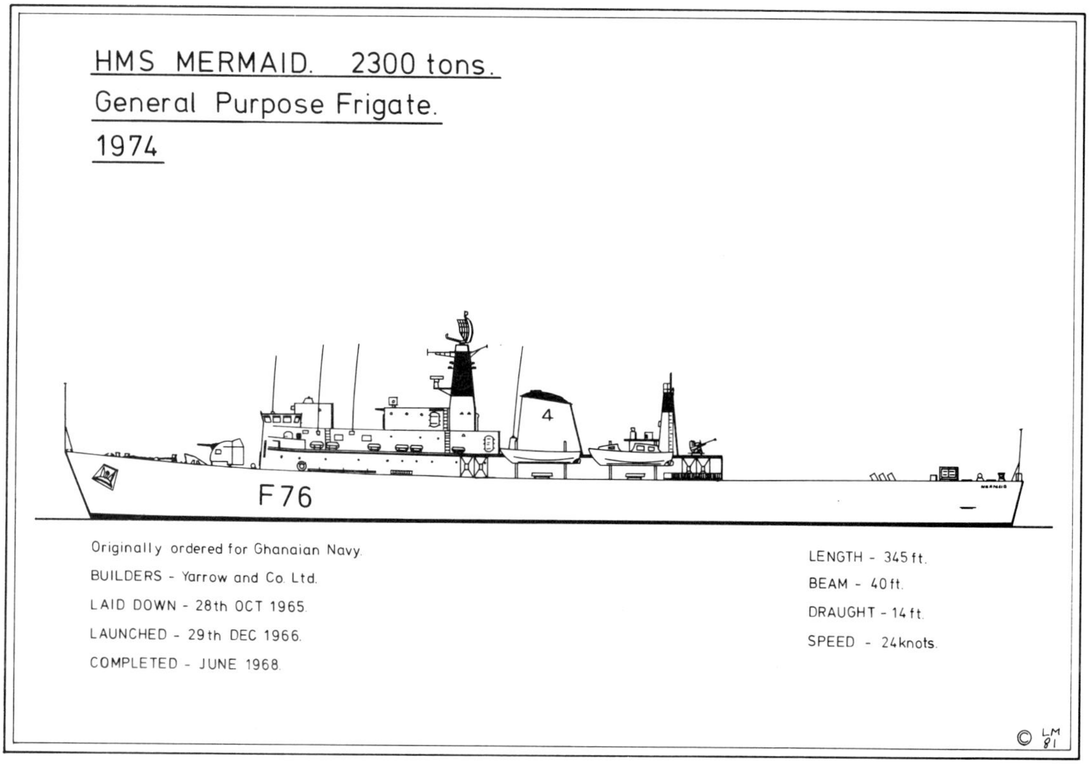

because of the relatively low technical capability of the customer navy. Forward of the bridge was a Mk XIX twin 4in AA mounting while four single 40mm AA guns were mounted on the upper superstructure abreast the masts. A Squid AS mortar was situated in a well aft, similar to the arrangement of the Limbo in the 'Leander' class frigates. Sonar Types 170 and 176 were carried. The long quarterdeck could serve as a helicopter landing platform although no hangar or other facilities were provided for sustained helicopter operations. Gunnery control was provided by a simple tachymetric director mounted abaft the bridge and a Plessey AWS-1 radar on the foremast provided the necessary warning system. A navigation radar was carried on a platform projecting forward of the foremast.

After swinging at anchor for several years, the ship was eventually purchased by the British Government for use by the Royal Navy and the ship was transferred in April 1972 to Portsmouth Dockyard and then in the following October to Chatham Dockyard. Here she was refitted to bring her up to Royal Navy standards and was finally commissioned on 16 May 1973. Her purchase from Yarrow Shipbuilders was partly politically motivated: the Conservative Government, which had been elected in 1971, saw this as a way to increase the numerical strength of the Royal Navy, while at the same time providing an indirect cash subsidy to a company which was a vital component of the country's defence industry. Having been provided with the ship by the politicians, it was left to the RN to find a use for her.

She was named *Mermaid*, a name previously carried by a 'Black Swan' class frigate, and after working up was dispatched to the Far East where she was based on Singapore. Her relatively unsophisticated armament and equipment made her unsuitable for front line duties in European waters but she could provide a useful presence in the Far East, undertaking the standard routine of patrols and visits. At times she stood in as the guardship for Hong Kong during the absences of HMS *Chichester* and she also stood by at the end of the Vietnam war in case it should become necessary to evacuate British nationals from Saigon. Returning home in 1976, she was involved in an unfortunate collision with the minesweeper HMS *Fittleton* whilst taking part in a NATO exercise. *Fittleton* sank with the loss of several lives among her RNVR crew, although the *Mermaid* was not seriously damaged. One of her last tasks in RN service was to carry out trials on a moving target indicator system which was a device enabling the radar to pick out small moving targets against the background clutter on the radar screen caused by reflections from the sea surface. When she paid off in 1977, the *Mermaid* had the distinction of being the last ship in the Royal Navy to carry the Mk XIX gun mounting which had been in service for over 30 years as the main AA armament of many types of ships before being replaced by the Mk VI twin 4.5in mounting.

In April 1977 *Mermaid* was transferred to the Malaysian Navy and was renamed *Hang Tuah*. She replaced another ex-British 'Loch' class frigate which had also been named *Hang Tuah* and following a refit by Vosper Thornycroft she sailed for Malaysia in August 1977. Retaining her RN pendant number, F76, she is still in service at the time of writing.

Name	No	Builders	Laid Down	Launched	Completed
Mermaid	F76	Yarrow Shipbuilders, Scotstoun	28/10/65	29/12/66	7/6/68

Note: Commissioned Royal Navy 16 May 1973.

Data: As built
Displacement: 2,300 tons standard; 2,520 tons full load
Length: 340ft oa
Beam: 40ft
Draught: 12ft
Guns: 2×4in AA (1×2) in Mk XIX twin mounting 4×40mm AA (4×1)
AS weapons: 1×Squid three-barrelled mortar
Machinery: 8×Admiralty Standard Range (ASR1) diesels driving two shafts with controllable pitch propellers giving a total of 12,400shp (16,000bhp)
Speed: 24kts
Oil Fuel: 230tons
Complement: 177 in Royal Navy service

86
The last 4in DP guns in service with the Royal Navy. This view shows the Mk XIX turret with the left and right handed ship's crest on the gun tampons. The angled face of the bridge, a feature of most modern warships, cuts down internal reflections at night. *Author*

5 Gas Turbines and Guided Missiles

'Amazon' Class (Type 21) GP Frigates

The decision of the Labour government in 1966 to phase out the Royal Navy's aircraft carriers led not only to the cancellation of CVA-01 (a large fleet carrier of 55,000 tons), but also of three of the four planned Type 82 destroyers which were intended to escort the new carrier. At that time the smaller Type 42 destroyers, which were to replace the Type 82 design, were at a very early stage of development, as were the advanced Type 22 frigates, which were to be the follow on replacement for the 'Leander' class. The net result was that a large gap had appeared in the Navy's shipbuilding programme and, if the Navy was to have sufficient modern fleet escorts in the 1970s a new type was needed urgently. The Royal Navy ship design departments were fully occupied with work on the Type 42 and 22 designs and so, in order to prevent an unacceptable workload on these departments, commercial companies were invited to tender suitable designs. Vosper Thornycroft offered a development of its Mk 5 and Mk 7 frigate designs which had been ordered by various foreign navies and this formed the basis of a contract for the design and development of a new frigate type for the Royal Navy. The contract for the new type, designated Type 21, was awarded to Vosper Thornycroft on 27 February 1968, and Yarrow Ltd, the Clydeside-based warship builder, was nominated to assist in the design stage and participate in the building programme.

The new Type 21 frigates turned out to be a handsome design with a sharply raked bow and streamlined modern looks which won almost universal approval. From the technical point of view, the major feature was that they were the first major warships designed from the start to be entirely propelled by gas turbines. The installation was a COGOG arrangement whose design benefited from the experience gained with HMS *Exmouth* (qv). Two Rolls-Royce Olympus gas turbines producing a total of 50,000shp provided the main propulsion giving a maximum speed of 32kts at full load. For cruising, two Rolls-Royce Tyne engines produced 8,500shp which gave a speed of 18kts. One Olympus and one Tyne were connected to each of two shafts which drove controllable pitch propellers. This arrangement endowed the ship with an exceptional degree of flexibility and manoeuvrability. In the event of combat damage the ship could run on one shaft if necessary and each shaft could be driven by either of the engines attached to that shaft (although both engines could not be coupled simultaneously). Although main engine performance was monitored and controlled from a compartment adjacent to the enginerooms, main engine functions could be directly controlled from the bridge by aircraft style throttles. The turbine exhausts were trunked through a broad squat funnel which contributed so much to the ships' distinctive appearance. Intakes and associated filter systems were mounted either side of the superstructure just forward of the funnel.

These frigates were designed, like the 'Tribal' class, as general purpose vessels and consequently carried a mixed armament. Introduced for the first time in a frigate was the new Mk 8 automatic 4.5in gun which had first entered service aboard the Type 82 destroyer, HMS *Bristol.* This gun had been developed from the British Army's Abbot self-propelled artillery piece and, adapted for shipboard use, featured an automatic loading system which gave a sustained fire rate of 25 rounds per minute. At the base of the mounting was a 'ready use' magazine holding 15 rounds and these could be fired by remote control without the turret being manned. More sustained firing required the gun to be manned in order to maintain the supply of ammunition. The 55 calibre barrel threw a 25.5kg projectile to a range of 22km (14 miles). Maximum elevation of the barrel was 55° which meant that the gun was mainly intended for use against surface or shore targets, with a limited capability against aircraft. The only other guns fitted were the standard pair of single 20mm guns mounted on either side of the bridge.

For defence against air attack, a quadruple Seacat launcher was mounted on the roof of the helicopter hangar and was controlled by two GWS24 fire control systems mounted abaft the bridge and abaft the funnel. A pair of Knebworth/Corvus chaff dispensers was fitted forward of the bridge for ECM purposes.

No ship-mounted AS weapons were fitted originally because the ship's Wasp helicopter was envisaged as the main weapons delivery system. Detection and ranging of submarine targets was carried out by Sonars Type 184M and Type 162M.

Compared to earlier designs, a major but less obvious advance was in the provision of advanced electronics and computers to assist in the operation and running of the ship. Computer Assisted Action Information System (CAAIS) was fitted and this was based on the Ferranti 1600B computer. Six Deccascan CA1600 display consoles with Ferranti tracker ball and keyboards were installed in the operations room. Each display is normally used for one specific task, such as ASW helicopter direction and control, but each display can accept data from any of the ship's sensor systems and can take over functions from any other display as necessary. CAAIS can be programmed to assist in target selection and recommend the best weapon to use in response. It can also be used to provide attack data for Exocet missiles (when carried) which use pre-programmed target information for the initial phase of flight, and also for helicopter-vectored attacks. The fire control section of the GWS24 Seacat system was the Ferranti WSA4 which embodied another Ferranti FM1600B computer. The WSA4 could also control the 4.5in gun, if necessary at the same time as a Seacat engagement. Two Type 912 (Italian Selenia Orion RTN10X) radars provided sensor data for the system and their aerials were mounted in front of the foremast and atop the hangar. The forward aerial is normally used for controlling the gun whilst the after aerial is normally used in conjunction with the Seacat, for which purpose it carries a boresighted TV camera. The TV picture is displayed at the Seacat operator's position in the operations room and is used for the guidance of the missile in flight. Other radars fitted included a Type 992Q (surveillance and target indicator), a Type 978 (navigation), and a Cossor Type 1010 IFF interrogator.

Apart from the quantum increase in fighting efficiency, the fitting of extensive electronics (including electronic engine control systems) had another far reaching effect in that the number of men required to man the ship was substantially reduced. Total complement was only 177 which compared favourably with the 250 or more required to man a 'Tribal' or 'Leander' class frigate.

In a pleasing link with the past, the ships were allocated names beginning with the letter A and most were in fact named after the 'A' class destroyers built between the wars. The original *Amazon* was a private venture design by J. I. Thornycroft, built at the request of the Admiralty in 1925 and which formed the basis of subsequent destroyer design up to the outbreak of World War 2. The new *Amazon*, first of the Type 21 frigates and nameship of the class, was launched in 1971 by HRH Princess Anne and entered service in 1974.

HMS ARROW. 2,750 tons.
Type 21 General Purpose Frigate.
1980.

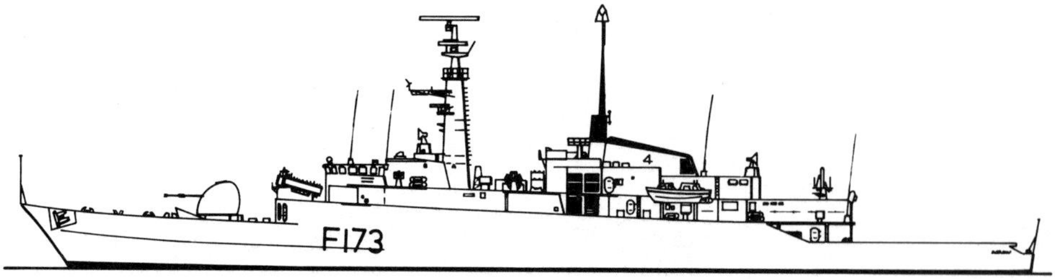

BUILDERS - Yarrow (Shipbuilders) Ltd, Glasgow.
LAID DOWN - 28th SEP 1972
LAUNCHED - 5th FEB 1974
COMPLETED - 29th JUL 1976

LENGTH - 384 ft. o.a.
BEAM - 41·8 ft.
DRAUGHT - 14·5 ft.
SPEED - 32 Knots.

© LM 82

87
HMS *Amazon*, the lead Type 21, with her Lynx helicopter preparing to land. As originally designed, these ships were criticised as being too lightly armed given their size and cost. The Type 912 radar, with boresighted TV camera, can be seen just abaft the funnel and formed part of the GWS24 Seacat missile system. *HMS Osprey*

88
HMS *Active* was the last of three Type 21s built at Vosper Thornycroft's Woolston yard. Completed in 1977, she was equipped to carry Exocet missiles mounted on launchers in front of the bridge. The Corvus chaff launchers were displaced to a position on the superstructure abreast the foremast. *HMS Osprey*

The design was subject to some criticism on the grounds that it was underarmed in relation to its size and cost, and several modifications were made to counter this deficiency. The major improvement was the installation of the Exocet missile system on all vessels after the first three (ie all except *Amazon*, *Antelope* and *Ambuscade*). This work was done while the vessels were completing and it was intended that the earlier vessels should be retrofitted with Exocet at their mid-life refits. To date this has not been done and indeed, *Antelope* was sunk in the Falklands without being equipped with the Exocet system. In those ships which were completed with the missile system the installation consisted of four fixed canister launchers mounted in pairs, angled inwards, forward of the bridge. The Corvus chaff launchers previously positioned here were displaced to the upper superstructure abaft the foremast. To protect the bridge structure, blast deflectors were fitted to the forward face of the superstructure. No reloads for the missiles were carried.

It was also planned that the last four ships should be equipped with the new Seawolf missile system instead of the original Seacat installation, but this plan was dropped due to cost considerations and also to topweight and stability problems associated with the greater weight of the new missile system. As it was, all the ships of the class needed extra permanent ballast as a result of equipment fitted over and above the original design.

The first ships to complete were originally equipped with a Wasp HAS1 helicopter pending the introduction of the newer Lynx HAS2 for which the ship was designed. Successful flight trials of the Lynx were conducted aboard HMS *Amazon* in July 1977 and the first ship's flight formed in 1978 with all ships of the class being so equipped as more Lynx became available. While the Lynx much improved the AS capability of the ship because it could carry a heavier weapon load over a greater range than the Wasp, there would still be times when the ship would not be able to attack a submarine because the helicopter was unserviceable or could not operate due to weather conditions. To rectify this defect a programme was put in hand to equip the class with the Plessey STWS-1 AS torpedo system. Two triple-tubed launching systems were fitted on the weather deck either side of the hangar. *Ardent* and *Avenger* were fitted with the AS torpedo tubes while building and again it was the intention that all of the class would be so equipped as the opportunity arose. Not all have yet mounted the STWS-1, with *Amazon* at least still waiting to receive hers.

Several items of electronic equipment have also been added during the ships' careers. The original design made provision for carrying the SCOT aerials and their protective domes on two platforms just in front of the mainmast. However, this equipment had only become available in the last few years and no ships of the class carried the aerials when completed, although all operational ships have now been so fitted. *Ardent* and *Avenger* were completed with a comprehensive ESM aerial array carried around the top of the foremast, but below the main radar platform. Other ships of the class are being progressively modified to incorporate this equipment but both *Arrow* and *Alacrity* went through the Falklands operations without being modified.

Generally speaking, the Type 21 frigates have been very popular with their crews. Being relatively modern their accommodation and messing arrangements are of a very high standard and their rakish good looks engender a feeling of pride in the ship. They have been employed in the normal peacetime tasks of a Royal Navy frigate including training, showing the flag and security patrols. *Alacrity* was one of the first Royal Navy ships to visit China for many years when she accompanied a task force of several ships, including HMS *Coventry*, to Shanghai in the autumn of 1980. Several ships, including *Active*, *Ardent* and *Ambuscade*, were deployed to the Persian Gulf area from late 1980 in order to protect the interests of British shipping in the area following the outbreak of war between Iraq and Iran.

All this activity turned out to be but a prelude to the most intensive and dangerous naval actions since the end of World War 2. Seven of the class were involved in the operations for the recovery of the Falkland Islands following their occupation by Argentinian forces on 2 April 1982. These were *Avenger, Ardent, Antelope, Arrow* and *Alacrity;* while *Active* and *Ambuscade* were also involved in supporting operations. *Amazon* missed out on the action as she was deployed to the Middle and Far East for four months and returned to Plymouth in late June 1982.

Antelope, *Arrow* and *Alacrity* sailed in early April as part of the escort of the main task force and accompanying merchant ships including the liner *Canberra*. Operations against the Falklands commenced on 1 May with the bombing of Port Stanley but, on 4 May, HMS *Sheffield* was hit by an Exocet missile launched from an Etendard strike aircraft. Although the missile did not explode, burning fuel caused a major fire which defied all attempts to extinguish it and gradually destroyed the ship. HMS *Arrow* went alongside the *Sheffield* to assist in firefighting efforts, and, when it became apparent that the fire was uncontrollable, to embark survivors. During this period an Argentinian submarine was detected in the vicinity and a torpedo was fired at *Arrow* and *Sheffield*, although, luckily, it missed. After several hours, *Sheffield* was abandoned and *Arrow* withdrew having rescued 236

89
HMS *Alacrity*, completed in 1977, shows the standard radar fit of the Type 21 design. At the top of the foremast is the Type 992Q surveillance radar; below and sharing the same platform is the Type 1010 IFF interrogator; a Type 1006 navigation radar is on the projecting platform halfway up the mast; Type 912 radars for the weapons direction system (WSA4) are fore and aft; and HF/DF is at the top of the mainmast. *MoD (Navy)*

90
The outbreak of war between Iran and Iraq in 1980 led to the establishment of a British naval presence in the area. HMS *Ardent* was employed on this duty in early 1981 and is seen here on station with a Union Jack painted on the roof of the bridge. One of the last two of the class completed, she carries ESM equipment on the foremast below the main radar platform, AS torpedo tubes abreast the hangar and SCOT aerials on platforms just forward of the funnels. ***Fleet Photographic Unit***

survivors from a total ship's company of approximately 300. Following the landings at San Carlos on 21 May, *Arrow* was engaged for the following two weeks in providing air defence and gunfire support for the ships in the area and the troops ashore. Later she was involved in bombardment opperations in support of the final attacks against Port Stanley. The ship suffered no major damage and claimed three enemy aircraft shot down as well as several gun emplacements and radar sites destroyed during shore bombardments. Returning to Plymouth on 7 August, she was greeted by an enthusiastic crowd of relations and wellwishers and also by a dramatic flypast of the Royal Air Force's Red Arrows display team trailing coloured smoke over the ship. The ship and the Red Arrows had formed a happy association over the years and the RAF team were pleased to be able to welcome their adopted ship as she returned from war.

HMS *Alacrity*, after escorting the Task Force to the Falklands, was employed on operations in preparation for the main invasion. On at least one occasion she landed men of the Royal Marine's Special Boat Squadron (SBS) to carry out reconnaissance of potential landing sites. On the night of 10 May the ship sailed through the Falklands Sound in an attempt to establish Argentinian positions and while thus engaged she came across an unidentified merchant ship which was immediately engaged with gunfire. After only a few minutes the merchant ship blew up in a sheet of flame and sank shortly afterwards. It was later established that the ship concerned with the Argentinian transport *Islas de Los Estados* which had been carrying a cargo of aviation fuel. Following the landings at San Carlos on 21 May, *Alacrity* was one of the ships escorting the *Atlantic Conveyor* just north of the Falklands when she was hit by Exocet missiles intended for the carrier *Hermes*. The missiles had been deflected by the carrier's countermeasures but had then locked on to the *Atlantic Conveyor*. Once again, an uncontrollable fire broke out and *Alacrity* went alongside to assist firefighting attempts and then to rescue survivors. Two of the ship's divers spent a considerable time in the extremely cold water and at great risk to their own lives in order to assist crew members from the *Atlantic Conveyor* who had taken to the water to escape the fires on the ship. *Alacrity* was one of the first ships to return from the Falklands, arriving back in Plymouth on 4 June and having suffered only superficial damage to her bows caused when going alongside the *Atlantic Conveyor*. She had been attacked from the air at least 10 times and on one occasion an Argentinian aircraft placed two bombs only 10ft on either side of the ship. Despite this, and a number of Exocet attacks, on her return to Plymouth the major item up for repair was the gun barrel which was worn out after firing more than 500 4.5in shells!

The third ship of the original trio, HMS *Antelope*, was not so fortunate. Escorting the landing force, which included the assault ships *Fearless* and *Intrepid* as well as the *Canberra* and other merchant ships, into Falkland Sound and San Carlos Water she survived the heavy air attacks on the first day. On Saturday, 22 May, there was a lull in the Argentinian attacks but the next day brought a renewal of the air offensive. British forces claimed six aircraft shot down plus three more probables. During this raid, a 500lb bomb hit the *Antelope* and, although it did not explode, it lodged in the engineroom. With the cessation of the air raids, the ship was moved to a quiet anchorage and almost all her crew was evacuated while efforts were made to defuse the bomb. During the night the bomb exploded, killing Staff Sergeant James Prescott of the Royal Engineers who was involved in the work on the bomb and who was awarded a posthumous Conspicuous Gallantry Medal in recognition of his bravery on this occasion. Warrant Officer John Phillips, another Royal Engineer, was seriously injured in the explosion along with six others. He received a DSC for his valiant efforts to save the ship.

The explosion of the bomb, positioned as it was in the bowels of the ship, caused serious damage and started a raging fire. Although several other ships and helicopters assisted the struggle against the fire and the all-enveloping smoke, the ship was quickly gutted and on the afternoon of the following day, 24 May, she broke her back and sank. Fortunately, apart from the bomb disposal team, there were no casualties among her crew as they had all been transferred to other ships.

Unhappily, *Antelope* was not the first or only Type 21 to be sunk. On 21 May, the first day of the landings, HMS *Ardent* was detached to assist in the bombardment of the Argentinian airstrip at Goose Green. Here, in the more open waters of the Falkland Sound, she was subjected to a series of heavy air attacks by Pucaras, Skyhawks and Mirages. During these attacks a pair of Skyhawks succeeded in placing two 500lb bombs on the after section of the ship, disabling the Seacat system and causing an outbreak of fire. Damage control teams succeeded in controlling the fires but then the ship was attacked again by three more Skyhawks and two more bombs hit the side of the ship causing further damage and starting more fires. Although reduced to firing machine guns and 20mm cannon, the ship's crew fought on as the ship was subjected to further attacks. The ship's canteen manager manned a machine gun during this phase and succeeded in hitting one of the attackers. For this action, and the inspiration he provided to others, he was later awarded a DSM. Meanwhile the ship was dying as the fires took hold and the mortally damaged ship settled in the water. The ship's captain, Cdr Alan

91
Almost the entire class was involved in the Falklands war. This is one of the last photographs of the ill fated *Antelope* as she heads south with the Task Force, taken as she approached HMS *Fearless* for a RAS (replenishment at sea). She has been updated with the addition of AS torpedo tubes aft, the white domed SCOT aerials amidships, and ESM equipment on the foremast. In common with *Amazon* and *Ambuscade*, she was never refitted to carry Exocets. *HMS Fearless*

92
HMS *Antelope* at San Carlos on the morning of 24 May 1982, following the explosion of the bomb which had lodged in her engine room. There is a gaping hole in the ship's side abreast the engine room, the foremast has disappeared and whole midships section has been gutted by fire. The hull is already sagging and later that day she broke her back and sank. *HMS Fearless*

93
HMS *Ardent* lies low in the water and on fire aft in Falkland Sound following successive air attacks. Her hangar and stern are wrecked and the normally stabilised Type 992Q radar aerial lies over at a drunken angle. *Central Office of Information*

West (later to receive the DSC), reluctantly gave the order to anchor and abandon ship. The performance of this ship and her crew were in the finest traditions of the Royal Navy and it is sad to recall that 22 men were killed and more than 30 injured during her last fierce battle.

Fortunately, *Ardent* and *Antelope* were the only losses sustained by British frigates during the Falklands campaign. By comparison, *Ambuscade* had a fairly straightforward war. Leaving Plymouth on 9 April 1982, she proceeded to Gibraltar where she arrived on the 13th. On 3 May she left Gibraltar in company with other ships and sailed for the Falklands, stopping at Ascension Island en route, in order to join up with the main invasion force. Between 21 May and 15 June she was engaged in support of the San Carlos landings and other operations. She was then detached to South Georgia carrying reliefs for the troops already ashore there, and then returned to Plymouth calling at Ascension Island on the way. By the time she docked at Devonport on 26 July, she had been at sea for 83 days, had steamed 29,226 nautical miles, fired 500 4.5in shells and her helicopter had made 377 deck landings.

A late arrival at the war was HMS *Avenger* which did not leave the UK until 10 May and arrived in the Falklands on the 25th, claiming her 15-day passage as a record for any ship involved in the task force operations. Proceeding to Falkland Sound she was a welcome replacement for the losses already suffered and she assisted in the continuing defence of the landing force against the valiant efforts of the still potent Argentine Air Force. Her divers salvaged a 20mm gun from the wreck of the *Antelope* and this was remounted on *Avenger* to increase her AA fire. Later she assisted in the final bombardments of Port Stanley and after the surrender stayed in the islands to assist in the postwar operations. On the day after the surrender she made the first landing in the West Falklands and picked up 900 Argentinian prisoners for transport to the main POW camp at Port Stanley. She eventually returned home in mid-September.

Also leaving the UK on 10 May was HMS *Active* and, in company with the other ships of the second group, arrived in the Total Exclusion Zone (TEZ) just a few hours after the sinking of HMS *Coventry*. *Active* quickly lived up to her name and during daylight hours was deployed as part of the escort screen for the main Task Force stationed between 150 and 180 miles east of Port Stanley. At night she was detached to escort resupply convoys to San Carlos or to carry out shore bombardments prior to the capture of Port Stanley. Inbound convoys normally departed from the edge of the TEZ at approximately 1800 and followed set routes along the north coast of East Falkland to arrive at San Carlos by 1000 the next day. Outbound convoys departed at 2200 to reach the Battle Group by 1100. Escorts normally exchanged convoys at approximately 0300 at a designated crossover point. Shore bombardments were normally carried out between 0200 and 0600 in order to deny the Argentinian forces around Stanley the maximum amount of sleep. On the night of 13/14 June, with a calm sea and a full moon, HMS *Active* and three other ships fired over 1,000 rounds on to the Moody Brook and Tubledown Mount area. This action contributed greatly to the subsequent Argentine surrender. *Active* then remained in the Falklands area for another four weeks before finally returning to the UK on 3 August. I am indebted to Cdr P. C. B Canter, RN, (CO HMS *Active*) for the detailed information set out above.

The Type 21 frigates were probably involved in some of the fiercest fighting of the war and were certainly tested to the utmost. Several sources have criticised the design in the light of the loss of the *Antelope* and *Ardent* but, although there may be some justification for this in respect of the properties of the aluminium alloys used in the superstructure when subjected to the intense heat of the fires, on the whole the ships have proved sturdy and reliable vessels. *Ardent* in paricular absorbed a tremendous amount of damage before being finally abandoned and it is doubtful if any other comparable contemporary warship type could have taken similar damage and have survived. No doubt the lessons of the Falkland war will be applied to future ships, but at the time the Type 21 frigates showed that, manned by the finest navy in the world, they could give a good account of themselves.

Name	No	Builders	Laid Down	Launched	Completed
Amazon	F169	Vosper Thornycroft, Woolston	6/11/69	26/4/71	11/5/74
Antelope	F170	Vosper Thornycroft, Woolston	23/3/71	16/3/72	19/7/75
Active	F171	Vosper Thornycroft, Woolston	23/7/71	23/11/72	17/6/77
Ambuscade	F172	Yarrow, Scotstoun	1/9/71	18/1/73	5/9/75
Arrow	F173	Yarrow, Scotstoun	28/9/72	5/2/74	29/7/76
Alacrity	F174	Yarrow, Scotstoun	5/3/73	18/9/74	2/7/77
Ardent	F184	Yarrow, Scotstoun	26/2/74	9/5/75	13/10/77
Avenger	F185	Yarrow, Scotstoun	30/10/74	20/11/75	15/4/78

Data: *Ardent* as built
Displacement: 2,750 tons standard; 3,250 tons full load
Length: 384ft oa
Beam: 41.8ft
Draught: 14.5ft
Guns: 1×4.5in Mk 8 automatic
2×20mm (2×1)
Missiles; 1×quadruple GWL Mk 20 Seacat Launcher
4×MM38 Exocet
Torpedoes: 6×12.75in (2×3) Plessey STWS-1 AS torpedo tubes
Aircraft: 1×Westland Lynx Mk 2
Machinery: COGOG. Two Rolls-Royce Olympus TM3 gas turbines, 25,000shp each. Two Rolls-Royce Tyne RMIA gas turbines 4,250shp each
Speed: 32kts (Olympus), 18kts (Tyne)
Complement: 177 (13 officers and 164 men). Accommodation for up to 192

'Broadsword' Class (Type 22) AS Frigates

The development of a successor to the excellent 'Leander' class frigates proved to be a long drawn out affair. Initial design efforts in the early 1960s centred on an enlarged 'Leander' carrying the Sea Dart AA missile which was under development at the time. The resulting general purpose escort vessel eventually grew in size and capability and finally became the Type 82 fleet escort destroyer which was designed to act as an escort to the new fast aircraft carrier (CVA-01). With the cancellation of the carrier in the February Defence White Paper, 1966, plans to build four Type 82 vessels were cancelled and only one, HMS *Bristol*, was completed. The loss of CVA-01 and the subsequent decision to phase out the rest of the aircraft carriers meant that by the mid-1970s the RN would have no effective defence against air attack and as a result top priority was given to the design and development of an air defence escort vessel which would be equipped with the Sea Dart system. The outcome of this effort was the Type 42 destroyer and the first example, HMS *Sheffield*, was commissioned in February 1975. A total of 14 ships have been ordered and they now carry the main responsibility for the air defence of the fleet.

With the priority accorded to the Type 42, work on the 'Leander' replacement proceeded slowly and, as already related, the privately designed Type 21 was produced as a stopgap measure. By the early 1970s the new design, now designated Type 22, was more or less complete but the first vessel of the class was not laid down until February 1975, with others being laid down at approximately yearly intervals.

The specification for the Type 22 called for a vessel capable of sustained AS operations, but with a general purpose capability also. An early decision was made that the class would be gas turbine powered and in fact the machinery installation was identical to that of the Type 42 destroyers which produced beneficial operating economies for the Navy and meant that a common spares holding could be utilised.

Although it is likely that consideration was given to the installation of the Ikara system, the main AS weapon finally selected was the Lynx helicopter. The Lynx's development started in 1967 and the first army version flew in March 1971 — the first naval version flying in May 1972. It represented a great improvement over the Wasp and could carry a greater load of weapons and sensors over greater distances. Also, being twin-engined, it could return to its parent vessel in the event of a single engine failure. All previous helicopter-equipped Royal Navy frigates had carried only one helicopter which meant that if the helicopter was unserviceable or was being refuelled or rearmed then the ship was bereft of its main AS weapon. Consequently it was decided that the Type 22 would carry two Lynx helicopters in a double hangar. A normal flight-deck was positioned over the stern and was large enough to allow one Lynx to land or take off. The second Lynx, if aboard, had to be stowed in the hangar to allow flightdeck operations to proceed.

The Type 22 was also designed to carry the Plessey STWS-1 triple AS torpedo launchers which were positioned on either beam abaft the funnel. Originally intended to fire the standard 12.75in homing torpedo, the system will also be able to fire the new Stingray lightweight torpedo when this comes into service. The Lynx helicopters will also be able to carry the Stingray and the two systems together give the Type 22 an outstanding AS capability.

Detection and tracking of submarine targets is carried out by a Type 2016 multi-frequency panoramic sonar. Other sonars are carried to give the precise information required for the attack phase using the helicopters or the ship-launched torpedoes.

The ability to maintain high speeds in a rough sea is a major requirement for modern AS vessels and to achieve this the hull of the Type 22 closely follows the lines of the 'Leander' class which was renowned for its seakeeping qualities. The hull is basically flush-decked with the characteristic raised forecastle as in the

94
HMS *Broadsword* was the prototype Type 22 frigate and is seen here still in her builder's hands with the Yarrow company's house flag at the foremast. The exhaust stacks above the funnel are a prominent feature.
Yarrow (Shipbuilders) Ltd

95
The inclusion of two separate GWS25 Seawolf systems gave the Type 22 an unrivalled short range self-defence capability which was well tested in the Falklands with outstandingly successful results. This dramatic picture shows a Seawolf at the moment of launch from HMS *Broadsword's* after six-round launcher during a test firing. *British Aerospace*

96
HMS *Battleaxe* leaves the Clyde following her completion in 1980. She carries the combined Type 967/968 radar at the top of the foremast, a Type 1006 navigation radar and two Type 910 missile tracking radars.
Yarrow (Shipbuilders) Ltd

HMS BATTLEAXE. 3,500 tons.

Type 22 Frigate.

1981.

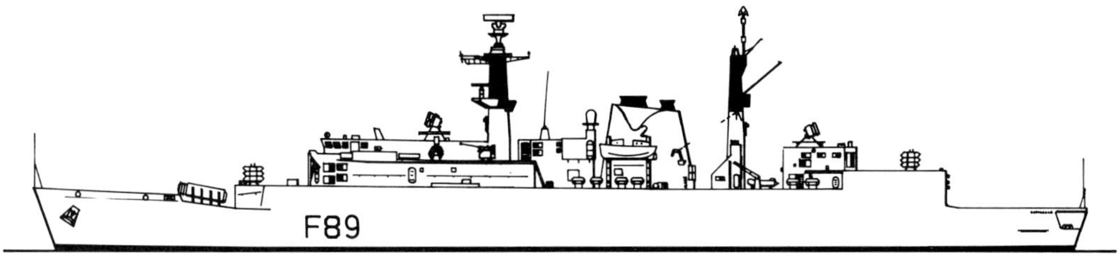

BUILDERS - Yarrow (Shipbuilders) Ltd., Scotstoun.
LAID DOWN - 4th FEB 1976
LAUNCHED - 12th MAY 1977
COMPLETED - 28th MAR 1980

LENGTH - 430 ft. o.a.
BEAM - 48·5 ft.
DRAUGHT - 14 ft.
SPEED - 30 knots.

'Leanders'. A superstructure deck, extending from the full width of the ship, stretches from the break of the forecastle to the hangar aft. This has provided a considerable volume of internal space for the extensive computers, weapon control systems and improved accommodation which are all features of any modern warship. The upper superstructure, masts and funnel have been kept as clean as possible with only essential weapon launchers, aerials and deck fittings being mounted outside the main superstructure blocks. This makes the ship easier to clean down if affected by nuclear fallout and also provides less radar reflective surfaces for missile guidance systems to lock on to.

To carry out the general purpose requirements of the design the ship is equipped with two missile systems. For use against surface targets four Exocet container launchers, angled inward in pairs, are carried on the forecastle deck. Two sextuple launchers for the Seawolf missile are carried, one on the hangar roof and the other forward of the bridge. Together with their tracking and guidance radars and control system, the Seawolf missiles constitute the GWS25 missile system and provide the ship with a most effective defence against aircraft and missiles.

Other weapons carried include two Mk 9 40mm Bofors mountings carried abreast the foremast and the standard multiple rocket launchers of the Knebworth/Corvus decoy system. At the time of their inception, the Type 22 frigates were the first major warships in the Royal Navy to dispense with the gun as part of their main armament; the 40mm guns were really only intended for peacetime patrol duties although they also represented a last ditch defence against missiles. In the field of engineering the class were also of interest in that they were the first British warships designed to metric standards instead of the old Imperial measures.

As is only to be expected these days, the Type 22 carries an extensive range of radar and electronic equipment. At the top of the foremast is the combined aerial for the Type 967/968 radar carried on a fully stabilised mounting. This equipment was first tested aboard HMS *Penelope* and is now also fitted to those 'Leander' class ships converted to carry the Seawolf missile. The 967/968 acts as an air and surface surveillance system and provides target information for the Seawolf tracking radars and also for the Exocet guidance system. As has been mentioned previously, the Exocet missile is provided with an updated target position before it is launched and flies most of the distance to the target using this pre-programmed information before switching on its own radar for final positioning. In this context it is interesting to note that current Royal Navy experience has shown that the Lynx helicopters, equipped as they are with the excellent Ferranti Seaspray radar, have proved most useful in providing targeting data for the Exocet; either giving information on targets over the radar horizon or else providing target information on normal targets so that the parent vessel does not need to betray its position by transmitting with its own radar. Coupled with the fact that the Lynx is now being equipped with the Sea Skua air-to-surface missile, the Type 22 now displays an anti-ship capacity not equalled by previous frigates.

For Seawolf guidance, the Type 910 guidance and tracking radar systems are carried, one atop the bridge structure and the other on the hangar structure aft. Below the main radar platform on the foremast are the sensors for a comprehensive ESM outfit while the mainmast carries HF/DF equipment at the mast top as well as more ESM equipment. Flying platforms are provided just forward of the funnel to carry the SCOT aerials although these were not always fitted on completion. The whole sensor and weapons fit is controlled by the ship's computerised Action Information System (AIO) which is a further development of the Computer Assisted Information System (CAAIS) fitted in earlier frigates. One other radar is carried; a Type 1006 navigation and short range surveillance radar with its aerial mounted on a small platform projecting forward and to port of the foremast.

The ship is powered by a COGOG arrangement of two Rolls-Royce Olympus marine turbines coupled with two Rolls-Royce Tyne gas turbines for cruising power. The installation gives the ship a cruising speed of 18kts using the Tynes, while maximum speed with the Olympus engines is 30kts. Great care has been taken in the design of the ship to ensure that the engine units can be easily removed and replaced so that a policy of 'upkeep by exchange' can be implemented. Four diesel-powered one-megawatt generators are carried, two forward of the main engines and two aft of them, to ensure a reliable supply of electrical power (440V, three-phase, 60Hz). The electrical supply system is duplicated and either system can be driven by any two generators to meet the full load requirement of the ship. In this way the ship's electrical power system can be maintained despite considerable battle damage: a vital factor considering a modern warship's absolute dependence on electronic systems.

The extensive use of electronics and computers has meant that the manning complement required for the ship is considerably less than would previously have been expected for a ship of this size and complexity. In fact the total of 250 men is about the same as the original complement of the early 'Leander' class, despite the fact that the Type 22 is nearly twice the displacement and carries a much more sophisticated armament. All internal space is air conditioned and a high standard of accommodation is provided for all crew members. Extensive use is made of modular furniture constructed from aluminium and GRP, and modern fireproof laminates provided a light and airy decor to the messdecks, although some would say that the result gives a cold and clinical appearance.

The lead ship of the class, *Broadsword*, was handed over to the RN at Plymouth in April 1979 just over three years after she was laid down. This represented a very creditable performance by the builders, Yarrow Shipbuilders, considering the complexity of the design and the inevitable problems connected with the construction of the first ship of a new class. The second vessel, *Battleaxe*, was also completed in just over three years and commissioned in March 1980, but the next two took nearer four years to complete. In service, the main role of the Type 22 is to act as leader of an AS task force for which its excellent communication facilities make it ideally suited. They can also combine with the larger ASW cruisers ('Invincible' class) to form a powerful ASW force which would be tasked with the closing off of the Greenland-Iceland-UK gap to the passage of Soviet submarines positioning to attack vital trans-Atlantic convoys.

In 1980 it was announced that the fifth and subsequent members of the class would be lengthened to provide extra internal space which would be mainly occupied by additional sonar equipment, both active and passive. *Boxer*, the first to be so modified, was laid down in 1979 and launched in 1981. Inspection of published plans shows that as well as a lengthened hull, the new design features a sharply raked bow which suggests that an American pattern bow-mounted sonar has been incorporated. It has also been stated that the lengthened vessels will be equipped with the newly developed towed passive sonar array. This sophisticated underwater listening device, evolved by the US Navy, promises to give a considerable increase in the range at which submarine targets can be detected while at the same time being less likely to betray the position of the surface vessel. The extra space required by the computerised target processor accounts for some of the extra volume created by the lengthening of the later Type 22s.

It was originally intended to build a significant number of Type 22 frigates (a figure of 14 has been mentioned by some sources) but the Defence White Paper introduced by Defence Minister John Nott in July 1981 appeared to spell the end of plans to continue building the class as they were deemed too expensive. It was announced that one more Type 22 would be ordered in addition to the six already approved at the time of the White Paper, but no more would be subsequently built. Even the seventh one

97

A stern view of *Brilliant* showing the flightdeck and hangar which could accommodate two Lynx helicopters, although in peacetime only one was normally embarked. *Brilliant's* Lynx helicopters were responsible for the initial hits on the Argentine submarine *Santa Fe* during the operations to recover South Georgia in April 1982. *HMS Osprey*

98

The Plessey STWS-1 AS torpedo system as fitted to the Type 22 and other RN frigates. Capable of firing the standard Mk 44 and 46 homing torpedoes, as well as the new British Stingray lightweight torpedo, the launcher is trained and operated by remote control from the ship's operations room. *Author*

Sketch plan of stretched Type 22 frigate. *Yarrow (Shipbuilders) Ltd*

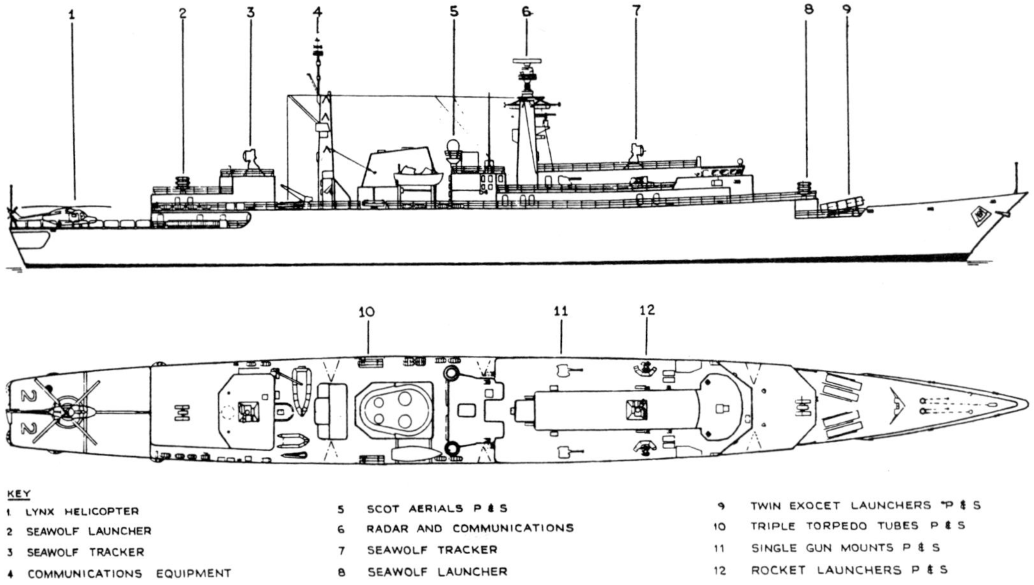

ordered was really little more than a sop to the Navy to make up for the decision to sell the carrier *Invincible*. However, the die was cast and it had been decided in government circles that it could no longer afford to construct large and sophisticated ships in any significant numbers and that subsequent frigates would be of a much simpler, and therefore cheaper, design. Already, as an economy measure, those Type 22 frigates in service were only equipped with one Lynx helicopter instead of the planned two, although it was planned to embark the extra helicopter in wartime. As it happened, the Type 22 went to war much earlier than anybody expected.

When the Falklands were invaded in early April 1982, *Brilliant* and *Broadsword* were among the first ships of the task force to sail, acting as close escorts to the two carriers *Hermes* and *Invincible*. *Brilliant* was soon in action. Equipped now with two Lynx helicopters she took part in the operations to recapture South Georgia and her two helicopters took part in the attack on the Argentinian submarine *Santa Fe*. Leaving South Georgia she proceeded to rejoin the main body of the task force and resume her duties as part of the defence screen of the two carriers. On 12 May, while engaged on this task, she was attacked by a wave of Argentinian Skyhawks and her Seawolf missiles shot down two of them while a third was observed crashing into the sea as it tried to avoid another Seawolf. This action was a significant milestone in warship development as it was the first operational use of the Seawolf missile and the success rate fully justified the effort and expense involved in this rapid reaction system. The Seawolf system is automatic in action, detecting and identifying targets, training and launching missiles to counter perceived threats without the intervention of human operators. So good did the system prove itself to be in combat conditions that it was said, with more than a grain of truth, that on many occasions the first warning of impending attack was the 'whoosh' as a Seawolf left its launcher.

Just before the main invasion at San Carlos, *Brilliant* was involved in the rescue of survivors from the Sea King helicopter which crashed in the sea while transferring SAS personnel between ships as part of the preparations for the main landings. On the day of the landings her aircraft direction team were responsible for vectoring Sea Harriers on many successful interceptions of Argentinian Skyhawks and Mirages. During the next few days she assisted in the defence of the beachhead and although near-missed by several bombs and hit by aircraft cannon fire she suffered no serious damage and only three minor casualties. On 25 May, *Brilliant* was on hand when the *Atlantic Conveyor* was hit and sunk by an Exocet

99
HMS *Brazen* is the fourth Type 22 in service and her completion was brought forward in case she should be required during the Falkland conflict. She commissioned at Plymouth on 2 July 1982, too late to see action, but will no doubt be deployed to the South Atlantic as part of a continuing British naval presence in the area. Note how, as the ship heels in the turn, the stabilised Type 967/968 aerial remains parallel with the horizon. *Yarrow (Shipbuilders) Ltd*

100
The launch of HMS *Boxer*, the fifth Type 22 and the first of the stretched Batch 2. Most of the extra 41ft lengthening of the hull occurs in the midship section where it provides more space for accommodation and extra equipment, as well as possible increases in weapons carried. *Yarrow (Shipbuilders) Ltd*

missile and once again was involved in rescuing survivors, 25 of whom were brought on board. In the closing days of the campaign in mid-June she acted as escort to the merchant ships *St Edmund*, *Container Bezant* and *Europic Ferry*, which were carrying vitally needed Chinook helicopters. While *Brilliant* stood by, the Chinooks were assembled and distributed among the ships before flying off together to the Falklands. Following her exploits in the South Atlantic, *Brilliant* set sail for home and arrived at her home port of Plymouth to a rapturous welcome on 13 August 1982.

Broadsword was on her way to the Middle East to take part in Gulf patrol necessitated by the Iran-Iraq war when she was redirected to accompany the task force south to the Falklands. Although not involved in the South Georgia operations, she nevertheless had a very active war. While attacked several times from the air in the days immediately following the San Carlos landings, her luck held out until 25 May when she was operating in close company with the Type 42 destroyer *Coventry*. Several waves of Skyhawks attacked both ships and one bomb ricocheted off the sea and ripped through the stern and flight deck, destroying a Lynx helicopter parked there. Fortunately the bomb did not explode and the damage was later repaired with the ship remaining operational in the meantime. The *Coventry* did not fare so well and several bombs hit her on the port side causing her quickly to heel over and sink. *Broadsword* immediately moved in and was able to rescue most of the survivors. During the Falkland operations, *Broadsword* claimed at least three enemy aircraft destroyed and despite being attacked more than a dozen times she sustained only 12 minor casualties. She arrived back in Plymouth on 23 August to the by then traditional welcome by thousands of well wishers and a flotilla of small craft following the ship to her berth.

It is believed HMS *Battleaxe* was also involved in the Falkland operations, but at the time of writing no details have been released. She was with other ships taking part in Exercise 'Springtrain 82' and entered Gibraltar on 24 March 1982. From there she may have accompanied the task force south and was probably engaged as a close escort for one or both of the carriers. Just after the close of hostilities, the fourth ship of the class, HMS *Brazen*, commissioned for service on 2 July 1982. Her completion had been brought forward as a result of a splendid effort by Yarrow Shipbuilders in case she should be needed in the Falklands.

The Type 22 frigate emerged from the Falkland campaign with an excellent reputation. The Seawolf system was now combat-proven and the ships had stood up well to the dual test of enemy action and heavy weather. Already, in February 1982, Mr Nott had announced that it had been decided to order an eighth ship of the class as a result of an offer by Yarrow to cut the price of the ship by £6million. Following the success of the other ships in the Falklands, it was further announced by the minister in parliament that it had been decided to order another (the ninth) Type 22 as a move towards replacing the war losses.

In the white paper published in December 1982 entitled *The Falklands Campaign: The Lessons*, it was announced that a total of five new Type 22 frigates would be built to replace the losses in the Falklands although this announcement included the ninth ship already ordered. Also announced in the same document was the information that three of the five ships would be of a new Batch III design which would differ from earlier versions in that it would carry the Mk 8 automatic 4.5in gun. Other details of this version have yet to be revealed but it will take advantage of the extra space provided by the stretched hull of the Batch II ships. It is quite possible that both Batch II and Batch III ships may be equipped with the twin 30mm AA mounting now being fitted to the Type 42 destroyers as a result of Falklands experience and this mounting would replace the single 40mm guns already carried.

Yarrow shipbuilders have revealed that the seventh ship, HMS *Brave* (a Batch II ship) will be powered by a combination of Rolls-Royce marine Spey and Tyne turbines instead of the standard Olympus/Tyne installation. This will be the first application of the Spey powerplant to a British warship but subsequent Type 22s will revert to the Olympus. The installation in HMS *Brave* will provide operating information and experience which will be of benefit to the projected Type 23 frigate now under development and which will be powered by the Spey engine.

The first eight Type 22 frigates (four Batch I and four Batch II) will be constructed by the Yarrow Shipbuilders Ltd at their Clydeside yard but the last two Batch II ships will be built by Swan Hunter Shipbuilders on the Tyne. This will leave Yarrow free to continue work on the Batch III ships and also the first of the new Type 23 frigates.

The Type 22 is undoubtedly the largest and best equipped frigate to see service with the Royal Navy and it is now unlikely that they will ever be surpassed given the policy of reverting to smaller and simpler designs. Thus they may be taken to represent the pinnacle of British frigate development with an all round capability which will undoubtedly be lacking from the next generation of designs. Admittedly, this has only been achieved at great financial cost but given the size and nature of the Soviet submarine threat it would seem a dangerous policy to force the Royal Navy to give up quality for the sake of balancing the books.

Name	No	Laid Down	Launched	Completed
Broadsword	F88	7/2/75	12/5/76	3/5/79
Battleaxe	F89	4/2/76	12/5/77	28/3/80
Brilliant	F90	25/3/77	15/12/78	15/5/81
Brazen	F91	18/8/78	4/3/80	2/7/82
Boxer	F92	1/11/79	17/6/81	
Beaver	F93	20/6/80	8/5/82	
Brave	F94	5/4/82		

Eighth ship was due to be laid down week commencing 7 March 1983. All built by Yarrow Ltd, Scotstoun.

Data: As built
Displacement: 3,500 tons standard; 4,000 tons full load
Length: 430ft oa
Beam: 48½ft
Draught: 19ft
Guns: 2×40mm AA (2×1) on Mk 9 mountings
Missiles: 4×MM38 Exocet launchers (no reloads) 12×Seawolf launchers (2×6)
Torpedoes: 6×12.75in torpedo tubes (2×3) firing AS homing torpedoes (Plessey STWS-1 system)
Aircraft: 2×Westland Lynx HAS2 helicopters
Machinery: COGOG. Two Rolls-Royce TM3B Olympus Gas Turbines producing a total of 56,000bhp. Two Rolls-Royce Tyne RM1A gas turbines producing a total of 8,500bhp. Drive through non-reversible gearboxes and controllable pitch propellers
Speed: 30kts (Olympus); 18kts (Tynes)
Complement: 250

Type 23 and Future Frigate Designs

With the Type 22 'Broadsword' class frigates the Royal Navy has probably reached the limit as far as size and cost is concerned. The Type 22 is a very successful design, as its performance in the Falklands proved. Although the spectacular successes of the Seawolf system hit the headlines, the Royal Navy is reported to be very pleased with the performance of the Type 2016 sonar which proved to be most reliable despite being in continuous operational use for many months in some of the most adverse sea conditions in the world. The Lynx helicopters also proved themselves in action and used their Sea Skua guided missiles with considerable success against a variety of surface targets: *Brilliant's* Lynx was instrumental in the disabling of the Argentinian submarine *Santa Fe*. Fortunately the ship's ability to absorb battle damage was not severely tested and some modifications may be expected in this department as a result of Falklands experience.

The Type 22 ships were not alone in proving themselves in the difficult and dangerous South Atlantic actions and perhaps the most remarkable exploits were those of the two Type 12 frigates *Plymouth* and *Yarmouth*. Although the basic design was over 30 years old and the ships themselves over 20 years in service, these two ships showed themselves almost the equal of later designs in action. This highlighted a trend in Royal Navy thinking which had begun to gain ground at the beginning of this decade and which was considering whether the interests of the RN would be better served by a frigate type which was smaller, simpler and cheaper than the current Type 22 design.

By late 1978 the only major warships under construction for the RN were the 'Invincible' class carriers, Type 42 destroyers, Type 22 frigates and nuclear-powered hunter killer submarines. Although these were all fine ships of their type, only a limited number could be built with the funds available from a sorely pressed defence budget. Strangely enough, many of the ships under construction or ordered at the time had been provided for by a Labour government which saw a naval shipbuilding programme as a good way of keeping down unemployment in traditional industries where much of their voting support came from. The RN was also faced with policies which required the dispatch of ships outside the European theatre to meet commitments such as the Gulf of Oman patrol. To maintain two ships on station for a patrol such as this requires at least six ships and sometimes more if refits are taken into acocunt. Consequently it was felt that a cheaper and simpler design was required to back up the Type 22 and to provide the RN with the numerical strength which it needed. Preliminary design efforts were started in conjunction with British shipbuilders, under the designation Type 23.

The shipbuilding industry welcomed the idea of a

return to more moderate dimensions as it was being found that, although the Type 22 was an excellent design, it was too expensive to be a viable proposition in terms of export sales to foreign navies. In contrast to earlier British frigate designs, the Type 21 ('Amazon' class) design had not attracted any foreign sales despite early high hopes of the builders. In an increasingly competitive world, British yards had lost out to foreign builders, particularly the Italians with their 'Lupo' class frigate which gained many orders from navies which had previously bought British. Yarrow Shipbuilders had a design study, designated Type 24, which was suitable for export and which the company had hoped that the RN would buy in order to increase its sales prospects. With the advent of the Type 23 requirement for a smaller and simpler RN frigate, work on the Type 24 ceased without any orders being secured.

The Conservative Government, elected in 1979, came to power promising a real increase in defence spending. However, even they fell prey to the desire to equip our armed forces with what could be afforded instead of what was actually required. By July 1981, the Defence Minister (Mr John Nott) was ready to present his now notorious White Paper which, as well was proposing sweeping cuts in the strength of the active fleet, also announced the end of the Type 22 building programme. The future of British frigate construction was to rest with the projected Type 23 design which appealed to the government because of its low unit cost which was cited as being £90million as against the £130million of a Type 22.

At this stage the Type 23 was seen as a simple design mainly intended as a platform for the American-developed towed passive sonar array. The ship would carry a lightweight missile system for self defence and would have landing and refuelling facilities for a helicopter but no hangar. It was envisaged that each squadron of Type 23 frigates would be accompanied by a new design of fleet auxiliaries which would provide hangar and repair facilities for the helicopters from the frigates. This scheme was surely a non-starter as, although it would keep down the unit cost of the frigates, the operational support problems would place a severe constraint on the deployment of each individual frigate.

The choice of a self-defence missile for the ships was fairly straightforward as the Seawolf really had no rival, but the choice of the supporting radar system caused a political storm which could have sunk a battleship, let alone a frigate! British Aerospace, manufacturers of the Seawolf missile, had designed a new lightweight system designated VM40 which employed a new twin missile launcher and a new lightweight tracking radar. The problem was that the radar was designed and built by Hollandse Signaalapparaten (a Dutch company) and at a time of increasing unemployment it was felt in some quarters that the contract should have gone to a British company. The Marconi company offered their Type 805SW system which, taking advantage of new techniques, was able to offer a 60% reduction on the total weight of the whole installation. Another potential political decision was the choice of gun to be carried, although in fact at one time it was seriously considered that the ship did not need a gun. When the requirement for a gun was accepted one of the major contenders was the Oto-Melara 76mm automatic which had been installed on some of the Dutch 'Leander' frigates during modernisation and which was manufactured in Italy.

When announced in the 1981 White Paper, it was stated that the Type 23 frigate would be ordered fairly quickly and in suitable numbers but there has been considerable delay and as yet none have been ordered. In July 1982 a further announcement was made regarding naval policy in the wake of the Falklands war and more details of the Type 23 design emerged. It became apparent that the new frigate would be more substantial than at first proposed, although it would be smaller than the Type 22 at around 2,800 tons (ie slightly larger than the 'Leander' class) and cost would be less at around the previously announced £90million. The ship is to be armed with the lightweight Seawolf system (radar unspecified), a 4.5in gun, anti-ship missiles and AS homing torpedoes. The gun will probably be the proven Mk 8 mounting already carried in the Type 21 frigates and very successfully used in the Falklands, particularly for ship-to-shore bombardment. Anti-ship missiles will be either the MM40 (an improved and longer ranged Exocet) or the British Aerospace P5T missile which is the subject of a development contract at present.

The ship will have a hangar and flightdeck to carry and operate the EH101 helicopter. This is a joint Anglo-Italian project intended as a replacement for the Sea King although it is slightly smaller in size. (Details of the EH101 are included in Appendix 4.) The ship's propulsion system also breaks new ground as it will consist of a diesel-electric plant for long range operation and also for quietness. Two Rolls-Royce Spey marine gas turbines will provide the necessary power for high speeds. This power arrangement is unique for a British warship although CODOG arrangements have been used by several foreign designs.

Now under detailed development, it is expected that the first Type 23 will be ordered in 1984 building up to an order rate of three per year thereafter. Even if this timetable is adhered to, it means that the first of the class will not be completed until 1988 and may even take longer. In the meantime, if the planned withdrawal from service of some current frigates goes ahead, the strength of the Royal Navy will be severely depleted.

It is obvious that the Type 23 design has progressed from being a simple weapons' platform, cheap to produce, and has grown into a sophisticated general purpose frigate. While the new design may well turn out to be a well balanced and powerful ship, it must be worth considering whether it would not be cheaper in the long run to continue building and improving the existing Type 22 ships. By the time the Type 23 is in service it is doubtful if the cost of developing and building a completely new design will have proved to be less than the cost of building a proven and existing design.

There is probably a very good case for building a small, say 2,000-ton, frigate carrying a small helicopter; perhaps armed with automatic guns and a lightweight self-defence missile system. Such a ship could be built in fair numbers and be used for patrol duties in out of theatre operations (to coin a current phrase). They could supplement the larger purpose-designed Type 22 and provide local numerical superiority for convoy and task force defence when needed. The requirement for a naval force to remain in the South Atlantic will probably turn out to be a long term commitment and the number of ships needed for this will be a considerable strain on the Navy's resources. A small economic frigate would be suitable for this job, releasing larger ships for service in the Eastern Atlantic where the main task of the Royal Navy remains.

Of course, the lessons to be learnt from the Falklands war will be debated long and hard. Already a trend for British warships to be equipped with more light AA weapons is apparent, and any new frigate is likely to be so armed. In general terms the performance of British surface-to-air missiles was well up to expectations with the Seawolf in particular gaining some spectacular successes. However, the supposedly obsolescent Seacat proved remarkably useful and since the end of the war the Royal Navy has placed a large order for more of these missiles which would indicate that it will remain in service with the fleet for many years yet. Although the Type 23 will certainly carry Seawolf missiles, the launcher configuration has yet to be decided. The lightweight VM40 system at present includes the two-round conventional launcher, but British Aerospace are also offering a vertical launch system where the missiles are fired vertically directly from their containers which are built into the hull or superstructure. For this method of launch the missile is fitted with an additional boost motor and immediately after launch the missile cants over to the direction of the target. This system does away with the complexity of a conventional launcher with its associated loading systems and magazines, giving the ship designer greater flexibility in the arrangement of on board weapon systems.

Another missile which would be a possible candidate for use on a future frigate would be the British Aerospace Lightweight Sea Dart. This is a smaller and containerised version of the Sea Dart missile carried by the Type 42 destroyers. In its lightweight version the Sea Dart can be used against air or surface targets and the shipboard command and guidance system is simplified so that it could be installed on a frigate-sized ship. The fact that this missile can be used against surface targets is a valuable bonus as it could mean that a frigate would only need to carry one type of missile instead of two (eg Seawolf and Exocet), and this could be one way of keeping size and cost down.

Two frigates, *Ardent* and *Antelope*, were lost in the Falklands and as a result considerable doubt has been raised as to the suitability of aluminium alloys for use in major portions of the superstructure. Although these materials provide considerable benefits in weight saving, it is now likely that aluminium will only be used on minor structures such as masts, funnels and gunshields but not on those structures whose failure could weaken the structure of the ship or hamper damage control operations. All this is not to say that the use of aluminium was a major factor in the losses. HMS *Sheffield* was lost after a fire caused by the impact of an Exocet missile which failed to explode. Although some aluminium had been used in the construction of *Sheffield*, her main internal structure and framing was mostly steel and photographs of the ship taken after the fire had burnt itself out show that the main shell of the hull and superstructure was intact. Reports would seem to indicate that the large amount of combustible material on board, such as PVC insulation on electrical cables, coupled with the unfortunate circulation of heat and fumes by the ventilation system, had a considerable bearing on the difficulty of controlling fires on board warships. This is obviously a field where future designs will benefit from experiences in the Falklands.

The success of the Exocet missile highlighted the need for efficient countermeasures against such weapons and, although the standard Corvus system of rocket-launched chaff decoys had some success in deflecting or decoying missiles, continued development of new systems is needed. Recently, Type 42 destroyers returning to the Falklands for guardship duties have been equipped with deck-mounted decoy launchers mounted abeam the bridge. Plessey also have a new system under development which improves on the Corvus system by having automatic fusing of the rocket heads before they are launched instead of the present manual setting. This means that clouds of chaff can be set up in pre-determined patterns and locations in order to present the maximum confusion to the incoming missile warhead and also lessen the risk of the missile being merely deflected on to another target (as appears to have happened to the *Atlantic Conveyor*).

Finally, when looking at future development, it is interesting to note that it is now proposed to equip the Type 23 with a mixed propulsion system. The choice of the marine version of the Rolls-Royce Spey engine is no surprise. This engine has been under development for many years and the aircraft version of it must be one of the most successful engines ever built by Rolls-Royce. It is used on Royal Navy Phantoms, the American Corsair II, as well as a wide range of civil and military aircraft. With this background it is very likely that the Spey will prove to be exceptionally reliable in marine service. The choice of a diesel-electric power train as the main propulsion system is somewhat surprising in view of the Navy's wholehearted support of the gas turbine concept in which field it has been a great pioneer and innovator (see Appendix 3). However the diesel engine has many useful attributes including relatively low fuel consumption at the type of power ratings required for normal frigate cruising speeds.

In the Type 23, it may be that the Speys are also used as turbo generators driving the same electric motor or motors as the diesel and this could result in the elimination of some of the heavy gearboxes used in the usual COGAG arrangement thus saving weight in the overall installation.

Given the political situation in this country it is difficult to forecast the likely pattern of warship construction. However, if presently declared plans are adhered to, then the Navy can look forward to perhaps a dozen Type 22 frigates in service at the end of the decade with an increasing number of Type 23 coming into service at the same time. If plans to build three Type 23 a year are fulfilled, it may be that the class will be as numerous as the highly successful 'Leander' class frigates. It must be a matter of concern that the Type 23 is unlikely to be in service until 1988 and it is therefore vital to the well being of the Royal Navy and the country that the programme is not delayed any more.

Whatever the outcome of the shipbuilding programme, the country as a whole will be able to rely (as it has always done) on the fact that those ships which are built will be manned by the finest navy in the world. It behoves this country to ensure that the crews of these ships are provided with the best designs available so that if they ever have to be put to the test on our behalf, they can get on with the job having been provided with enough of the right kind of ships. The Falklands operations at least had the effect of alerting much public and political opinion to the need for this country to maintain a strong Royal Navy and to pursue a prudent maritime strategy. Let it be hoped that this new awareness coupled with the lessons learnt in the recent conflict will lead to a resurgence in the strength and capability of the Royal Navy.

Appendices

1 RN Warship Type Designations

With the introduction of new frigate designs in the postwar period, the Royal Navy adopted a system of Type numbers to designate the various designs. The Type number allocated depended on the main function of the ship concerned and the sequence of numbers were as follows:

0 to 40	Anti-submarine escorts.
41 to 60	Anti-aircraft escorts.
61 to 80	Aircraft direction escorts.
81 to 99	General purpose escorts.

Originally the Type numbers were intended to be applied to frigate designs but, with the lessening distinction between frigates and destroyers, some numbers were also allocated to destroyers. The following list gives all known type numbers allocated to date including those allocated to destroyers.

Type 11 Diesel-powered design for an AS frigate to complement Types 41 and 61. Abandoned in favour of the Type 12.

Type 12 Steam-powered fast AS frigate. 'Whitby' and 'Rothesay' classes.

Improved Type 12 'Leander' class general purpose frigates developed from basic Type 12 design.

Type 14 'Blackwood' class utility AS frigate.

Type 15 Full conversion of wartime destroyers to fast AS frigates.

Type 16 Limited conversion of wartime destroyers to fast AS frigates.

Type 17 Designation applied to design for a third rate AS vessel smaller and slower than the Type 14. Armed with one Limbo and a single 40mm gun. Designation later applied to another study for a very large AS frigate. No details available.

Type 18 Possibly applied to later versions of 'T' class conversions with frigate type bridge. Alternatively may have been the designation for projected conversion of 'N' class destroyers to fast AS frigates.

Type 19 Projected high speed escort with a similar armament to the 'Whitby' class, but with a speed of 43kts. Presumably meant to combat the high underwater speed of nuclear powered submarines but the introduction of torpedo carrying helicopters aboard frigates made high surface speeds unnecessary.

Type 21 'Amazon' class gas turbine-powered patrol frigates.

Type 22 'Broadsword' class gas turbine-powered AS frigate. 'Leander' replacement.

Type 23 Follow on design from Type 22. Intended to be simpler and cheaper with possible export potential.

Type 24 Commercial design by Yarrow, intended mainly for export. Not built.

Type 41 'Jaguar' class AA frigates.

Type 42 'Sheffield' class air defence guided missile destroyers. Designation also applied to a design in 1954 for a steam powered escort armed with three single, automatic 4in guns. Intended mainly for North Sea and coastal duties.

Type 43 Large guided missile destroyer armed with Seadart and Seawolf. Not built.

Type 44 AA escort vessel. No details available.

Type 61 'Salisbury' class aircraft direction frigates.

Type 62 Projected conversion of 'M' class destroyers, presumably along the lines of the later 'Weapon' and 'Battle' class destroyers converted to radar picket ships.

Type 81 'Tribal' class general purpose frigates.

Type 82 Projected class of four general purpose fleet escorts. Only one, HMS *Bristol*, built.

2 Frigate Pendant Numbers

At the end of World War 2 all Royal Navy escort vessels were carrying pendant numbers with flags K (frigates and corvettes), L ('Hunt' class escort destroyers) and U (sloops) superior. In 1947/48 all these groups of vessels were reclassified as frigates and given a pendant number with flag F superior. In most cases this merely involved a change of prefix letter whilst the ship retained its original number. For example, the frigate *Loch Craggie* changed from K609 to F609.Where such a straightforward change would have resulted in two ships carrying the same number, a multiple of 100 was added or subtracted to one ship's number in order to prevent the double allocation. Thus the 'Hunt' class destroyer *Whaddon*, previously L45, became F145 while the sloop *Wild Goose* changed from U45 to F45. The following list gives all frigate pendant numbers allocated since the introduction of the present system in 1948. Where the same number has been allocated to more than one ship, the ships are listed in order of allocation. The class of each frigate is also given in brackets except where this is obvious from the name (eg 'Loch' or 'Castle' classes).

F02	*Liddesdale* (Hunt)
F05	*Atherstone* (Hunt)
F06	*Bigbury Bay*
F07	*Acteon* (Black Swan)
F08	*Exmoor* (Hunt)
	Urania (Type 15)
F09	*Easton* (Hunt)
	Troubridge (Type 15)
F10	*Aurora* (Leander)
F12	*Bamborough Castle*
	Achilles (Leander)
F14	*Beaufort* (Hunt)
	Leopard (Type 41)
F15	*Eggesford* (Hunt)
	Euryalus (Leander)
F16	*Stevenstone* (Hunt)
	Diomede (Leander)
F17	*Ulysses* (Type 15)
F18	*Flamingo* (Black Swan)
	Galatea (Leander)
F19	*Terpsichore* (Type 16)
F20	*Snipe* (Black Swan)
F21	*Dart* (River)
F22	*Wheatland* (Hunt)
F23	*Teazer* (Type 16)
F25	*Southdown* (Hunt)
F27	*Lynx* (Type 41)
F28	*Wren* (Black Swan)
	Cleopatra (Leander)
F29	*Whimbrel* (Black Swan)
	Verulam (Type 15)
F30	*Mermaid* (Black Swan)
F31	*Panther* (Type 41)
F32	*Salisbury* (Type 61)
F33	*Opossum* (Black Swan)
F34	*Puma* (Type 41)
F35	*Enard Bay*
F36	*Whitby* (Type 12)
F37	*Jaguar* (Type 41)
F38	*Cygnet* (Black Swan)
	Arethusa (Leander)
F39	*Hind* (Black Swan)
	Naiad (Leander)
F40	*Sirius* (Leander)
F41	*Volage* (Type 15)
F42	*Modeste* (Black Swan)
	Phoebe (Leander)
F43	*Torquay* (Type 12)
F44	*Tenacious* (Type 16)
F45	*Wild Goose* (Black Swan)
	Minerva (Leander)
F47	*Fleetwood* (Sloop)
	Danae (Leander)
F48	*Dundas* (Type 14)
F49	*Pheasant* (Black Swan)
F50	*Rochester* (Sloop)
	Venus (Type 15)
F51	*Grafton* (Type 14)
F52	*Juno* (Leander)
F53	*Undaunted* (Type 15)
F54	*Hardy* (Type 14)
F55	*Silverton* (Hunt)
F56	*Test* (River)
	Petard (Type 16)
	Argonaut (Leander)
F57	*Black Swan*
	Andromeda (Leander)
F58	*Hart* (Black Swan)
	Hermione (Leander)
F59	*Zetland* (Hunt))
	Chichester (Type 61)
F60	*Alacrity* (Black Swan)
	Jupiter (Leander)
F61	*Llandaff* (Type 61)
F62	*Pellew* (Type 14)
F63	*Scarborough* (Type 12)
F64	*Nereide* (Black Swan)
F65	*Tenby* (Type 12)
F66	*Starling* (Black Swan)
F67	*Tyrian* (Type 16)
F69	*Redpole* (Black Swan)
	Bacchante (Leander)
F70	*Farndale* (Hunt)
	Apollo (Leander)
F71	*Sparrow* (Black Swan)
	Scylla (Leander)
F72	*Wizard* (Type 15)
	Ariadne (Leander)
F73	*Eastbourne* (Type 12)
F75	*Haydon* (Hunt)
F75	*Charybdis* (Leander)
F76	*Virago* (Type 15)
	Mermaid (1973)
F77	*Blackpool* (Type 12)
F78	*Cottesmore* (Hunt)
	Blackwood (Type 14)
F79	*Brissenden* (Hunt)
F80	*Duncan* (Type 14)
F81	*Stork* (Black Swan)
F82	*Magpie* (Black Swan)
F83	*Ulster* (Type 15)
F84	*Exmouth* (Type 14)
F85	*Arabis* (Flower)
	Keppel (Type 14)
F86	*Pelican* (Sloop)
F87	*Eglinton* (Hunt)
F88	*Lamerton* (Hunt)
	Malcolm (Type 14)
	Broadsword (Type 22)
F89	*Allington Castle*
	Battleaxe (Type 22)
F90	*Woodcock* (Black Swan)
	Brilliant (Type 22)
F91	*Murray* (Type 14)
	Brazen (Type 22)
F92	*Exe* (River)
	Boxer (Type 22)
F93	*Vigilant* (Type 15)
	Beaver (Type 22)
F94	*Palliser* (Type 14)
F96	*Peacock* (Black Swan)
F97	*Russell* (Type 14)
F98	*Orwell* (Type 16)
F99	*Lincoln* (Type 61)
F101	*Yarmouth* (Type 12)
F102	*Zest* (Type 15)
F103	*Arbutus* (Flower)
	Lowestoft (Type 12)
F104	*Dido* (Leander)
F105	*Alnwick Castle*
F106	*Brighton* (Type 12)
F107	*Rothesay* (Type 12)
F108	*Londonderry* (Type 12)
F109	*Leander* (Leander)
F112	*Albrighton* (Hunt)

F113 *Falmouth* (Type 12)
F114 *Ajax* (Leander)
F115 *Berwick* (Type 12)
F116 *Amethyst* (Black Swan)
F117 *Ashanti* (Tribal)
F118 *Tallybont* (Hunt)
F119 *Eskimo* (Tribal)
F120 *Garth* (Hunt)
F121 *Tumult* (Type 16)
F122 *Ghurka* (Tribal)
F123 *Crane* (Black Swan)
F124 *Zulu* (Tribal)
F125 *Mohawk* (Tribal)
F126 *Bedale* (Hunt)
Plymouth (Type 12)
F127 *Penelope* (Leander)
F128 *Wilton* (Hunt)
F129 *Rhyl* (Type 12)
F130 *Blankney* (Hunt)
F131 *Chiddingfold* (Hunt)
Nubian (Tribal)
F132 *Belvoir* (Hunt)
F133 *Tartar* (Tribal)
F134 *Bicester* (Hunt)
F135 *Cattistock* (Hunt)
F137 *Hambledon* (Hunt)
F138 *Rapid* (Type 15)
F141 *Undine* (Type 15)
F142 *Brockelsby* (Hunt)
F143 *Blackmore* (Hunt)
F145 *Whaddon* (Hunt)
F146 *Cleveland* (Hunt)
F148 *Holderness* (Hunt)
F150 *Bleasdale* (Hunt)
F152 *Cowdray* (Hunt)
F154 *Cotswold* (Hunt)
F155 *Ballinderry* (River)
F156 *Tuscan* (Type 16)
F157 *Wrangler* (Type 15)
F158 *Quantock* (Hunt)
F159 *Wakeful* (Type 15)
F162 *Croome* (Hunt)
F169 *Paladin* (Type 16)
Amazon (Type 21)
F170 *Antelope* (Type 21)
F171 *Calpe* (Hunt)
Active (Type 21)
F172 *Ambuscade* (Type 21)
F173 *Arrow* (Type 21)
F174 *Middleton* (Hunt)
Alacrity (Type 21)
F176 *Brecon* (Hunt)
F182 *Meynell* (Hunt)
F184 *Ardent* (Type 21)
F185 *Relentless* (Type 15)
Avenger (Type 21)
F187 *Whirlwind* (Type 15)
F189 *Termagent* (Type 16)
F190 *Ledbury* (Hunt)
F191 *Rocket* (Type 15)
F192 *Pytchley* (Hunt)
F195 *Roebuck* (Type 15)
F196 *Cowslip* (Flower)
Urchin (Type 15)
F197 *Grenville* (Type 15)
F198 *Oakley* (Hunt)
F199 *Tetcott* (Hunt)
F200 *Ursa* (Type 15)
F206 *Avondale* (Hunt)
F215 *Nith* (River)
F217 *Swale* (River)
F219 *Ness* (River)
F221 *Chelmer* (River)
F222 *Teviot* (River)
F224 *Rother* (River)
F230 *Wear* (River)
F232 *Tay* (River)
F235 *Jed* (River)
F241 *Kale* (River)
F246 *Spey* (River)
F248 *Waveney* (River)
F252 *Helford* (River)
F253 *Helmsdale* (River)
F254 *Ettrick* (River)
F257 *Derg* (River)
F269 *Meon* (River)
F270 *Nene* (River)
F271 *Plym* (River)
F272 *Tavy* (River)
F286 *Amberley Castle*
F293 *Tees* (River)
F294 *Towey* (River)
F295 *Usk* (River)
F355 *Hadleigh Castle*
F356 *Odzani* (River)
F362 *Portchester Castle*
F365 *Lochy* (River)
F367 *Taff* (River)
F371 *Wye* (River)
F372 *Rushen Castle*
F379 *Carisbrooke Castle*
F383 *Flint Castle*
F384 *Leeds Castle*
F386 *Hedingham Castle*
F387 *Berkeley Castle*
F388 *Dumbarton Castle*
F389 *Knaresborough Castle*
F390 *Loch Fada*
F391 *Loch Killin*
F397 *Launceston Castle*
F399 *Tintagel Castle*
F413 *Farnham Castle*
F417 *Halladale* (River)
F420 *Kenilworth Castle*
F423 *Largo Bay*
F425 *Loch Dunvegan*
F428 *Loch Alvie*
F429 *Loch Fyne*
F431 *Loch Tarbert*
F433 *Loch Insh*
F434 *Loch Quoich*
F436 *Surprise* (Bay)
F437 *Loch Lomond*
F449 *Pevensey Castle*
F523 *Dovey* (River)
F525 *Ribble* (River)
F530 *Oakham Castle*
F600 *St Brides Bay*
F603 *Loch Arkaig*
F604 *Start Bay*
F605 *Tremadoc Bay*
F608 *Padstow Bay*
F609 *Loch Craggie*
F615 *Widemouth Bay*
F616 *Wigtown Bay*
F619 *Loch Glendhu*
F620 *Loch Gorm*
F622 *Burghead Bay*
F628 *Loch Killisport*
F630 *Cardigan Bay*
F633 *Whitsand Bay*
F634 *St Austell Bay*
F636 *Carnarvon Bay*
F639 *Loch More*
F644 *Cawsand Bay*
F645 *Loch Ruthven*
F647 *Alert* (Bay)
F648 *Loch Scavaig*
F650 *Porlock Bay*
F651 *Veryan Bay*
F655 *Loch Tralaig*
F658 *Loch Veyatie*
F690 *Caistor Castle*
F691 *Lancaster Castle*
F692 *Oxford Castle*
F693 *Morpeth Castle*

Notes: Only Royal Navy vessels are listed above. Ships of Commonwealth navies were also allocated new numbers with Flag 'F' superior, but these are not included.

3 RN Gas Turbine Development

One of the major technical developments of World War 2 was the evolution of the gas turbine as a practical power plant for aircraft, either as a pure turbojet or as a turboprop. The Royal Navy was quick to perceive the possibilities of this new powerplant in the field of warship propulsion and shortly after the end of the war it was decided to convert a motor gunboat (MGB2009) to gas turbine propulsion in order to test the practicality of such an installation. The engine used was an aircraft powerplant modified for marine use; the Metropolitan Vickers Gatric. This engine was of axial flow design, with a nine-stage compressor and a four-stage turbine driving the gearbox. MGB2009 ran for four years and provided much useful data on the operation of gas turbines at sea.

In 1948, a successor to the Gatric was ordered. This was an adaptation of the Metropolitan Vickers Beryl, another axial flow aircraft engine which was also the power plant for the Saunders Roe twin jet flying boat fighter which was under development at the same time. This engine drove a separate power turbine and produced 4,800bhp on a shore test rig. Two G2s were installed in the two 'Bold' class fast patrol boats (*Bold Pioneer*, *Bold Pathfinder*) which were completed in 1951/52 but the results were not very satisfactory as numerous serious teething problems were encountered. However, this is the price of progress and several useful lessons were learnt from the operation of these vessels.

Capitalising on the experience gained with the previous vessels, designs were drawn up in the mid-1950s for a new class of fast patrol boat using Bristol Siddeley Proteus gas turbines. These were again aircraft engines and powered the Britannia airliner which in service was probably one of the most fuel efficient aircraft of its time although it was eclipsed in performance by the contemporary pure jet airliners. The new boats, the 'Brave' class, employed three Proteus engines of 3,500hp each giving a maximum speed of over 50kts and a cruising speed of 44kts. Only two vessels were completed for the Royal Navy, *Brave Swordsman* and *Brave Borderer,* but their spectacular performance led to export orders from several countries for similar craft. Several of the foreign orders specified auxilliary diesel engines for cruising to overcome the relatively low endurance of the purely gas turbine powered vessels. This arrangement was known as CODOG (combined diesel or gas turbine).

All the foregoing designs employed aircraft engines which had a low specific weight (ie high power to weight ratio) but were expensive on fuel. In 1946, Rolls-Royce was contracted to design and develop a gas turbine plant specifically designed for marine use and suitable for powering a 200-ton gunboat. The outcome of this contract was the RM60 powerplant which probably had one of the most complex cycles ever evolved for a gas turbine. Commencing with a low pressure axial compressor, the air was led through an intercooler, a first stage centrifugal compressor, another intercooler, a second stage centrifugal compressor, heat exchanger, combustion chamber, three single-stage turbines (one for each compressor stage), and a two-stage power turbine. The result must have been a thermodynamacist's nightmare! The object of all this complexity was to achieve a flat fuel consumption curve (ie an even increase in fuel consumption with increasing power settings). Two RM60 units were installed in HMS *Grey Goose*, a war-built steam gunboat which commissioned in 1955 for trials. In service the RM60 proved to be an excellent powerplant, particularly in respect of fuel consumption but the complexity of the design led to high development costs and no further work on the design was carried out following completion of the trials aboard *Grey Goose.*

While development of the RM60 continued, a contract was placed with English Electric for a gas turbine unit designated EL60A. This was a much more straightforward unit than the RM60 and was intended for installation in the frigate *Hotham* which was an American-built vessel of the 'Captain' class. *Hotham*'s normal powerplant was a two shaft turbo-electric system and the intention was to replace one of the steam turbines in order that a direct comparison of the steam and gas turbine plants could be made. Although the *Hotham* was taken in hand for conversion, development of the EL60 was abandoned in 1952 after shore trials showed that the plant was overweight and not flexible enough in operation. The *Hotham* was returned to the United States and scrapped.

In 1954 design work commenced on the Type 81 general purpose frigates and it was decided to incorporate a mixed steam and gas turbine plant which was also under development for a destroyer design which eventually became the 'County' class guided missile destroyers. The new plant envisaged a 12,500shp steam turbine for normal and cruising purposes and a 7,500shp gas turbine as a boost engine for maximum speed and emergency manoeuvring. This arrangement was known as COSAG (combined steam and gas turbine). The gas turbine was a development by AEI (amalgamated with English Electric) and designated G6. In operational use the system was highly successful and the G6 proved capable of more extended periods of running than was envisaged in the original concept of a boost engine.

101
HMS *Bold Pathfinder* was one of two gas turbine powered experimental fast patrol boats. She is armed with two lightweight 4.5in guns adapted from an army design for a howitzer. The G2 gas turbine engine proved troublesome and both vessels saw limited service. *Bold Pioneer*, the other ship of the class, was scrapped in 1958 and *Bold Pathfinder* lingered on until listed for disposal in 1962. *MoD Navy*

102
The Type 81 was the first frigate design to incorporate a gas turbine, which accounted for the two funnel layout; the turbine exhausted through the after funnel and the boilers for the steam turbine exhausted through the fore funnel. *Fleet Photographic Unit*

103
The first all gas turbine design of frigate in any navy was the Type 21, exemplified here by HMS *Ardent*. Her engines were all adaptations of well proven aviation turbine engines. *Yarrow (Shipbuilders) Ltd*

As a result of the success of the installation in the 'County' and 'Tribal' class vessels, thoughts turned to the possibility of all gas turbine-powered vessels and to test this concept it was decided to convert a Type 14 frigate. Development of gas turbines purely for marine use had proved very expensive so it was decided to revert to the practice of modifying existing aero engines for warship use. The most powerful aircraft engine available was the Olympus which powered the Vulcan heavy bomber and in later versions the supersonic TSR2. With the addition of a power turbine stage, and modified for marine use, an Olympus power plant was installed in HMS *Exmouth* (Type 14 frigate). Also installed were two Proteus gas turbines rated at 3,250shp each for cruising power. The Olympus was derated to 15,000shp as the hull of the Type 14 was not capable of absorbing more. The installation was completed in 1968 and the ship was subsequently employed on trials to test the viability of the concept. However, even before the *Exmouth* commenced her trials, the Royal Navy was already convinced of the advantages of gas turbine propulsion and in 1967 decided that all major warships would be gas turbine-powered.

The first vessel to be designed from the start for all gas turbine propulsion was the Type 21 frigates designed by Thornycroft to naval requirements. This class of vessel employed the Olympus for high speed work and two marine versions of the Rolls-Royce Tyne turboprop, another aircraft engine which powered the Vanguard airliner among others. The two Tynes, rated at 4,250shp each, gave the ship a cruising speed of 18kts while the Olympus, now rated at 25,000shp, allowed a maximum speed of 32kts.

The Tyne/Olympus combination proved reliable and efficient in operation and was specified for all subsequent designs including the Type 22 frigate and Type 42 destroyer, as well as the through deck cruisers ordered in the early 1970s powered by four Olympus engines. Thus in 25 years the gas turbine has progressed from an experimental curiosity to the main means of propulsion of a modern warship.

The advantages of the gas turbine as a warship propulsion plant are numerous. They are slightly more economic on fuel than an equivalent steam plant and are easier to control, replying almost simultaneously to changes of power settings. This in turn leads to less engineroom staff required on watch, a factor which is also helped by the fact that the complete engine module can be easily removed and replaced which means that on-board maintenance is reduced. The fact that major repairs and overhauls can be carried out ashore while another engine is installed in the ship means that the amount of time a ship needs to spend in dockyard hands is sharply reduced. In fact, as was shown in the Falkland Islands, large ships such as the carrier *Invincible* can actually carry out an engine change while at sea. Of course this is not possible in a smaller ship such as a frigate but it does illustrate the advantages of the modular concept of the gas turbine. The Type 42 destroyer HMS *Southampton* changed one of her Tyne units while at anchor alongside the repair ship *Stena Seaspread* in the relative calm of San Carlos Water, showing that with limited facilities this sort of work can be carried out when required.

Another advantage lies in the fact that most marine gas turbines are modified versions of existing aero engine designs which means that the cost of initial design and development has already been absorbed by the aerospace industry, thus reducing the total cost of the engine programme as far as the Navy is concerned. Additionally the necessary industrial base for the production of engines and spares is guaranteed.

There are some disadvantages which cannot be ignored, especially by the warship designer. Gas turbines are very sensitive to the environment in which they operate and consequently extensive air ducting and filters are necessary for both the intake and the exhaust gases. This ducting can take up a lot of internal space amidships and experience has shown that this also leads to problems in containing fires caused by battle damage as the large open ducts can provide considerable draughting for such fires. This may have been a factor in the loss of the *Antelope* — although it must be said that a bomb exploding deep in the engineroom of a ship is bound to cause considerable damage.

Exhausts from gas turbines are considerably hotter than in a steam turbine installation and so provision has to be made to keep masts and aerials away from the exhaust. Also the flow of hot gases aft could seriously affect helicopter operations from the flightdeck and careful design of funnel and superstructure is needed to avoid problems. One solution to this problem was the 'Loxton bends' or 'elephant ears' which were fitted to the funnel of HMS *Sheffield.* However in this particular case they were found not to be necessary and were not fitted to subsequent Type 42 ships. Another point to bear in mind is that the hotter gases will increase the ships infra-red signature which under certain circumstances would make it easier to detect and track the ship and could be used as a homing point by an anti-ship missile although at present no operational anti-ship missile uses this form of homing. (Several under development use thermal imaging to detect and home on to the target).

Future Royal Navy use of the gas turbine centres on the Rolls-Royce SM 1A turbine based on the successful Spey aero engine. This lies between the Tyne and the Olympus in terms of power rating (17,000hp) but is considerably smaller and lighter than the Olympus. It is expected that the forthcoming

Type 23 frigate will include two Spey units, but cruising power will be provided by a diesel engine in a CODOG arrangement. It is certainly true that at the power outputs required at typical frigate cruising speeds there is little to choose in terms of flexibility and cost of installation, while the diesel engine shows considerable savings in fuel consumption. It will be interesting to see if in fact the Type 23 is built as planned or whether in fact it will end up with three Spey units. In any event, the gas turbine is well established as the prime powerplant for all Royal Navy surface combat vessels and this state of affairs is likely to remain at least to the end of the century.

4 Frigates and Helicopters

As far back as 1943 the Royal Navy had seen the potentialities of the helicopter as a useful extension to shipborne airpower when an order was placed for the Sikorsky R-4 helicopter then under development in the United States. Some machines were used for trials during the war and the first Royal Navy helicopter squadron, No 771, formed at Portland in September 1945. Although a shore-based unit, it was an R-4 Hoverfly Mk 1 from this squadron which made the first landing on a frigate. The ship was the *Helmsdale*, a 'River' class frigate adapted for training purposes, and a series of trials were carried out to determine the suitability of the helicopter for anti-submarine warfare. The trials took place in late 1946 and one of the main findings was that a considerably more powerful machine was going to be needed if it was to be capable of operating under a reasonable range of weather conditions and carry a worthwhile load of weapons and equipment. Although the Navy went on to develop the helicopter as a potent AS weapon, initial efforts were directed towards larger helicopters which could only operate from the decks of aircraft carriers.

In the late 1940s and early 1950s the Saunders Roe company developed the Skeeter light helicopter for the Army and a version of this was proposed for naval use (Skeeter Mk 5) but again power was lacking and the design was dropped. In the meantime the Fairey company had developed its Ultra Light design which was powered by a gas turbine exhausting through nozzles at the rotor tips. After this design was turned down by the Army it was demonstrated to the Navy in the hope of gaining a production order. Trials were conducted from a landing platform constructed on the stern of the Type 15 frigate *Grenville* in September 1957. Much useful data was obtained on the operation of light helicopters from small flightdecks but the Fairey Ultra Light was still too small for naval requirements.

Following its experience with the Skeeter, the Saunders Roe company instigated design of a turbine powered helicopter using many features of the Skeeter. The new design, designated P531-0, first flew on 20 July 1958, powered by a 300shp Turbomeca Turmo 600 engine. After the initial trials the Royal Navy ordered three P531-0/N helicopters for further trails and tests aboard ship. By this time the Navy had a firm requirement for a torpedo carrying helicopter to operate from small warships. This was due to the fact that shipboard weapon systems could not operate at the long ranges at which modern sonar equipment could detect and track submarines. Thus the MATCH (manned torpedo carrying helicopter) concept was born, and in late 1959 the P531 prototypes carried out a series of trials to determine the type's suitability for the new role. The trials were conducted aboard another Type 15 frigate, *Undaunted*, which also had a small flightdeck constructed over the quarterdeck. As a result of these trials the P531 was ordered in quantity for the Royal Navy from the Westland company which had by then taken over development of the aircraft from Saunders Roe. The production version, named Wasp, was powered by a Blackburn Nimbus engine rated at 700shp and featured a larger cabin than that of the P531 prototype. As a result of the trials aboard *Undaunted*, the Wasp was fitted with a four-wheel fully castoring undercarriage instead of the skids of the earlier version. A total of 98 Wasps was delivered to the Royal Navy and, flown by detached flights of No 829 Squadron, they were operated by 'Tribal', 'Leander', 'Rothesay' and Type 21 class frigates. The first ship's flight formed aboard HMS *Leander* on 11 November 1963, with other flights forming as aircraft became available.

By the late 1960s the helicopter was established as an integral part of a frigate's armament and following presentations from Westlands a naval version of their WG13 was ordered in prototype form in 1967. This order was part of a larger deal involving Anglo-French production of three helicopter types for both countries. These were the Puma, a medium capacity troop carrying helicopter to be produced under French leadership; the Gazelle, a light helicopter mainly for army use and again produced under French leadership; and the Lynx (WG13) produced under Westland's leadership for both the British and French armed forces. The first naval Lynx flew in May 1972 and it was immediately obvious that the type had considerable potential. Thanks to its new 'rigid rotor' it was fast and very manoeuvrable, and could carry a wide range of weapons including Mk 44 and 46 torpedoes as well as AS12 and Sea Skua missiles. An initial order for 60 was placed and the first ship's flight formed in 1978 aboard HMS *Sirius*, an Exocet 'Leander' class frigate. Subsequently, all Type 21 class frigates, as well as many 'Leander' class were equipped with the new type while the Type 22 frigate was designed from the outset to carry two Lynx helicopters. The Wasp is gradually being withdrawn from service as it is replaced by Lynx. Probably the last frigates to carry the Wasp will be the Ikara converted 'Leanders' as these ships have not had their flight deck size increased to operate the larger Lynx.

Looking to the future, it has been stated that the new Type 23 frigates, now in the design stage, will be equipped to carry and operate the Westland/Augusta EH101. This is a new design being developed by Westland and the Italian company Augusta which, like Westland, have produced their own versions of several American helicopters including the Sea King. A joint company, European Helicopters, has been set up to design and market the EH101 which is slightly smaller than a Sea King but will be able to carry a 50% greater load. The Royal Navy version will be equipped with a Ferranti Blue Kestrel search radar, and advanced sonobuoy information processing equipment. It will be able to carry current AS torpedoes including the new Stingray lightweight torpedo. Power will be provided by either three General Electric T-700 turboshafts or three Rolls-Royce RTM321 engines. Maximum all up weight will be in the region of 28,500lb (13,000kg) and disposable load will be 13,200lb (6,000kg) making it by far the largest helicopter to operate from a British frigate. As an AS weapon the EH101 should be a great improvement on both the Lynx and the Sea King but it will probably not be so manoeuvrable as the Lynx and therefore perhaps not so useful in the anti-ship role.

Brief specifications of helicopter types operated from Royal Navy frigates are given below.

Sikorsky R-4 Hoverfly Mk 1
Rotor Diameter: 38ft
Length: 35ft 3in
Max weight: 2,530lb
Max speed: 80mph
Max range: 220 miles
Powered by: One Warner Super Scarab R-550-1 seven cylinder radial engine, 180hp
Crew: 2
Total: 52 supplied to UK for use by RN and RAF

Fairey Ultra Light
Rotor Diameter: 28ft 3½in
Length: 15ft 8in
Max weight: 1,900lb
Max Speed: 95mph
Max range: 185 miles
Powered by: One Blackburn Turbomeca Palouste turbine, 252lb static thrust, driving two-bladed rotor through tip nozzles
Crew: 2

Saunders Roe P531-0/N
Rotor diameter: 32ft 3in
Length: 30ft 4in
Max weight: 4,000lb
Max speed: 132mph
Max range: 242 miles
Powered by: One Blackburn Turbomeca Turmo 600, 300shp
Crew: Five seats, normal crew two

Westland Wasp HAS1
Rotor diameter: 32ft 3in
Length: 30ft 4in
Max weight: 5,500lb
Max speed: 120mph
Max range: 270 miles
Powered by: One Blackburn (later Rolls-Royce) Nimbus turbine engine, 710shp
Crew: Five seats, normal crew 2

Westland WG13 Lynx HAS2
Rotor diameter: 42ft
Length: 39ft 1¼in
Max weight: 9,500lb
Max speed: 207mph
Max range: 391 miles
Powered by: Two Rolls-Royce BS360 Gem turboshafts, 900shp each
Crew: Two, can carry up to 10 troops. Later versions equipped with MAD and dipping sonar, to give limited AS detection capability

Westland/Augusta EH101
Max weight: 28,500lb
Max speed: 200mph
Max range: 1,100nm
Powered by: Three General Electric T-700 turboshafts, each 1,700shp

104
The sole example of the Fairey Ultra Light helicopter which carried out deck landing trials aboard HMS *Grenville* in 1958. Note the compact size of the fuselage and the absence of a tail rotor which was not required as the tip nozzle powered main rotor produced no torque.

105
One of the three Saunders Roe P531-0/N prototypes carrying out deck landing trials aboard HMS *Ashanti* in 1962. The suction pad landing gear was an experimental attempt to evolve a suitable undercarriage for operations from a small flightdeck. The idea was that the suction pads would grip the deck upon landing while reverse pressure would caused the pads to act like small hovercraft so that the helicopter could be moved easily around the deck. Eventually a four-wheel castoring undercarriage was adopted for the Westland Wasp which was developed from the P531 design. *Westland Helicopters*

106
An early production Wasp HAS1 lifting off from the deck of a 'Leander' class frigate. The Wasp had a more powerful engine then the earlier P531 prototypes and also featured a folding tailboom to assist stowage in small hangars. Note the Limbo AS mortar and VDS gear on the frigate's quarterdeck. *Westland Helicopters*

107
HMS *Brilliant's* Lynx on display in 1982, equipped with a Mk 46 lightweight AS torpedo and MAD gear on an outrigger boom. The MAD (Magnetic Anomaly Detector) equipment is trailed some way behind the aircraft on the end of a length of wire which could be reeled in by remote control. The Lynx can also carry the Sea Skua missile, giving it an effective anti-ship capability, and will also carry the new Stingray torpedo. *Author*

108
A manufacturer's model of the projected EH-101 design which is a joint Westland (UK) and Augusta (Italy) undertaking. Smaller than the current Sea King but carrying a greater operational load, the EH-101 will be operated from the forthcoming Type 23 frigates. The radome under the nose will house the Ferranti Blue Kestrel radar. *Westland Helicopters*

5 Frigates in Falklands Task Force Operations

The following is a list of Royal Navy frigates known to have taken part in the operations to recover the Falkland Islands following their invasion by Argentine forces in April 1982.

(a) Recovery of South Georgia
HMS *Brilliant*, HMS *Plymouth.*

(b) Main actions around Falkland Islands
HMS *Brilliant*, HMS *Broadsword* (Type 22 frigates)
HMS *Plymouth*, HMS *Yarmouth* ('Rothesay' class)
HMS *Alacrity*, HMS *Ambuscade*, HMS *Antelope* (sunk 24/5/82 San Carlos), HMS *Ardent* (sunk 21/5/82 Falkland Sound), HMS *Arrow*, HMS *Avenger* (Type 21 frigates)
HMS *Andromeda*, HMS *Argonaut*, HMS *Minerva*, HMS *Penelope*, HMS *Diomede* ('Leander' class).

(c) Recovery of South Thule
HMS *Yarmouth*

At the cessation of hostilities, several ships were en route to the South Atlantic or were preparing to depart. Among these were the frigates HMS *Battleaxe*, HMS *Danae* and HMS *Amazon* which escorted the carrier *Illustrious* on her way south to relieve HMS *Invincible.* HMS *Apollo*, a 'Leander' class frigate, was also in the Falklands zone just after the war and sustained damage to her hull while on patrol due to severe weather conditions.

109
Frigates in the Falklands. The ill fated HMS *Antelope* passes ahead of the 'Leander' class frigate HMS *Minerva* as she enters San Carlos Water. Note *Minerva's* Seacat launchers and director trained to port in anticipation of imminent air attack. *MoD Navy*

Bibliography

The following books have provided a considerable amount of background information as well as the facts and figures necessary in compiling a book such as this.

Edgar J. March; *British Destroyers 1892-1953*; Seeley Service and Co, 1966.

Denis Archer (Ed); *Jane's Pocket Book of Naval Armament* (No 9 in a series); Macdonald and Jane's Publishers Ltd, 1976.

Jean Labayle Couhat (Ed); *Combat Fleets of the World 1978/79*; Arms and Armour Press, 1978.

Capt John E. Moore RN, FRGS (Ed); *Jane's Fighting Ships* (Various editions 1945-1982); Jane's Yearbooks.

H. T. Lenton; *Warships of the British and Commonwealth Navies*; Ian Allan Ltd, 1969 (2nd Edition).

Norman Friedman; *Modern Warship Design and Development*; Conway Maritime Press, 1978.

Raymond V. B. Blackman, AMINA, AIMarE; *The World's Warships*; Macdonald 1960, 1963, 1969.

Laurence Dunn, Assoc RINA; *British Warships*; Longacre Press Ltd, 1962.

H. T. Lenton; *British Fleet and Escort Destroyers* (two vols); Macdonald and Co (Publishers) Ltd, 1970.

110
HMS *Chichester* was one of 26 frigates of various types built under a major construction programme started in 1951. The effect of electronics on warship design is clearly shown in this photograph taken shortly after she was completed in 1958. *Wright and Logan*

John Young; *A Dictionary of Ships of the Royal Navy of the Second World War*; Patrick Stephens Ltd, 1975.

H. T. Lenton; *British Warships*; Ian Allan Ltd, Sixth Edition 1962.

Peter Elliott; *Allied Escort Ships of World War II*; Macdonald and Jane's, London, 1977.

Transactions of the Institute of Naval Architects, Vols 89 and 116; Royal Institute of Naval Architects, London, 1947 and 1974.

Owen Thetford; *British Naval Aircraft Since 1912*; Putnam, London, Fourth Edition, 1978.

Lt-Cdr J. M. Milne; *Flashing Blades over the Sea*; Maritime Books, Liskeard, 1980.

H. T. Lenton; *British Escort Ships*; Macdonald and Jane's, 1974.

Mike Critchley; *British Warships Since 1945 (Part 3 Destroyers)*; Maritime Books, Liskeard, 1982.

The following magazines and periodicals are devoted to warships or publish articles of interest connected with warships and their history and development. They have, again, proved useful in carrying out research for this book.

Warship published quarterly by Conway Maritime Press.

Flight International published weekly by IPC Transport Press Ltd.

Ships Monthly published monthly by Waterway Productions Ltd.

Armed Forces published monthly by Ian Allan Ltd.

Navy News published monthly by *Navy News*, HMS *Nelson*, Portsmouth.

Navy International published monthly by Maritime World Ltd.